W9-ATS-331

THE PRIVATE WORLD *OF*
THE DUKE *AND* DUCHESS *OF* WINDSOR

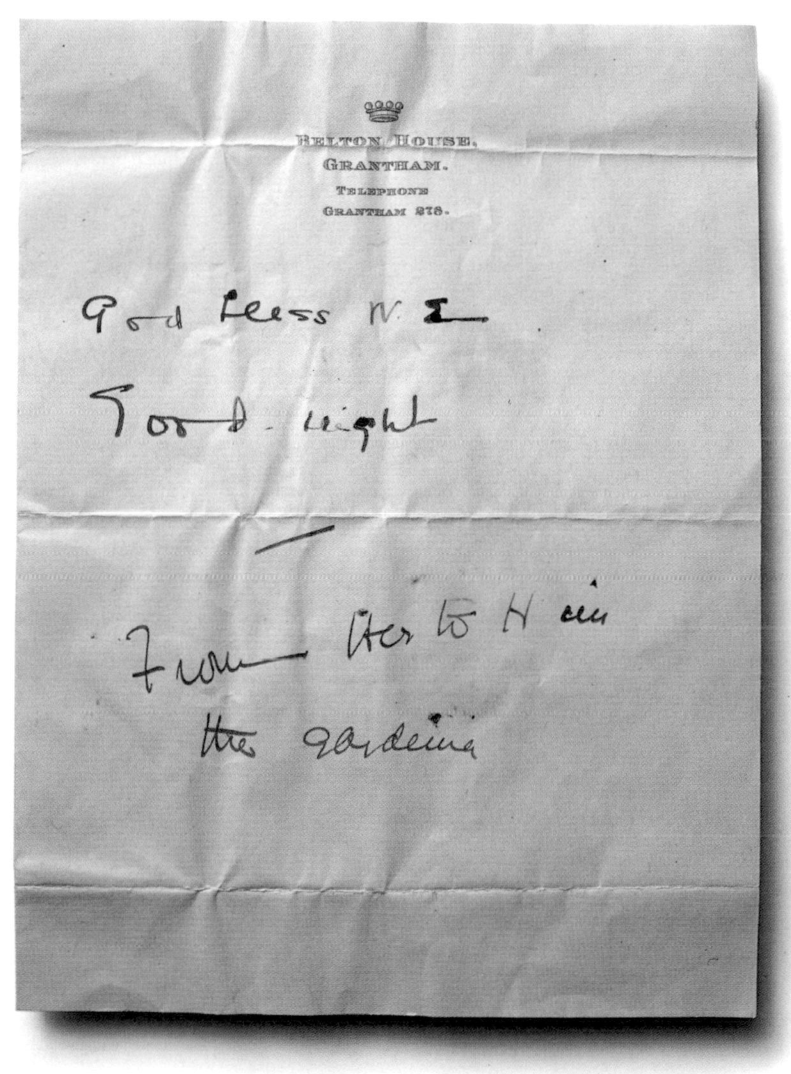

BELTON HOUSE,
GRANTHAM.
TELEPHONE
GRANTHAM 278.

God bless W.E.

Good-night

From Her to H in
the gardenia

CAFÉ

THE PRIVATE WORLD *OF* *THE* DUKE *AND* DUCHESS *OF* WINDSOR

HUGO VICKERS

INTRODUCTION *BY* JOSEPH FRIEDMAN

ABBEVILLE PRESS PUBLISHERS
NEW YORK LONDON PARIS

First published in the United States of America in 1996 by
Abbeville Press, 488 Madison Avenue, New York, N.Y. 10022

First published in Great Britain in 1995 by
Harrods Publishing
55 Park Lane, London W1Y 3DB

First edition
1 3 5 7 9 10 8 6 4 2

ISBN 0-7892-0226-3

Main photography by Fritz von der Schulenburg

Editorial Coordinator: Christiane Sherwen
Editor: Sebastian Wormell
Design: Carroll Associates, Kenneth Carroll and Roy Davison
Additional photography by David Timmis
Production: Deer Park Productions

Picture origination by Precise Litho Ltd, London
Printed and bound by Arnoldo Mondadori Editore, Verona, Italy

Notes on Names

The Duke of Windsor underwent eight name changes in the course of his life. He began as His Royal Highness Prince Edward of York. In 1901, on the death of his great-grandmother, he became Prince Edward of Cornwall and York. He was soon Prince Edward of Wales. Then in 1910, when his father became King, he automatically became The Duke of Cornwall. In 1911 he was created Prince of Wales, and in 1936 he succeeded to the throne as King Edward VIII. In the Abdication broadcast he was introduced as His Royal Highness Prince Edward, and on 8 March 1937 he was given the title of Duke of Windsor by Letters Patent. Christened Edward Albert Christian George Andrew Patrick David, he was always called David in his family. In this book he is the Prince in the early part, the King in 1936 and the Duke thereafter.

FRONT COVER, ABOVE: *The Prince of Wales, London, 1923, and Wallis Spencer, New York, 1921: the future Duke and Duchess of Windsor, long before they met for the first time.* BELOW: *The villa in the Route du Champ d'Entraînement, on the edge of the Bois de Boulogne in Paris, which was the final home of the Duke and Duchess.*

BACK COVER, ABOVE: *Cecil Beaton portraits: Wallis Simpson, November 1936, shortly before the Abdication, and the Duke of Windsor, May 1937, on the eve of his wedding.* BELOW: *A corner of the upstairs boudoir in the Windsors' Paris house. The Duchess's bedroom is glimpsed through the doorway on the right.*

HALF-TITLE: *A note to the Prince of Wales sent with a gardenia. It was written by Wallis Simpson during a weekend at Belton House, Lord Brownlow's country seat, 1935.* FRONTISPIECE: *Wallis Spencer and Ethel Noyes in France, 1924.* TITLE PAGE: *Portrait of the Duke of Windsor by Dorothy Wilding, 1943. This was one of the Duchess's favourite photographs of her husband.* OPPOSITE: *The Duke's gold-mounted briar pipe, a Christmas present from the Duchess, 1940.* ENDPAPERS: *Labels on the underside of a mahogany games table in the Duke of Windsor's collection.*

CONTENTS

INTRODUCTION

THE RESTORATION OF THE WINDSOR RESIDENCE

When, in 1986, the Duchess of Windsor died in Paris, some fourteen years after the Duke, the future of their house and collection in the Bois de Boulogne seemed uncertain. The house itself had been held by the Windsors on a lease from the City of Paris. The contents, including all the Windsors' personal belongings, had been left by the Duchess to her Trustees to be sold for the benefit of the Institut Pasteur. Within days, interested parties were approaching the City of Paris with a view to obtaining the lease of the mansion.

A unique ensemble of architecture, decoration and artefacts, together with personal papers, photographs, and other documents bearing on the lives of the two leading figures in one of the most remarkable stories of the century was about to be dispersed, and would probably have been lost without record but for the intervention of Mr Mohamed Al Fayed, the international businessman and philanthropist. Mr Al Fayed took on the task of saving, documenting and restoring the house and its contents.

Born in Egypt, Mohamed Al Fayed had made his home in England and France. He had already established a high reputation in the field of architectural conservation, masterminding the award-winning refurbishment of the Paris Ritz, as well as an extensive programme designed to restore Harrods, the great London store, to its original Edwardian splendour. However, the restoration of the

PREVIOUS PAGES, LEFT: *The two-storeyed Entrance Hall of the Windsor Villa. The marbled commode below the staircase is typical of designs by Syrie Maugham, one of the fashionable decorators who advised the Windsors in the 1930s.* RIGHT: *Many books were in need of repair, including this one, a present from Lord and Lady Brownlow.*

TOP RIGHT: *The entrance front of the villa in 1986. During the Duchess's long illness the shuttered house had become a mournful place.* OPPOSITE PAGE: *The* trompe l'oeil *ceiling in the Hall was created for the house, but the lantern with Prince of Wales feathers came from the Duke's beloved Fort Belvedere, and the banner had hung above his stall in St George's Chapel, Windsor.* TOP LEFT: *During the restoration the ceiling was cleaned and repaired.* ABOVE: *One of a set of elaborate sconces incorporating the Royal Arms of the Stuarts, supplied by Jansen, the Paris firm responsible for most of the interior decoration.* LEFT: *The hall furnishings include a* bureau plat *in Louis XV style and two fine carved wooden* torchères.

Windsor Residence was a project of particular complexity, requiring great sensitivity and unusual skill.

The Windsor Residence itself had originally been built around the turn of the century, but the interior was a creation of the 1950s, when the Windsors first moved here. This alone made the project unusual. The restoration of so modern an interior was almost unprecedented, and although Mr Al Fayed would later initiate a similar project, to refurbish the celebrated Dorchester Hotel suite decorated by Oliver Messel, at the Windsor Residence he was breaking new ground.

The relatively recent date of the Windsor Residence in turn brought unusual benefits. The accurate restoration of older buildings is often hampered by a lack of documentary and physical evidence. Architectural and decorative elements have been lost, and in the absence of adequate documentation, guesswork comes into play, creating problems of historical authenticity. In the case of the Windsor Residence, the physical and documentary evidence could not have been more complete.

The house was in serious need of attention, as were the contents, since they had suffered from long neglect during the Duchess's final illness. But with the exception of items of furniture bequeathed by the Duchess to Versailles, and a quantity of jewellery sold with spectacular success through Sotheby's, virtually every object from the Windsors' collection was still in place. Any doubts could quickly be settled by reference to the Windsors' remarkable archive of photographs, which provided a detailed record of the appearance of the house throughout their occupancy, and the first-hand testimony of living witnesses. Former guests revisited the house and offered vital clues, as did the remaining, devoted members of the Duke and Duchess's household staff, who had been retained by Mr Al Fayed. By a remarkable coincidence the Duke's former valet, Sydney Johnson, who left the Windsors' service following his master's death, had subsequently joined Mr Al Fayed's personal staff and thus found himself once more in a house which for him held such vivid memories.

Some features of the decoration could be conserved and restored; others had to be recreated. In many cases it was possible to trace and involve the very same craftsmen

TOP: *In the course of the restoration, the ground-floor office was converted into a museum room. The Duke kept with him the wall-map showing his world tours as Prince of Wales. Two more museum rooms were created in the basement of the villa.* ABOVE: *A view from the Hall gallery during refurbishment, looking towards the front entrance of the villa.* RIGHT: *A detail of the Duke's late-eighteenth-century mahogany desk, which had been in his study at York House, showing its scuffed and damaged state prior to restoration.*

who had originally worked on the house for the Windsors, drawing on their unrivalled knowledge and expertise. The firm of Hamot, celebrated carpet manufacturers of Paris and Aubusson, restored the carpet they had originally supplied for the Salon, woven in silver with ostrich-feather plumes reminiscent of the Prince of Wales emblem, and at the same time produced an exact replica of the carpet they had made for the Duke of Windsor's bedroom, working from original cards and other documents in their archives. Another company, L.O.R.D., successors to the furniture-making division of Maison Jansen, the Windsors' principal decorators, was entrusted with the task of repairing the furniture which they and their predecessors had originally supplied not only for the house at the Bois de Boulogne but for the Windsors' earlier Paris residence in the Boulevard Suchet. Particularly thrilling was the moment when the original painter and gilder returned to take up his brushes. Now in his seventies, he was accompanied by his son, who had worked with him here before as a teenage apprentice, and who was now joined in turn by his own teenage son, to begin work on the restoration of a scheme of decoration which was among his family's proudest achievements.

ABOVE: *The Duke's former chauffeur, Gregorio Martin, with the cache of photographs discovered in the Duke's bathtub in 1988.* LEFT: *Pre-restoration. The painted marbling in the Entrance Hall was worn and dirty.* BELOW: *The visitor's first view of the Salon from the Entrance Hall. In the centre is the table at which the Instrument of Abdication was signed in December 1936.* BELOW LEFT: *Two belt-clasps, part of the Duke's collection of military memorabilia.*

The scale and scope of the restoration were impressive. All essential services had to be replaced, a major undertaking requiring complete rewiring, replumbing, and the installation of a conservation-based heating and humidification system. Significant structural works were required, including underpinning, re-roofing, and the creation of a suite of basement galleries for the display of treasures from the collection of the Duke and Duchess. Every item was carefully labelled and removed to the Ritz storehouses for safekeeping. Only when the major construction activity was complete could work begin on the restoration of the interiors and their contents. Their unusual range and diversity called for the involvement of specialist conservators in almost every field and from all parts of Europe.

Most remarkable perhaps is the fact that the restoration was undertaken on the personal initiative of a private individual. All who visited the Windsor Residence in the period following the Duchess's death remember the atmosphere of sadness and decay; it was hard to believe that the house could ever be restored to anything like its original appearance and spirit. Mr Al Fayed, however, saw that with adequate support and proper direction, the Windsor Residence could be revived, and that the remaining contents could and should be properly preserved and recorded. He agreed to take the lease of the house from the City of Paris, and in separate negotiations he moved quickly to acquire the contents from the Duchess's trustees. Having then assembled his expert team of advisors and conservators, he immediately set to work

LEFT: *The cool colours of the Salon were inspired by the eighteenth-century Amalienburg Palace in Munich. The Aubusson carpet is decorated with ostrich feathers, heightened with silver.* TOP: *Some of the craftsmen who had worked on the decoration in the 1950s returned for the 1989 restoration.* ABOVE: *Brockhurst's unusual portrait of the Duchess, painted in 1939, stares out into the Salon from above the Library mantelpiece.* BOTTOM RIGHT: *The warm golden-yellow painted panelling in the Library was restored to its original brilliance.*

and no expense was spared in realizing his ambitious plans.

Mr Al Fayed, with his love of history, had grasped at once the unique importance of the house. Here after all was the residence of a former king who, although never crowned, had been sovereign of one of the world's most powerful nations and the head of a vast empire spanning the globe; a man who as Prince of Wales had been the object of unprecedented worldwide adulation, whose accession to the throne had been accompanied by great hopes, and whose abdication after less than a year had followed a constitutional crisis which seemed to threaten the very institution of the monarchy.

This was the home of a man who had been admired or reviled for sacrificing the highest honours to love, and who found that in marrying the woman of his choice he had given up not only his throne, but also his country and his family. Here for twenty years he had lived in exile with the Duchess. The couple were seldom apart. The Duchess through her gifts as a wife and hostess, created a magical atmosphere in which the Duke continued to live in regal style, surrounded by distinguished friends old and new.

The house itself commanded admiration. Within the walls of this secluded turn-of-the-century villa, the Windsors had created a sequence of interiors whose decoration epitomized the sophistication and glamour for which they were renowned. With the assistance of Stéphane Boudin, chief artistic director at Maison Jansen, then the foremost interior decorating company in France, and with advice from friends such as Elsie de Wolfe, another leading figure in interior decoration, they conjured up a world both intimate and grand, in a style uniquely their own.

Boudin's links with the Duke of Windsor went back to 1934. He had decorated two pre-war houses for the Duke and Duchess, one in Paris, the other in the South of France, and had developed an understanding of their way of life, while in their turn they trusted his judgement on questions of colour, materials and furnishings. Sumptuous yet restrained, with fine furniture and pictures, the house was unmistakably royal but free of excessive formality, with a theatrical touch characteristic of the Duchess, matched by an elegant

ABOVE: *Two views of the Dining Room, after and during restoration. Stéphane Boudin introduced the partition at the end of the room, with minstrels' galleries and mirrored recess, as well as the eighteenth-century chinoiserie wall-decorations. Boudin, a much sought-after decorator, was President of Jansen and responsible for many of most exciting features in the villa's decoration.* RIGHT: *The Library was used by the Windsors as their downstairs sitting room. The equestrian portrait of the Prince of Wales above the banquette is one of Munnings's best works.*

simplicity reflecting the tastes of the Duke.

The interiors of the Windsor Villa were among the finest surviving examples of post-war decoration, a unique blend of French, English and American influences. From the start, their restoration was conceived as important not only for their association with the Windsors but also for the light they shed on a rich and as yet neglected phase in the development of taste.

No less important than the house were the many collected possessions, great and small, still displayed in the principal rooms, as well as those, still more numerous, which had been carefully stored away. The latter came to light only gradually as the project evolved, and included the remarkable cache of photographs discovered in the Duke's bathtub several weeks after work began. The contents of the house were fascinating for the light they shed on the lives of the Windsors. Here were paintings, furniture and objects of great historical interest, some brought to France from England by the Duke, others belonging to the Duchess, others acquired by the couple during their years of marriage.

The furniture at the house united the best of England and the Continent. Furniture of the Louis XV and Louis XVI period was matched by a fine ensemble of eighteenth century English furniture that had been used by the Duke at St James's Palace and Fort Belvedere. Among the highlights was the handsome Chippendale-period writing table on which the Duke had signed the Instrument of Abdication — with a brass plaque recording the event. Other outstanding pieces included a painted commode formerly belonging to the decorator Syrie Maugham, and a rare group of tables and chairs specially designed for the Windsors by Maison Jansen. Reminders of the Duke's long years as Prince of Wales were much in evidence: in the Entrance Hall was a resplendent gilt-bronze chandelier decorated with the Prince of Wales feathers, while from the gallery opposite hung the Prince's Garter Banner, which had formerly hung in St George's Chapel, Windsor Castle.

The Duke and Duchess had enjoyed assembling and arranging their diverse collection of paintings. A whole wall of the library was given over to a magnificent portrait by Sir Alfred Munnings of the Duke when Prince of Wales, riding out on 'Forest Witch'. Above the chimney-piece in the same room was Gerald Brockhurst's hypnotic portrait of the Duchess, while in the adjoining Salon another portrait of the Duchess by her friend and protégé Étienne Drian hung alongside a formal portrait of the Duke's mother, Queen Mary. Here too was a landscape by Degas, a bathing scene by Dufy, and a screen print by Andy Warhol, testimony to the Windsors' broad interest as patrons and collectors. Dazzling flower pictures by Lorjou hung above the staircase, while in the Duchess's bathroom a mirror above the bath-tub framed a portrait of the Duchess in gouache by Cecil Beaton. The Duke's rooms were decorated with

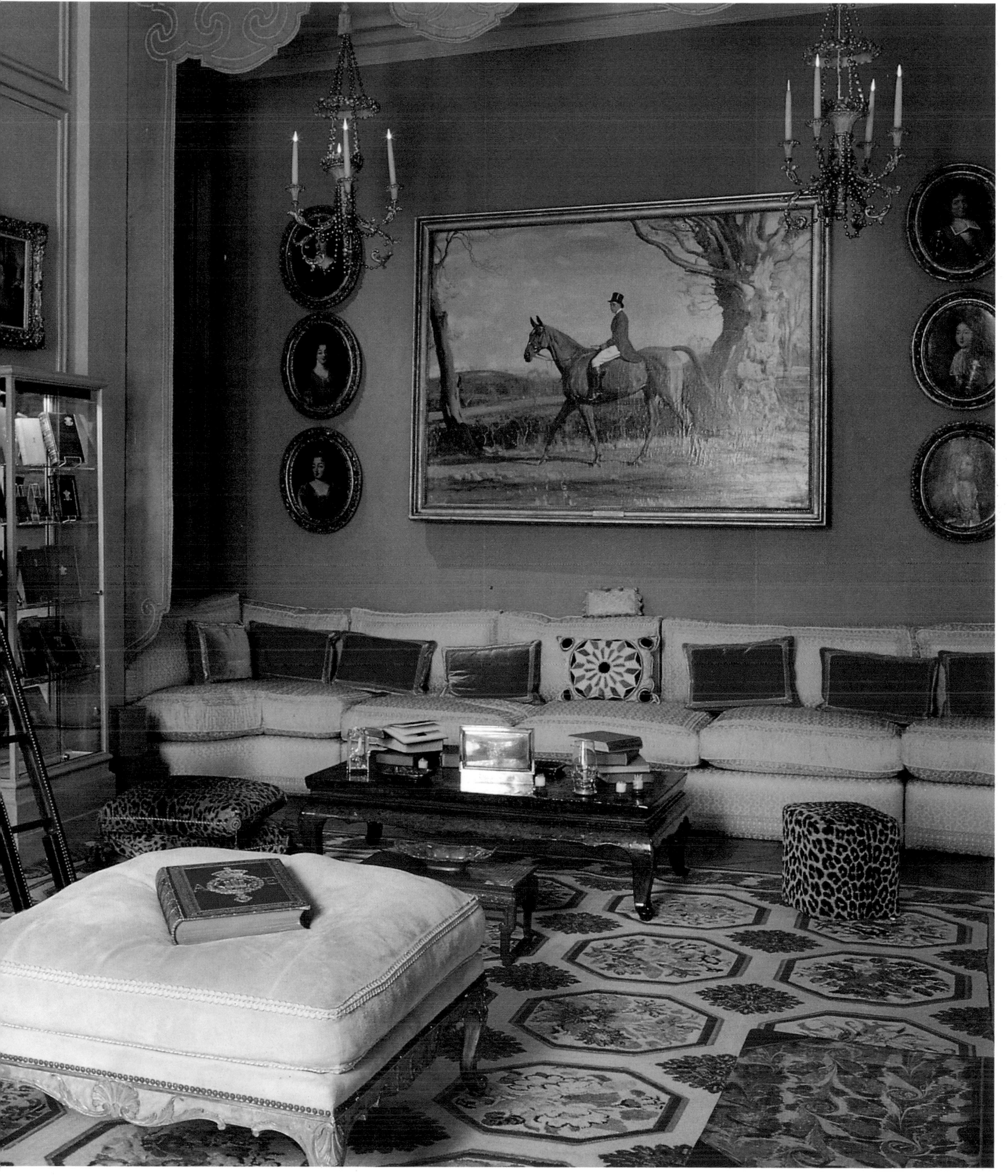

English military prints and topographical views, evidence of his enduring emotional ties to the country of his birth. Chief among these was a watercolour drawing of Fort Belvedere in Windsor Great Park, the Duke's favourite residence as Prince of Wales and King, signed by the architect Sir Jeffrey Wyatville and identified as a preliminary design for the remodelling of the Fort by King George IV in the early nineteenth century. Not the least of the treasures in the house was an exquisite portrait of a child, signed by the seventeenth-century Dutch painter Paulus Moreelse and dated 1634. In the course of Mr Al Fayed's restoration programme the painting was expertly cleaned, and research revealed that the portrait had come from the Royal Collection, having hung at one time at Hampton Court, and that the child was almost certainly Prince Gustavus of Bohemia, youngest son of the Winter Queen, Elizabeth Stuart, sister of King Charles I. Although the painting had occupied an important place in the Windsor Residence, Mr Al Fayed had the pleasant task of returning it to Her Majesty the Queen, and it now hangs once again among the treasures of the Royal Collection. Its place in the Paris house has been taken by a replica.

The Duchess of Windsor had a particular love of ceramics, and the collection was correspondingly strong in this area, with fine examples of Oriental and Western manufacture, including Meissen, Derby, Chelsea and Saint-Cloud. A personal note was struck by the large group of porcelain pug-dogs; pugs were the favourite pets of the Duke and Duchess in their later years. As a leading hostess, the Duchess had naturally assembled several fine dinner services, including a particularly elegant service bearing the Windsor cypher, produced by the Limoges factory shortly after the Second World War. Another important service was that brought to France from England by the Duke, a collection of over two hundred pieces bearing the mark of the Royal Copenhagen Porcelain Manufactory. In addition there was an extensive group of commemorative china ranging from souvenirs of Queen Victoria's Golden Jubilee in 1887 to cups, jugs, plates and other objects produced in anticipation of the Duke's own coronation as Edward VIII.

Accompanying these ceramics was a superb ensemble of glassware, including dishes, finger bowls, wine glasses, and other articles formerly used at the Windsors' legendary dinner parties, as well as a documented service of wine glasses produced around 1946 by the famous Lalique factory and engraved with the Windsor cypher. Another interesting item was a pair of claret jugs used by Edward VII when Prince of Wales at Oxford and given by Queen Alexandra to her

ABOVE: *A console in the Dining Room, one of the exuberant furnishings supplied by Jansen in 1939 for the Windsors' house in the Boulevard Suchet.* TOP RIGHT: *A copy was made of the portrait of Prince Gustavus of Bohemia by Paulus Moreelse. The original was expertly cleaned, before being returned to the Royal Collection.* BOTTOM RIGHT: *A few of the porcelain pug-dogs in the Duchess of Windsor's collection. The Windsors were fond of the breed, owning a total of nine pugs over the years.* OPPOSITE: *The Boudoir, the Windsors' first-floor sitting room, where warm reddish colours predominate.* OVERLEAF: *The Duchess wrote her letters in the Boudoir, at an eighteenth-century Chinese-style lacquer secretaire. Her Bedroom can be seen though the doorway beyond.*

IMPROVE
YOUR GOLF

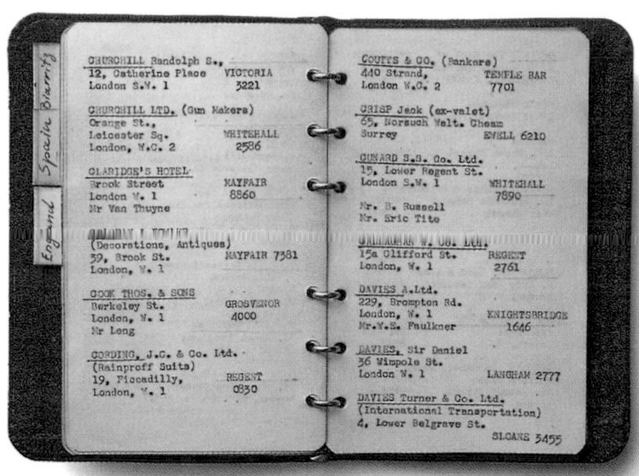

Spain Biarritz
England

CHURCHILL Randolph S.,
12, Catherine Place VICTORIA
London S.W. 1 3221

CHURCHILL LTD. (Gun Makers)
Orange St.,
Leicester Sq. WHITEHALL
London, W.C. 2 2586

CLARIDGE'S HOTEL
Brook Street MAYFAIR
London W. 1 8860
Mr Van Thuyne

[illegible]
(Decorations, Antiques)
59, Brook St. MAYFAIR 7381
London, W. 1

COOK THOS. & SONS
Berkeley St. GROSVENOR
London, W. 1 4000
Mr Long

CORDING, J.C. & Co. Ltd.
(Rainproff Suits)
19, Piccadilly, REGENT
London, W. 1 0830

COUTTS & CO. (Bankers)
440 Strand, TEMPLE BAR
London W.C. 2 7701

CRISP Jack (ex-valet)
65, Norsuch Welt. Cheam
Surrey EWELL 6210

CUNARD S.S. Co. Ltd.
15, Lower Regent St.
London S.W. 1 WHITEHALL
7890
Mr. B. Russell
Mr. Eric Tite

[illegible]
15a Clifford St. REGENT
London, W. 1 2761

DAVIES A.Ltd.
229, Brompton Rd.
London, W. 1 KNIGHTSBRIDGE
Mr.W.S. Faulkner 1646

DAVIES, Sir Daniel
36 Wimpole St.
London W. 1 LANGHAM 2777

DAVIES Turner & Co. Ltd.
(International Transportation)
4, Lower Belgrave St.
SLOANE 3455

grandson. Significant, and especially revealing of the Duke's feelings towards the past, was a large group of objects in glass bearing his cypher as King, together with others proclaiming his Coronation, all displayed in a cabinet on the first-floor landing. They included a remarkable engraved triangular decanter, its three sides commemorating the Jubilee of George V, the Abdication of Edward VIII and the Coronation of George VI.

The Windsors had likewise formed an extensive collection of silver and silver-gilt, most of which was stored in a two-storey strongroom in the basement. Here again were royal mementoes: a set of ashtrays from the Royal Yacht *Victoria and Albert*; a matchbox that had belonged to King Edward VII; the silver mug which Queen Victoria gave to her great-grandson for his first birthday present; a travelling clock that had belonged to the Duke's father; a set of four eighteenth-century dishes bearing the crowned royal cypher of King George III. There were souvenirs also of the Duke's years as Prince of Wales: gifts from his foreign tours; the sword he had worn at his father's Coronation; a cigarette case engraved with the Prince of Wales feathers. There were items bearing the cypher of King Edward VIII, made during his brief reign, including a rare set of silver-gilt match cases and a splendid gold memorandum case.

The Duchess had a more modest, but interesting, collection of her own, dating from the days before her marriage to the Duke and ranging from family heirlooms handed down from her grandmother, to gifts she had received on her marriage to Winfield Spencer. There were also wedding presents, such as the silver basket given by Winston Churchill, and mementoes

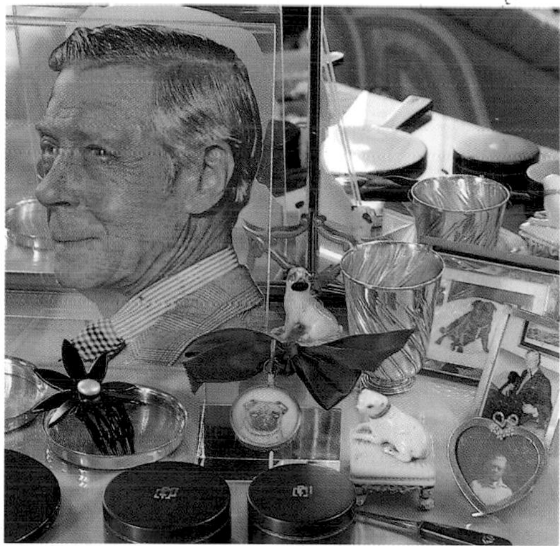

OPPOSITE: *The Duke's bed with its monogrammed bedspread was positioned beneath a tapestry woven with the arms of a Tudor Prince of Wales, just as it had been in his bedroom at Fort Belvedere.* LEFT: *The Duchess's Bedroom in her favourite 'Wallis' blue. Pugs in all forms are the leitmotiv of the Windsor Villa. The pets were treated like spoiled children, and were given the run of the house.* TOP: *A corner of the Duke's desk with his pipes and the cigar-case made for his grandfather, Edward VII.* ABOVE: *The Duchess's crowded dressing table. She cut the photograph of the Duke out of a magazine.* TOP LEFT: *An address book from the 1950s.*

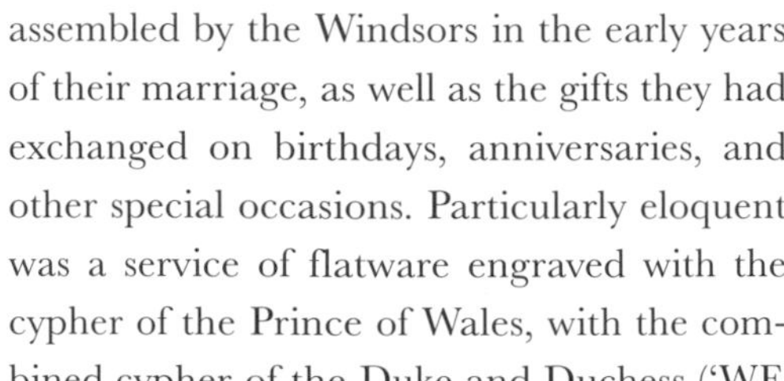

assembled by the Windsors in the early years of their marriage, as well as the gifts they had exchanged on birthdays, anniversaries, and other special occasions. Particularly eloquent was a service of flatware engraved with the cypher of the Prince of Wales, with the combined cypher of the Duke and Duchess ('WE') added later.

The Duchess was a leader of fashion on both sides of the Atlantic, a patron and friend of many of the great couturiers of her day, among them Christian Dior, Balenciaga, Yves Saint Laurent, Grès, Valentino and Givenchy. Her wardrobe kept pace with changing fashions. Some items dated back to the period before her marriage to the Duke, but most came from the colourful sixties and seventies, the last period when the Duchess was able to keep abreast of fashion. One of the most extraordinary experiences in visiting the Windsor Residence was to stand before the open wardrobes in the Duchess's Dressing Room, filled to overflowing with garments and accessories of every description.

The Duke too had been an influential figure in the history of fashion. He himself was fascinated by, and very knowledgeable about, the development of dress, and despite his reputation as an innovator, he had a conservative streak which grew stronger with the years. He seems seldom to have disposed of any item of dress, with the result that his wardrobe was quite outstandingly complete, extending back to the earliest years of his youth. Here were the midnight blue dinner suits; the buttons inscribed with the Duke's monogram; the ties specially lined to produce the famous 'Windsor knot'; the suits with coats made in London and trousers in New York. All had survived, untouched since the day the Duke had died. Alongside the items of civilian dress were others recalling the Duke's connections with the British Army:

TOP: *Repairing the ceiling in the Duchess's Dressing Room.* RIGHT: *The Duchess's Bathroom had been designed to resemble a fantastic tented pavilion. The decorative paintings by the theatrical designer Dimitri Bouchène are the dominant feature, but the gouache portrait above the bath was painted by Cecil Beaton in November 1936.* ABOVE: *The bathroom during restoration.* TOP RIGHT: *Always a Royal Prince, the Duke's cheques were printed with his cypher: the letter 'E' surmounted by a Royal coronet.*

badges, buttons, and other accessories representing all those regiments with which he had been associated as Prince of Wales, including his beloved Welsh Guards. Here too were the clothes he had worn while shooting, playing golf, and riding to hounds. A more varied and idiosyncratic wardrobe can hardly have been formed by any man this century.

Livery worn by the household staff had also survived. There was the black livery for day-wear in Paris, the grey livery used at the Moulin de la Tuilerie, and a third set of livery in scarlet worn on evenings when the Windsors entertained. All these uniforms were still hanging neatly in cupboards, accompanied by corresponding buttons in black, silver and gilt, each embossed with Duke of Windsor's arms.

Although not a bookish man, the Duke had assembled a fine library, with a bias to history, biography and politics. Housed in the Duke's bedroom and study, as well as in the Library on the ground floor, his books included many with handsome leather bindings bearing the Windsor cypher. There were also presentation volumes gathered on the Duke's tours as Prince of Wales and gifts from friends and admirers with dedications and inscriptions from leading figures in the world of politics, diplomacy and the arts, as well as members of the Duke's own family. Also represented were the books written by the Duke and Duchess, including the very first copy of the Duchess's memoirs, *The Heart Has Its Reasons*, inscribed with love to the Duke, and a complete collection of all the various editions of the Duke's autobiography, *A King's Story*, translated into more than a dozen languages.

TOP LEFT: *Three of the desk seals in the Windsors' collection: the Duchess of Windsor's gold and rock-crystal seal; a citrine seal with the cypher of King Edward VIII; and an enamelled silver seal of the Prince of Wales.* ABOVE: *The Hall closet contained the Duke's coats, hats, walking-sticks and golfing gear, left as they were at the time of his death.* LEFT: *Red lacquer* étagères *brought a splash of colour to the Duchess's dressing room. The Duchess was celebrated as a leader of fashion. Many colourful outfits in her wardrobes date from the sixties and seventies.* BELOW: *The orderly cupboards in the Duke's Dressing Room, showing the muted colours of his tweeds and rows of his special 'Windsor knot' ties.*

Most of the Duke's papers had been deposited in the Royal Archives at Windsor after his death, while other, more personal, letters and documents had been removed by the Duchess's lawyers, but certain of the Windsors' personal papers still remained. They included some love letters dating from their courtship, and an equally revealing group of Christmas and New Year Cards from various members of the British Royal Family. The collection ranged from the Letters Patent by which the former King was created Duke of Windsor, to driving licences, certificates and other personal documents, as well as scribbled notes and typescripts. A group of handwritten recipes had survived, together with menu cards recalling the exquisite dinners given by the Duchess. More poignantly, there was also a Buckingham Palace menu card from 1914 on which Queen Mary had jotted down the list of the Prince's brother officers in the Grenadier Guards who had lost their lives in the first bloody battles on the Western Front.

No less evocative were the programmes from concerts, plays, gala dinners and other entertainments, and a remarkable collection of newspaper cuttings from the British and American press dating back to the early part of the century, with extensive coverage of the foreign tours the Duke had made as Prince of Wales, as well as the dramatic events surrounding the Abdication.

The archive also contained a quantity of stationery which the Windsors had used at various times from houses in Paris and other residences, with the Duke and Duchess's various monograms, together with luggage tags, inventory labels, score sheets, playing cards, invitations and greeting cards, all in the unmistakable Windsor style.

Among these papers was a selection of rare recordings of speeches and interviews given at various times by the Duke, beginning with the broadcast he made on his Accession and includ-

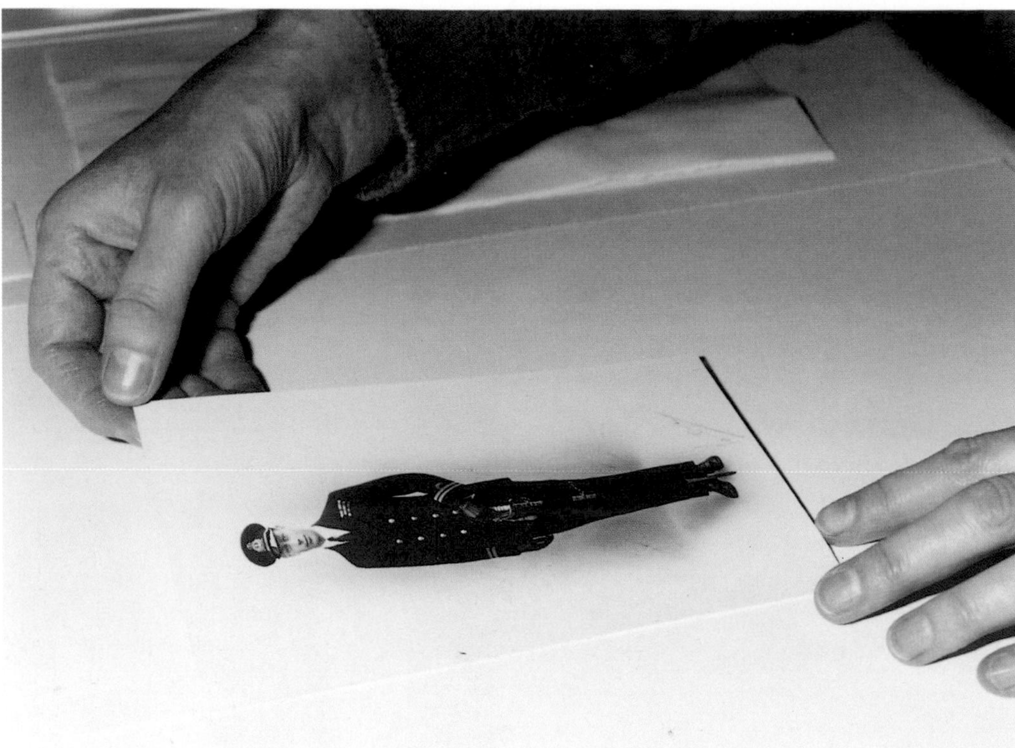

ABOVE: *All loose photographs were mounted on acid-free paper by the conservators.* LEFT: *There were also albums of newspaper cuttings requiring special attention. The albums shown here cover visits the Duke and Duchess made to the United States during their years in the Bahamas. Some of the other press cuttings in the collection are reproduced in the following chapters.*

ing his famous farewell speech to the empire. Musical recordings were a reminder of the the sort of light-hearted numbers which provided a characteristic background to the Windsors' celebrated parties.

Most remarkable of all was the collection of photographs, containing more than twelve thousand images, many of which had never before been published or seen outside the immediate circle of family and friends. These photographs, a selection of which is presented here for the first time, ranged in date from the mid-nineteenth century to the 1960s and 1970s, and covered virtually the whole of the Windsors' lives. Formal portraits were accompanied by intimate snapshots, many of them with personal inscriptions. The highlights include a unique group of photographs taken by the Duke himself during the First World War when he was serving in France, Italy and the Middle East, and a number of revealing photographs documenting the period the Duchess spent in China in the 1920s, as well as her early childhood in America. There was a sequence of snapshots taken on the notorious *Nahlin* cruise of 1936, and the couple's peregrinations in the aftermath of the Abdication. The collection also contained outstanding examples of the work of leading photographers such as Cecil Beaton, Dorothy Wilding, Horst and other major figures in the history of photography.

Under the direction of Mohamed Al Fayed, all these treasures were documented and restored. Through this book, and through television and video, the Windsor Residence and its riches have been given the broader public attention they deserve.

Mr Al Fayed also brought back to the house items that had been

1941
A PAPER FOR PEOPLE WHO THINK
With Crowd on Visit Here

he Duke and Duchess gave friendly and from trains. (Herald-American photo.)

SEP 28 1941
HERALD-AMERICAN

Duchess Calls Dress 'Refugee Rag'
BUT IT'S LATEST IN CITY

BY JANE MEYER.

Two views of the Duchess of Windsor, American-born bride of England's former king, as she appeared to throng that welcomed the distinguished visitors here.

THE CHICAGO DAILY NEWS
SEP 27 1941

EXTEND SMILING 'CHEERIO' TO CHICAGO

SEP 27 1941 The Duke and the Duchess of Windsor.

Thousands Greet Windsors; Brief Visit a 'Smash Hit'

BY GENE MORGAN.

Crowds Hail Windsors Here; Duke Tours Lake Front

CHICAGO DAILY NEWS SEPT. 27th.

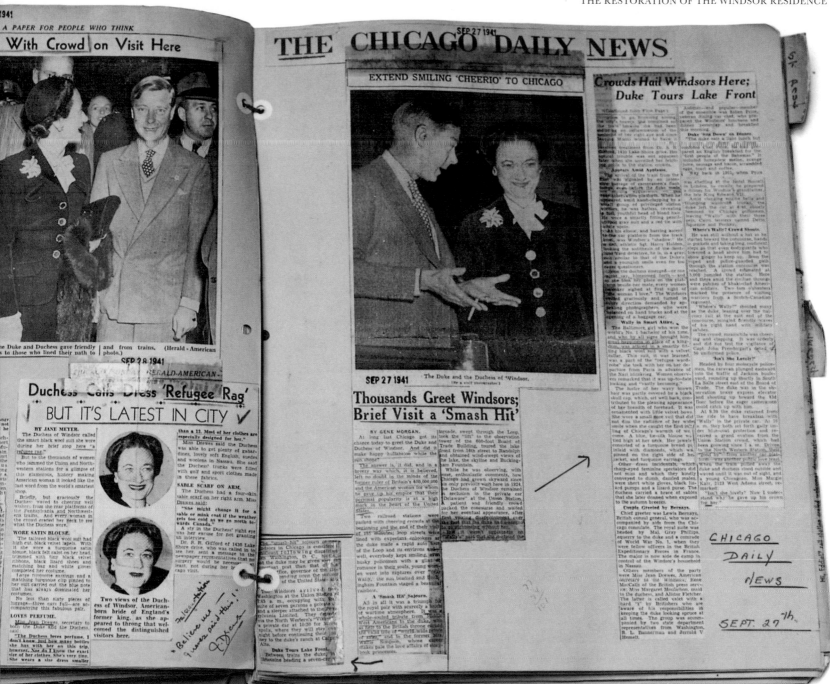

removed from the collection. When the Duchess's jewels were auctioned in Geneva, Mr Al Fayed was among the principal bidders and acquired a large number of pieces, subsequently reunited with the collection in Paris. They included a fascinating group of royal seals, some with the cypher of Edward VIII, and others that had belonged to Princes of Wales of the eighteenth and nineteenth centuries. Other items were acquired from former members of the Windsors' staff, and these too were reinstated.

The effect of all these riches can be overwhelming, yet the Windsor Residence is memorable above all for the modest yet illuminating tokens which seem to speak most eloquently of the Windsors' lives: a white satin box containing a piece of their wedding cake; a row of cushions in the Duchess's Bedroom modelled after her favourite pug-dogs; a rag doll by the Duke's bedside which he received as a child from his mother and which he took with him wherever he travelled. By taking care to preserve these objects of sentimental value, as well as the more spectacular treasures of the collection, Mr Al Fayed has made it possible to gain a deeper understanding of the personalities at the centre of a momentous love story.

The Miami Herald

Children's Hospital Goal Reached

Building Starts Today; Drive Workers Celebrate

MIAMI DAILY NEWS

To The Colonel

From

The Lieutenant Colonel

Dec 10th 1936.

PROLOGUE

WHY EDWARD WENT

ACME

ROMANTIC. *The Duke of Windsor, who gave up his throne for "the woman I love," is generally credited with the most romantic gesture of our time.*

There are some stories that will be told as long as history is related and the extraordinary drama of the Abdication in 1936 is one of them. It has been told in many different ways, with a variety of external influences colouring each account. On the surface the story is clear and straightforward. Britain had a King who had fallen in love with an American woman with two husbands living. At that time Britain and the Empire would not accept such a woman as Queen, and so the King went. Then come the questions. What were the King's real motives? Was he so abjectly in love that he could not face reigning without Wallis Simpson at his side? Did he want to be King at all? Or had he wanted to escape and found in the marriage issue a convenient bolt-hole? Was it perhaps the Government who wanted to rid Britain of their King for reasons quite unconnected with the marriage?

And what of Mrs Simpson? Was she a hard and scheming woman, bewitching Edward VIII with sorcery of various kinds? Did she want to be Queen? What did she think of the Abdication with the life-long implications that it held for her?

Though often told as a great love story, there is much about the Abdication that is terribly sad. The image of the much-loved King sailing away on a cold December night to an uncertain future, leaving behind him his vast and impressive inheritance, is a touching one. King Edward VIII, better known in his early life as the Prince of Wales, was a hugely popular figure. The people thought of him as a boyish figure, alert, smiling, slightly rakish, and a good contrast to the more austere, bearded figure of his father, King George V. He stayed up late, he danced, he rode to hounds, and risked his neck in point-to-points. He had emerged from the Great War with dignity, even honour, and embarked on an extensive programme of travel to the far corners of the British Empire.

His contact with his fellow soldiers had left him with a sympathy with the plight of the poor which none of his predecessors had reached. He liked informality and hated the aloofness that was expected of royalty. Nor did he like being thought of as a special person by virtue of his birth alone. Throughout his early life he had resented being treated differently from his contemporaries. He hated being kept from the front during the Great War, and he claimed not to have understood his father's constant imprecations: 'You must always remember who you are!' He often asked himself: 'But who was I?'

He had frequently spoken of his dread of becoming King, for he knew that his life would change and be more hemmed in by protocol. Even during his short reign in 1936, Edward VIII found that when he tried to throw open the windows to let in a bit of air, he was faced with frowning faces of disapproval.

Looking back, the Duke of Windsor was aware of the drawbacks of being a constitutional monarch. He explained in an article commissioned by the New York *Daily News* in 1966:

'Being a monarch, whether man or woman, in these egalitarian times can surely be one of the most frustrating and, over the duller stretches, the least stimulating jobs open to an educated, independent-minded person.

'Even a saint would on occasion find himself driven to exasperation by the taboos which invisibly and silently envelop

PREVIOUS PAGES, LEFT: *A troubled Prince: a portrait by Hugh Cecil in 1925.* BACKGROUND: *A loyal dedication written by a brother officer of the Welsh Guards in a book presented to Edward VIII on the day of his Abdication.* RIGHT: *The Duke of Windsor just before his wedding. Cecil Beaton's wedding photographs were flashed round the world.*
OPPOSITE: *Wallis Simpson's strained and unhappy face after she had fled from Britain during the Abdication crisis.* LEFT: *The public image: the Prince of Wales at the races.* ABOVE: *1916, Béthune. The 1914-18 War gave the Prince an opportunity to meet ordinary people for the first time. He claimed that in those four years he found his manhood.* TOP: *He felt a ready sympathy with the hardships of the working people in the twenties and thirties.*

The original Glamor Boy was Edward of Wales, now the Duke of Windsor. The Glamor Boys of today follow fairly closely in his steps as regards charm, humor, attractiveness. Since he became the Duke of Windsor and the husband of Wallis Simpson, Windsor has, of course, removed himself both physically and spiritually from the glamor group.

LEFT: *Queen Mary and George V were the embodiment of tradition and stability to their people. The old King was to die a few months after this photograph was taken in the autumn of 1935.* ABOVE: *The Prince of Wales with Mrs Simpson. In the public mind he was associated with the world of nightclubs and café society.*

OVERLEAF: *By the swimming pool at Fort Belvedere, the Prince of Wales's country retreat near Windsor. The Prince and Wallis are seated beside King George II of Greece (third left). At first, Wallis's husband, Ernest (right), was always one of the party.*

a Constitutional Monarchy. This is not meant in disrespect. It is only the way it looked to me from the inside.

'The Sovereign stands aloof from and above politics. He can, to be sure, be an extremely busy person. As Head of State, he consults with his Ministers, receives foreign ambassadors, interests himself in the Armed Forces, scans and signs an endless volume of state papers, holds investitures for honouring his subjects who have distinguished themselves in public service, gives audiences to all manner of people who presumably have something interesting to say that deserves the King's ear, opens Parliament, makes royal progresses to distant precincts of the Commonwealth, and one way or another, strives to give the impression of being interested in just about everything.

'Yet, day in day out, the King's or Queen's direct responsibility tends of necessity to be confined to fairly uncomplicated things.'[1]

The Duke had envisaged a new, modern sort of kingship. 'I tried to bring the monarchy into touch,' he told James Pope-Hennessy in 1958. 'Why, look at my grandfather [King Edward VII]. He'd just sit in an open landau, receive an address, snip a ribbon and declare something open, returning to Knowsley to dine with his girl friends. Didn't even leave the landau. I did my best to change all that.'[2]

From his first visit to the United States in 1919 the young Prince loved America, attracted by its freshness and freedom. He found life in America a marked contrast to the stuffy formality of his court life in England. It is significant that when he became King in 1936, the woman with whom he had been in love for some years was an American. Walter Monckton,

the astute lawyer who was his closest adviser during the Abdication crisis, was one of the best observers of the romance. He needed no convincing of the depth and intensity of the King's devotion to Mrs Simpson:'To him she was the perfect woman. She insisted that he should be at his best at all times, and he regarded her as his inspiration. It is a great mistake to assume that he was merely in love with her in the ordinary physical sense of the term. There was an intellectual companionship, and there is no doubt that his lonely nature found in her a spiritual comradeship. Many find any assertion of a religious side to the problem impossible to contemplate, but it was there. The King had the strongest standards which he set himself of right and wrong. They were often irritatingly unconventional. One sometimes felt that the God in whom he believed was a God who dealt him trumps all the time and put no inhibition on his main desires . . .'[3]

LEFT: *Wallis in 1938. The perfect woman? Edward VIII's admiration for Wallis Simpson knew no bounds: before their marriage and later, he showered her with gifts of extravagant jewellery to enhance the beauty he saw in her. He delighted in her conversation and her refreshing forthrightness; she became a sounding-board for his ideas and a standard for his behaviour.* ABOVE: *The King and Mrs Simpson, the* Nahlin *cruise, 1936.*

Such was the King's obsession that it seemed to him quite natural and right that he should be in love with another man's wife.

The King felt that he could not possibly take the Coronation Oath while the question of his marriage to Mrs Simpson was unresolved. When he discovered that the Government would not let him have his way by marrying the woman of his choice and remaining on the throne, he went, quietly, swiftly and without a backward glance. His loyalty to Mrs Simpson superseded anything he felt for anyone else. The British Empire, the Indian Empire, the realms and territories beyond the seas, the Royal Family, Queen Mary, the fate of his brother who succeeded him, and the lives of all those who died for King and country in the Great War were as nought compared to his devotion to this thin, elegant American woman, to whom he would remain slavishly devoted until his dying day.

Mrs Simpson was not a low-born American. She was a society girl from Baltimore with two unsuccessful marriages behind her and some sojourns in romantic places such as China, which gave her a cosmopolitan glamour and laid her open to suspicions of a life ill-spent. She arrived in Britain as the not especially interesting wife of Ernest Simpson but when she met the Prince of Wales, she knew how to treat him with exactly the right blend of gracious disdain to arouse his curiosity. As their relationship progressed, her confidence grew and she metamorphosed into a lady of fashion. As the Prince's favourite she received the homage of Society. The wisecracks became sharper, the wit quicker, and people testified that the room lit up when she entered it. She came to enjoy the luxury of the dinners and the weekends, the lavish presents of jewellery and flowers, the butlers who would arrive to help her entertain and the entrée the Prince gave her to a fascinating world peopled with men and women of style and achievement. At times she may have thought it possible, even rather exciting, to become the King's wife. It is almost certain that she was out of her depth, not at all understanding her position or the potential gravity of the situation and evidently assuming it would come to an end in due course. She did not have time to contemplate the issues — there was too much fun around her — and those who tried to raise them were invariably dismissed as bores.

It is unquestionable that Mrs Simpson loved being the Prince's friend, and in 1936 she

ABOVE: *Dapper, sprightly old age: the Duke and Duchess leaving a Paris restaurant in the late 1960s.* RIGHT: *The Duke and Duchess of Windsor were in the United States in the spring of 1970 to attend a dinner given in their honour by President Nixon. This photograph was taken in their suite at the Waldorf-Astoria, where they habitually stayed when in New York. The Duchess is wearing a dress by Givenchy, with her famous Cartier flamingo brooch.* BELOW: *Pottery figurines of the Duke and Duchess made in Czechoslovakia, late 1930s.*

enjoyed her role as the King's intimate confidante. Many people who knew her liked her for herself, though the British public, who only learned of her existence a week or so before the Abdication, gave her the cold shoulder from the first. There is plenty of evidence to suppose she was the person most horrified by the Abdication. As the gravity of the impending crisis became apparent, she did her best to extricate herself from the situation, but by then it was too late.

When she heard the ex-King's parting speech, she cowered under a rug in the Villa Lou Viei in Cannes and at the 'woman I love' sentence she fled from the room, crying: 'Did you hear what he said?'[4] Soon after the Abdication she wrote to Cecil Beaton, the photographer: 'I should like you to know and to believe me when I say I did everything in my power to prevent what I consider a great tragedy in many, many ways.'[5]

There were to be many disappointments for the Duke in the years after 1936. Not least of these was the running sore of exile from the country of his birth and especially the much-loved home he had made for himself at Fort Belvedere. Yet had the Duke of Windsor been woken at four o'clock in the morning, that hour when tired truths emerge despite themselves, and had he been asked: 'Do you love her?' he would always have said yes.

The Duchess's position was more complex. It is easy to appreciate her reluctance to become the wife of an exiled Duke of Windsor. She would never be admired for having made a grand romantic gesture. On the contrary, she was hated and blamed by many, and yet all her life she had to be gracefully grateful to her husband for his immense sacrifice. Her irritability with the Duke was well known. Yet accounts of their relationship suggest that, whilst their idle and aimless life, cut off from roots and family ties, may have left them dissatisfied with each other, there was a fondness, understanding and mutual dependence, built of time and familiarity. In a letter to the Duke after nearly twenty years of marriage, as she was leaving New York to join him, the Duchess wrote: 'Never will I be away from you so long again. Can't wait for Friday . . . I love you more and more . . . your Wallis.' And the Duke replied from France: 'It's been so long and lonely and it will be thrilling to have you back running the place again. I will even welcome getting into the line of your gunfire at breakfast time . . .'[6]

Thus the Duke and Duchess drifted together into dapper, sprightly old age, maintaining a certain *élan* and sparkle to impress the watching outside world, but with the Duchess gradually looking harder and more brittle, and the Duke looking sadder with his haunted spaniel eyes.

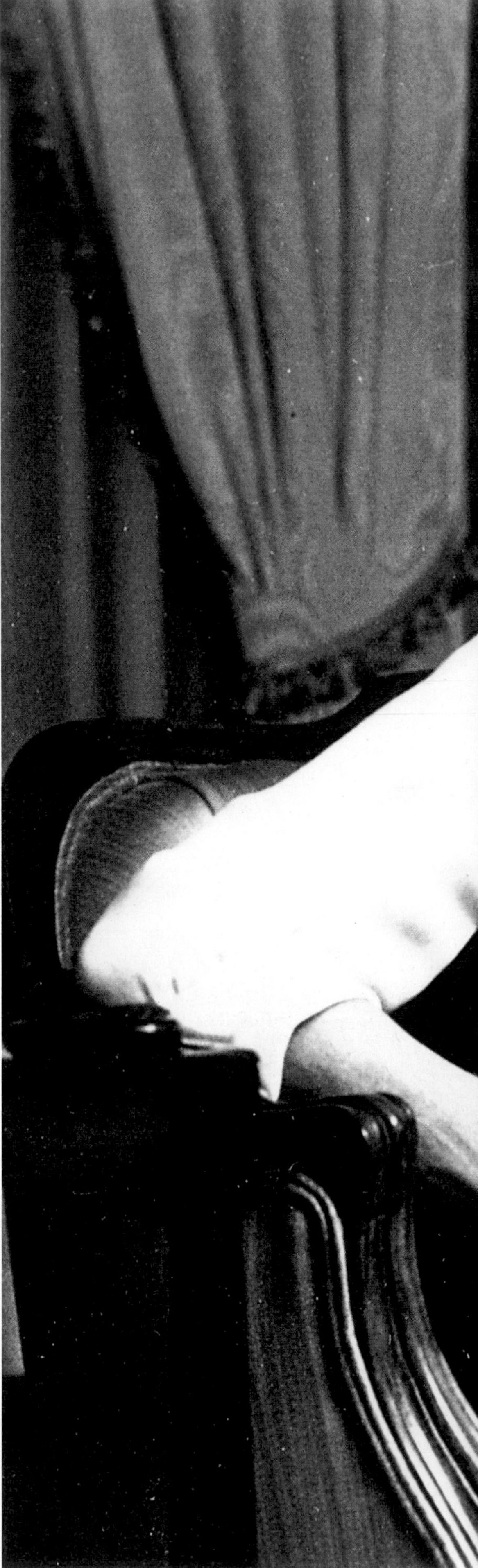

Photographers by Appointment to H.M. the

CHAPTER ONE

ROYAL FAMILY

PREVIOUS PAGES, LEFT: *Prince Edward of York with his great-grandmother, Queen Victoria ('Gangan').* BACKGROUND: *An inscription by Queen Victoria in a book she gave to Augusta, Duchess of Cambridge, another of Prince Edward's great-grandmothers.* RIGHT: *Prince Edward, July 1894, in the christening robes made for Queen Victoria's eldest child.*

THESE PAGES, RIGHT: *Prince Edward in the arms of his doting grandmother, Alexandra, Princess of Wales, 1895.* BELOW: *The extended Royal Family was the object of public fascination, as this crudely collaged picture postcard of about 1906 demonstrates. Prince Edward is second from the right in the front row.* OPPOSITE: *Three generations of kilted kings: Edward VII with his son, George V, and grandsons, Edward VIII and George VI, at Balmoral, 1902.*

OVERLEAF: *The young Prince Edward with his father's family, 1895; standing: The Duchess of Fife, the Prince of Wales (later Edward VII), the Duchess of York, Princess Maud and her husband, Prince Charles of Denmark; seated: The Duke of Fife, the Duke of York with Prince Edward, the Princess of Wales, and Princess Victoria.*

Prince Edward was born in the last decade of the Victorian era, just over a century ago, on 23 June 1894. He was the eldest great-grandson of the reigning monarch and first child of the Duke and Duchess of York, Prince George and the former Princess Victoria Mary of Teck. On the throne sat Queen Victoria, a magnificent matriarch, the mother of nine children, over forty grandchildren and a galaxy of great-grandchildren (a handful of those born around 1910 still survive today), widowed some thirty-two years, and soon to celebrate her Diamond Jubilee as sovereign.

Although the young Prince was nearly seven when Queen Victoria died, his memories of her were dim. He was taken to see her at Windsor, Balmoral and Osborne, the three residences she favoured during her long widowhood. He recalled her peregrinations to different parts of her estate, her journey undertaken in a low-slung carriage, and then by wheelchair, accompanied by a swarm of relations, ladies-in-waiting and Indian servants. 'What fascinated me most about "Gangan"', wrote the Duke of Windsor, 'was her habit of taking breakfast in little revolving huts mounted on turn-tables, so that they could be faced away from the wind.'[7] His maternal grandparents, the Duke and Duchess of Teck, he could not recall, as they died when he was very young. He was taken to see his other great-grandparents, King Christian IX and Queen Louise of Denmark, in 1898, but later remembered only the ferry-boats that conveyed the royal family across the Baltic to Copenhagen.

Prince Edward was too young when Queen Victoria died at Osborne in January 1901 to have any sense of the passing of an era. Instead he recalled the 'piercing cold, the interminable waits, and of feeling very lost among scores of sorrowing grown-up relatives — solemn Princes in varied uniforms and Princesses sobbing behind heavy crêpe veils.'[8]

7111 G
A ROYAL FAMILY PARTY.
ROTARY PHOTO. E.C.
BACK ROW: CROWN PRINCE OF SWEDEN. PRINCE ARTHUR OF CONNAUGHT. PRINCE ALEXANDER OF TECK WITH PRINCESS MAY, PRINCESS PATRICIA OF CONNAUGHT. DUKE OF CONNAUGHT. DUCHESS OF CONNAUGHT. PRINCE OF WALES. PRINCESS HENRY OF BATTENBERG. QUEEN OF SPAIN WITH INFANT JAIME, PRINCE ALEXANDER OF BATTENBERG. PRINCESS VICTORIA. PRINCE LEOPOLD OF BATTENBERG. PRINCE MAURICE OF BATTENBERG. (FRONT ROW) CROWN PRINCESS OF SWEDEN (PRINCESS MARGARET OF CONNAUGHT) WITH HER CHILDREN, PRINCESS OF WALES. PRINCESS ALEXANDER OF TECK WITH PRINCE RUPERT. QUEEN & KING OF NORWAY. PRINCE OLAF, QUEEN ALEXANDRA. KING EDWARD VII. PRINCE GEORGE. PRINCE JOHN. PRINCESS MARY OF WALES, KING OF SPAIN. INFANT HEIR, PRINCE HENRY OF WALES. PRINCE EDWARD OF WALES. PRINCE ALBERT OF WALES.

Victoria Mary
George. 1900. Edward

The Prince's parents departed soon after this for a prolonged tour of the Empire, leaving him (and his brothers and sister) in the care of his grandparents, King Edward VII and Queen Alexandra. The King was a story-book grandfather, large-tummied, bearded, genial, invariably puffing at a substantial cigar. He loved the boisterous antics of the young children and wallowed in their merriness with the same zest that he approached all forms of fun and entertaining. He sympathised with the children's dislike of their lessons, and did not hesitate to frustrate the attempts of their governess to return them to the schoolroom.

Of Edward VII, the Duke later wrote: '. . . the portrait of my grandfather seems bathed in perpetual sunlight. He was in his sixties, in the twilight of his life, when his personality began to mean something to me. Few men could match his vitality, his sheer *joie de vivre.* The Parisian term, *un bon boulevardier*, might have been invented for him. And while I can remember him, of course, as the regal figure of solemn ceremonies, I like best to recall him presiding over a well-laden table or making gallant gestures towards beautiful women.'[9]

Writing with hindsight, the Duke of Windsor wondered if his own reign might not have been rather like that of his grandfather, a king 'who enjoyed the society of witty men and beautiful women, who relished foreign travel and the savour of high diplomacy . . .'[10]

King Edward's death in 1910 was a matter of some sorrow for the young Prince. According to Lord Esher, the aide and confidant to several generations of royalty, King George, who now succeeded his father, came to the throne with the same sense of foreboding as most Princes of Wales experienced. He had dreaded the moment for some years, fearing he could not adequately fill his father's shoes.

The Prince came to know his elegant grandmother, Queen Alexandra, better in the long years of her widowhood. By his father's submissive generosity, Queen Alexandra remained in the 'Big House' at Sandringham until her death in 1925, and whenever he was at York Cottage, the Prince would walk over to see her. He admired her queenly dignity, her 'delicately-chiselled features, her high coiffure, and the grace of her manner', and loved her charm and genuine warmth of character.[11] She was a loving and indulgent grandmother, who believed only in happiness, universal and personal. In her vague and particularly feminine way, somewhat isolated from the general fray by her deafness, she allowed many of life's tiresome and difficult aspects to drift by unnoticed.

In his memoirs, the Duke of Windsor presented his father as a dour man of some severity, disapproving of his heir from an early age. His occasional arrival in the royal nursery was the cause for apprehension, as was a summons to his study, an austere room, very much the captain's cabin. The Duke saw his father as representing the values of both the Victorian and Edwardian eras. On the one hand, he had 'the Victorian's sense of probity, moral responsibility, and love of domesticity. He believed in God, in the invincibility of the Royal Navy, and the essential rightness of whatever was British.'[12] On the other hand this was tempered by more Edwardian tastes, a fondness for smart clothes, a love of sport in all forms: deer-stalking and fishing, the shooting of partridges and tigers. But the overall impression was of a man sternly dutiful and keenly punctual, who treated his children 'much as he regarded noisy midshipmen when he was captain of a cruiser — as young nuisances in constant need of correction.'[13]

In those early days, Queen Mary, then the Duchess of York, was a more sympathetic figure; only later did she come to represent an implacable force of duty in opposition to the

OPPOSITE: *Prince Edward with his parents, Osborne, 1900. The Duchess of York has signed formally with her full name 'Victoria Mary'; her son was always called David in the family. Osborne House on the Isle of Wight was a favourite residence of Queen Victoria. She died there on 22 January 1901.* ABOVE: *A Royal carriage passing by: The Princess of Wales (later Queen Alexandra), her daughter Princess Victoria, and Prince Edward of York returning from the Birthday Parade, around 1900.* LEFT: *Prince Edward cradling the infant Prince George, 1902.* BELOW: *'Mama', Princess May, Duchess of York, in 1897.*

Duke's wish for private happiness. Her aesthetic tastes set her apart from her husband's more philistine family. Such cultural interests as the Duke enjoyed were acquired at his mother's knee, during the hour she saved each night to rest in her boudoir. The children were called from the schoolroom at 6.30, and she read to them, while, for example, they crocheted woollen comforters for her charities.

Queen Mary's youth had not been easy. Princess May, as she was known, was the daughter of a marriage arranged by Queen Victoria between the impoverished Duke of Teck, himself the product of a morganatic union, and Princess Mary Adelaide, a grand-daughter of King George III. This much-loved Princess, with a warm heart in her ample bosom, was noted for her charitable works and her enormous girth (she was widely known as 'Fat Mary'). In their early married life the Tecks had been so short of money that they were obliged to leave London, spending the years between 1883 and 1885 in Florence to evade debt-collectors. It was here that the young Princess acquired her love of art, but she also learned the humiliation of being an exile and an impoverished outcast from the British Court. The vicissitudes of her early life made her venerate all the more the stability of the family into which she married.

As with her mother, it was Queen Victoria who ordained the life of Princess May. The old Queen decided that she would make a good Queen Consort and arranged a marriage between her and Prince Albert Victor, Duke of Clarence, the elder son of the Prince of Wales. The engagement was announced in December 1891. History was saved much trouble when her fiancé succumbed to violent influenza and died at Sandringham on 14 January 1892. Even at the time there were rumours about his dissolute behaviour and his sexual preferences, and he has since been the subject of lurid speculation. It is most likely, however, that he was merely rather dim.

QUEEN VICTORIA RECORDED IN HER DIARY THAT THE MONTH-OLD PRINCE EDWARD OF YORK WAS WELL BEHAVED DURING HIS CHRISTENING. HE WAS GIVEN THE NAMES EDWARD ALBERT CHRISTIAN GEORGE ANDREW PATRICK DAVID. ALL VICTORIA'S DESCENDANTS WERE NAMED AFTER HER LAMENTED HUSBAND, PRINCE ALBERT. EDWARD WAS FOR HIS PATERNAL GRANDFATHER AND CHRISTIAN FOR HIS ROYAL DANISH GRANDFATHER WHO WAS ALSO ONE OF THE TWELVE GODPARENTS. THE OTHER NAMES REPRESENTED THE PATRON SAINTS OF THE BRITISH ISLES. THE CUP AND SAUCER WERE A GIFT ON THAT OCCASION FROM HIS GREAT UNCLE AND GODFATHER, GEORGE, DUKE OF CAMBRIDGE.

BOTTOM: *Edward VII entertaining Czar Nicholas II and his family at Cowes in 1909. The striking physical resemblance between the Czar (seated, second left) and his cousin, the future George V (seated, second right), was often remarked. The young Prince Edward (right) was amazed at the strict security cordon which surrounded the Russian Imperial Family during the visit.*

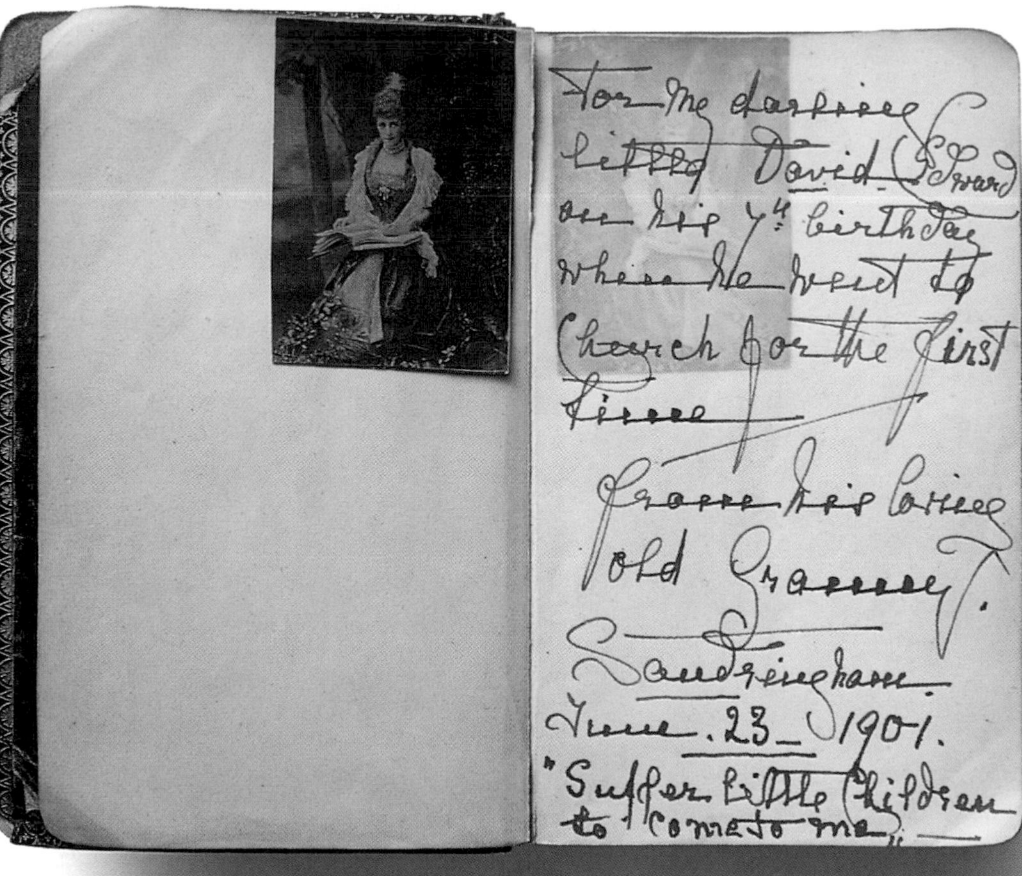

TOP LEFT: *A stern papa, a Christmas card from the Duke of York to his eldest son in 1899.* ABOVE: *'Loving old Granny', an inscription and photograph in a prayer book given to the Prince by Queen Alexandra for his birthday in 1907.* BOTTOM LEFT AND RIGHT: *Maternal grandparents, the warm-hearted Princess Mary Adelaide, Duchess of Teck, and the Duke of Teck. Both died before Prince Edward had a chance to know them.*

After a suitable period of mourning, Princess May was married to her fiancé's younger brother, Prince George, Duke of York, again with Queen Victoria's blessing. To modern eyes this replacing of one partner by another seems cold and calculating. But perhaps fate had been kind to her and there was genuine affection in the second betrothal. When James Pope-Hennessy, Queen Mary's biographer, visited Sandringham in the 1950s, the daughter of the Duke of Clarence's doctor told him that 'it was quite obvious that Princess May and Prince George were falling in love; when attending the Duke of Clarence in his bedroom that fatal time, he could see, out of the window, Princess May and Prince George pacing the gardens hand in hand.'[14] However, the Duke of Windsor doubted that his mother had ever been in love.[15]

Prince Edward was surrounded by a host of royal relations. Of the elderly sons and daughters of Queen Victoria, the Prince was particularly fond of his great-uncle Arthur, the Duke of Connaught, a 'revered figure' of his childhood: 'No other person of Royal birth that I have ever encountered seemed to blend in his own character such a tolerant understanding of human nature combined with a rigid sense of duty.'[16] Then there were his three paternal aunts. In later life, the Duke of Windsor said: 'Of my aunts, my father's sisters, you might say they could just read and write.' The eldest aunt was Princess Louise, Duchess of Fife, dismissed by Pope-Hennessy with the words: 'Her hold on reality was, like her health, imperfect.' Next came Princess Victoria, dubbed 'a bitch of the first order' by her nephew.[17] When they were grown up, 'the Snipe' (another nickname) never hesitated to report to the King any indiscretion she discovered.[18] The aunt he found the warmest was Maud, later Queen of Norway, whose health was also weak. She suffered from 'nagging neural-

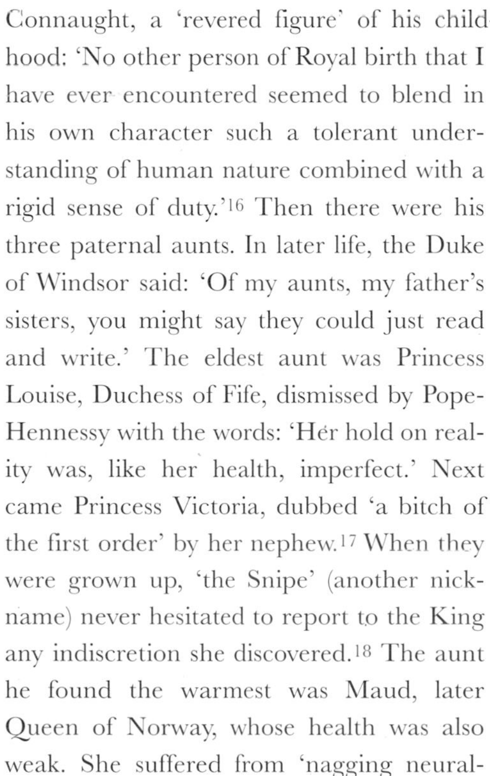

gia', disliked her adopted country, Norway, and spent most winters at her home, Appleton House, near Sandringham.

Casting the net wider, the Royal Family spread through cousins to every Royal House of Europe. In the course of his childhood the Prince met most of the crowned heads. In 1909 he met Czar Nicholas II of Russia, his godfather, for the only time. The young Prince was horrified at the great formality and considerable security that surrounded the Czar, who was almost the twin in looks to George V. The German Kaiser was a more familiar figure at the British court, making, from time to time, one of his 'spectacular descents on our little island'.[19] The Prince's clearest memories of him were fixed during a visit to the Königliches Schloss in Berlin, where the Kaiser sat astride a saddle at his desk, and appeared in a variety of glittering uniforms.

The Duke of Windsor's main playmates as a child were his brothers and sister, especially the older two, Prince Albert (Bertie), later Duke of York and George VI, born in 1895, and Princess Mary, later Countess of Harewood and Princess Royal, born in 1897. They began life sharing a bedroom with a nurse. Bertie joined his elder brother at the naval colleges of Osborne and Dartmouth and for many years they were close. The elder brother protected Bertie during the rigours of early naval training and in 1913, wrote of his departure: 'We have been so much together of late and I shall miss him terribly.'[20] He was always concerned for Mary too, feeling that she led a particularly restricted life at Buckingham Palace, and going to considerable lengths to encourage her to have more friends, and later to find her a suitable husband. (He did not approve of her even-

PRINCE EDWARD HAD BECOME ACQUAINTED WITH THE LONG AND ELABORATE CORONATION CEREMONY AT AN EARLY AGE. IN 1902 HE HAD BEEN PRESENT IN WESTMINSTER ABBEY WHEN HIS GRANDFATHER, EDWARD VII, WAS CROWNED. AS PRINCE OF WALES, WEARING THE ROBES OF THE ORDER OF THE GARTER, HE HAD PLAYED A SIGNIFICANT PART IN HIS FATHER'S CORONATION IN 1911. GEORGE V HAD BEEN MUCH MOVED WHEN HIS SON KNELT TO DO HOMAGE TO HIM. THE PRINCE KEPT AS MEMENTOES THE EMBROIDERED BADGES WORN BY HIS PAGES AT BOTH CORONATIONS. THE BADGE WORN BY LORD ASHLEY IN 1911 COMPRISED THE PRINCE OF WALES FEATHERS COUPLED WITH THE WELSH DRAGON. THIS UNUSUAL DESIGN REFLECTED A NEW EMPHASIS ON THE WELSH DIMENSION OF THE PRINCE'S ROLE, WHICH WAS UNDERLINED AT THE INVESTITURE CEREMONY AT CAERNARVON A FEW WEEKS LATER.

BELOW LEFT: *Queen Marie of Roumania (known in the family as 'Missie') had been the object of some affection from her cousin George V, before his marriage. A signed photograph of the Queen with her daughter Princess Ileana, 1919.* BELOW RIGHT: *Prince Edward with his younger brother Prince Albert (Bertie), Sandringham, 1903. They often played football with the village school.* OPPOSITE: *The three eldest children: Prince Edward and Prince Albert, with their sister, Princess Mary, in 1901.*

For David
from
Ileana
Missie
1919

tual choice, probably because her husband was so much older than she.)

The first three were followed by Prince Henry in 1900, Prince George in 1902, and in 1905 by Prince John. The Duke was never particularly close to Prince Henry, while Prince George became his favourite brother and ally in their adult years and they often travelled together. The youngest boy, Prince John, though he looks strong enough in photographs, suffered badly from epilepsy from early in his life. 'For this and other reasons',[21] he was kept apart from his family, living quietly at Wood Farm, Sandringham. In 1919, Prince John began to lose 'his frail grasp on reason' and died.[22] Queen Mary wrote of the 'great release' of his death, of his 'restless soul' and his 'poor little troubled spirit'.[23]

These then were the characters of the Duke of Windsor's childhood. Born to a life of royal service, his relations accepted their lot with equanimity. This was an epoch in which the hierarchy of class and the concept of duty went largely unchallenged. Members of the Royal Family were no less fallible then than they are now, but they were able to live out their private dramas without the scrutiny of the media. Personal happiness was not something they were brought up to aspire to or expect, the rules of conduct were strict and they accepted them.

The Duke of Windsor was to be one of the first to break free of this code and in so doing he lost the respect of his entire family. He believed in the mating of souls and felt that having found Wallis Simpson, his perfect woman, he should be allowed to share his life with her. He was aware that he was breaking certain well established rules, but he hoped that the goodness of her character, as he saw it, was such that these rules could be laid aside, and that his family would accept her. But his family could not understand this and as near as said he had gone mad.

He went his own way, but he never really broke free of the royal reins. Towards the end of his life, on one of his visits to Windsor, he spoke to the ghost-writers who hoped to collaborate with him on a projected book about his childhood. Viewing the past with what they called 'the prism of the independence which he had acquired at such painful cost', he found the curious priorities and foibles of his family, with all the 'inner turmoil along with their surface calm' both appealing and endearing. They were surprised how fascinated he was by everything royal around him.[24]

Even so, he declared: 'I had a *wretched* childhood! Of course, there were short periods of happiness but I remember it chiefly for the miserableness I had to keep to myself.'[25]

OPPOSITE: *Queen Alexandra with four of her grandchildren, Balmoral, 1904. The baby in her arms is Prince George; standing between Prince Edward and Princess Mary is Prince Henry.* ABOVE: *A 'revered figure' of prince Edward's childhood, his great-uncle, Prince Arthur, Duke of Connaught, photographed in 1920 in Grenadier Guards uniform.* LEFT: *Princess Mary, aged sixteen, with her whippet, Mosca, May 1913. Her elder brother thought his sister's life at Buckingham Palace was cruelly restricted.* BELOW: *Their youngest brother, the unfortunate Prince John. As his epileptic fits worsened, John was kept in seclusion at Sandringham. He died in January 1919, not long after this photograph was taken.*

For darling David
from his loving

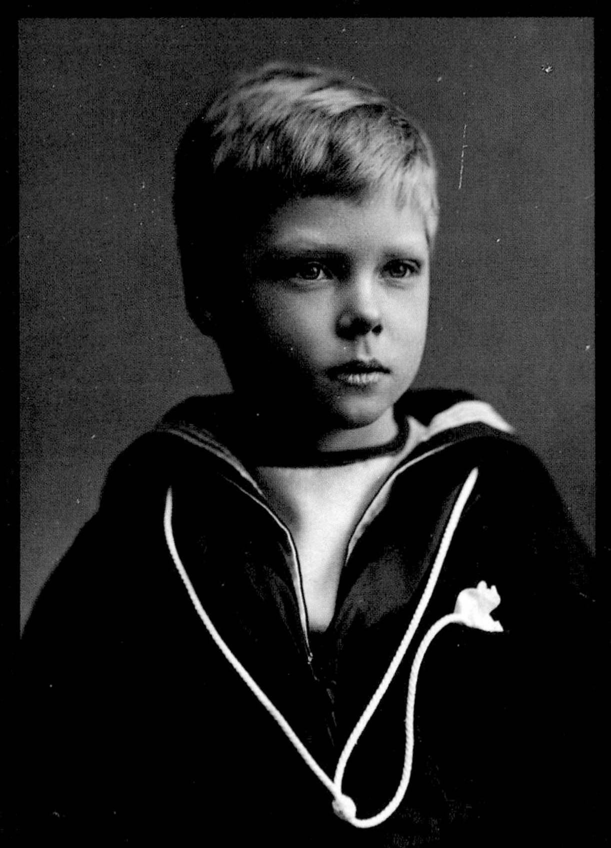

Mama

June 23d 1904.

CHAPTER TWO

MOULDING OF A PRINCE

PREVIOUS PAGES, LEFT: *Prince Edward of Wales 1901.* BACKGROUND: *An inscription in a book from his mother for his tenth birthday.* RIGHT: *One of the Royal desk seals which George V presented to his eldest son when he created him Prince of Wales.* THESE PAGES, RIGHT: *Boating trips on the Thames were part of the Prince's childhood.* BOTTOM: *A typical shooting party at Sandringham, 1908. Edward VII surrounded by family and friends. Mrs Keppel, the King's favourite mistress, is seated far right. At the other end of the row is Princess Victoria, with Prince Albert and Prince Edward.*

The Duke's 'wretched childhood' was spent largely at Sandringham, the Norfolk estate of King Edward VII. In those early days it took a three-hour train journey and then a three-mile drive in horse-drawn carriage to reach the house from London. The 'Big House', an imposing red-brick edifice, had been the domain of King Edward and Queen Alexandra since 1863. It was usually alive with guests from the echelons of smart society, intermingled with distinguished ambassadors and delegates from foreign lands, enjoying the grand dinner parties, bright conversation, shooting lunches and excursions to the racing stud.

But the Duke of York and his young family lived in another property on the estate, 'the glum little villa' called York Cottage, an unexpectedly modest residence for the heir to the throne and his growing family. Queen Mary's biographer, who visited it in 1956, described it as 'grotesquely ugly, unarchitected . . . all gables, and beams and little balconies, and hexagonal turrets.' It stood, he observed, 'on the rim of a melancholy, reed-infested pond.'[26]

In London the family lived at York House, St. James's Palace, a warren of rooms in that ancient palace, and then, in 1901, they moved next door to Marlborough House, their home until 1910. The young Prince was naturally a frequent visitor to Windsor Castle, one of the widowhood retreats of Queen Victoria. Revisiting the castle in the late 1950s, the Duke mused that the style of the monarchy had changed: 'There is one place, however, which changes hardly at all, and that is Windsor Castle. Here is a palace essentially English in character,

SADLY, THIS GIFT OF A SILVER TANKARD BY HIS GRANDPARENTS TO PRINCE EDWARD ON THE OCCASION OF HIS CONFIRMATION WAS PRESENTED BY QUEEN ALEXANDRA ALONE. EDWARD VII HAD DIED A MONTH BEFORE. QUEEN ALEXANDRA, ALTHOUGH IN DEEP MOURNING, MADE HER FIRST PUBLIC APPEARANCE AT THE PRIVATE CHAPEL IN WINDSOR FOR THE PRINCE'S CONFIRMATION SERVICE IN 1910. THE YOUNG EDWARD EXPLICITLY MODELLED HIMSELF ON HIS GOOD-LIVING BUT SHREWD GRANDFATHER AND NAMESAKE. TOGETHER WITH HIS GRANDMOTHER, ALEXANDRA, A WARM AND LOVING PRESENCE, THEY PROVIDED A WELCOME CONTRAST TO HIS SEVERE AND UNDEMONSTRATIVE PARENTS.

because it is lived in; so much more personal in its atmosphere, for all its bulk, than the Château de Versailles and other continental palaces, for all their past glories and classical splendours. I take pleasure in the way it broods, with an air of comfortable benevolence, down over the homely town of Windsor, while to the South spreads the spacious Great Park, with the Long Walk stretching three miles through the soft green English landscape and the meadows of the Home Park to the south, refreshed by the waters of the slowly winding Thames.'[27]

Interestingly, he chose not to live in the Castle during his brief reign, preferring the intimacy and relative freedom of his own creation, Fort Belvedere, at nearby Sunningdale. Buckingham Palace was a residence that held little appeal for him. He spent part of his youth there, until he moved to his own rooms at St James's Palace. He only moved back there as King in October 1936, making use of it until his Abdication in December of that year.

ABOVE: *Prince Edward (third right) in costume as one of the chorus of 'sisters, cousins and aunts' in a production of* HMS Pinafore *at the Royal Naval College, Dartmouth, November 1909.* BELOW: *At the wheel of a car outside the 'grotesquely ugly' York Cottage, Sandringham, around 1911. His tutor, Henry Hansell (wearing a flat cap), is seated behind him. This unpretentious villa on the Sandringham estate, was the Prince's main childhood home.*

The Royal Family retreated annually to Balmoral, the Gothic castle in Scotland, where they remained secluded during the summer months. When in Scotland, the Yorks lived at Abergeldie Castle, a small, rather upright little fourteenth-century castle a few minutes drive from the Balmoral estate (on the road to Birkhall). Queen Mary was not enthusiastic about Scotland. Very often the fruit in the walled garden never ripened, the flowers never seemed to be in season when the Yorks were there, and the weather veered more to pelting rain than to sunshine.

Their Scottish life afforded the Yorks the most protection from the public eye, though this was an age when their public engagements were not as widely covered by the press as they would be today. For the grown-ups life at Balmoral was a mixture of deer-stalking and grouse-shooting, picnics and expeditions. King George V became an

even better shot than his father. It was at Balmoral on 28 August 1922, shooting with eight others, that he bagged 1,178 grouse, 4 black game, 14 hares, one rabbit and a snipe, beating all previous records on a perfect day.[28]

A succession of nannies, governesses and tutors peopled the early world of the York children, including the much loved Charlotte 'Lala' Bill and the Alsatian governess, Mlle Helen Bricka. Frederick Finch was an important figure in their lives. He became their nursery footman after three years in their father's service. He graduated from 'nanny', to valet and finally to the Prince of Wales's first butler. Finch joined up as soldier-servant to the Prince at the beginning of the First World War. This continuity of service was important to his young master.

ABOVE: *Princes Albert, Henry and Edward being drilled by the footman, Findlay Cameron, Abergeldie Castle, 1903. Their French tutor, Gabriel Hua, stands in the doorway behind.* TOP: *In January 1909, Prince Edward (seated, right) was joined at the Royal Naval College, Osborne, by his younger brother, Prince Albert (seated, left). This photograph was taken not long after Bertie's arrival; Mr Hansell, the Princes' tutor, is seated next to the apprehensive new cadet.* RIGHT: *Charlotte 'Lala' Bill, with the nursery footman, Frederick Finch, outside Abergeldie Castle, 1917. Finch was to become the Prince's valet.* OPPOSITE: *Prince Edward with Captain Henry Campbell at the start of a three-month training tour in the battleship HMS* Hindustan, *October 1911.* OVERLEAF: *Shooting near Balmoral with stalker, C. Mackintosh, September 1910.*

Lord Esher noted that the young Prince Edward was charming, dignified and clever. 'His memory is remarkable — a family tradition,' he wrote in 1906, 'but the look of *Weltschmerz* in his eyes I cannot trace to any ancestor of the House of Hanover.'[29] Esher was not greatly impressed by the Prince's new tutor, Henry Hansell, a Norfolk-born schoolmaster and sportsman, who introduced a methodical if unimaginative routine to the private class room. As the boys were not to be sent to preparatory school, Hansell recreated a school atmosphere within the home, complete with blackboards and desks. French lessons were consigned to the black-bearded Gabriel Hua, who had done his best to teach French to the Prince's father, while German was taught by the wizened Professor Eugen Oswald.

In contrast to the dull discipline of the schoolroom, there were two kilted Scottish retainers, Forsyth and Cameron, who marshalled the youngsters into a squad from time to time, marched them about and taught them how to salute the Colour. They loved it.

It is doubtful whether the standard of the Prince's education would have secured him the place at the Royal Naval College, Osborne, for which his father had destined him. But in 1907 he went before the selection committee, who reported favourably, underwent the written examination, where he fared less well, but was given the benefit of the doubt, and became Cadet Prince Edward.

It was the first time he had left home, and tears duly coursed down his youthful cheeks. He was not yet thirteen. His father told him bracing naval tales on their way down to Osborne from London, and then admonished him: 'Now that you are leaving home, David, and going out into the world, always remember that I am your best friend.'[30] It is unlikely that the young Prince had much faith in the understanding of his tough father.

Life at Osborne was grim, according to the Duke of Windsor's later recollection. As the rather over-protected son of a royal house, he was teased and bullied by his contemporaries. Once they poured red ink on his

ABOVE: *The six children of George V and Queen Mary, 1916; back row: Prince Albert, the Prince of Wales, Prince Henry; front row: Prince John, Princess Mary, Prince George.* RIGHT: *Beagling near Oxford, 1912. The Prince's boundless energy found an outlet in strenuous sports.* BELOW: *Visiting the Schneider family's armaments factory, during his educational visit to France, June 1912.*

hair so that he was forced to miss 'quarters,' or evening parade. Another time they pushed his head out of the window and rammed the window down on his neck in mock execution. The college regime was austere. Waking in the morning was done to a series of gongs, which summoned the boys from bed to prayers and into a freezing shower. But in this harsh world he did adequately well, and Lord Esher noted that he lost his shyness and learned good manners.

Prince Edward was joined at Osborne by his next brother, Prince Albert, in 1909, but soon afterwards he progressed to the senior establishment, the Royal Naval College, Dartmouth. Although life here was more dignified, there were still petty persecutions. Exams remained a problem, but the young prince gained confidence and made some friends. Dartmouth also afforded some chance for him to expend his prodigious energy in boating, swimming and amateur theatricals. When on leave he rode, hunted and enjoyed other traditional sports.

In 1910, Queen Mary complained to Esher that her sixteen-year-old son was childish and backward in his learning.[31] She left discipline to her husband and did not intervene much between father and son. She found that if she did, her son resented it. The boy, previously terrified of his father, now seems to have had something of a change of heart declaring: 'You know, I think Father now is quite a nice man.'

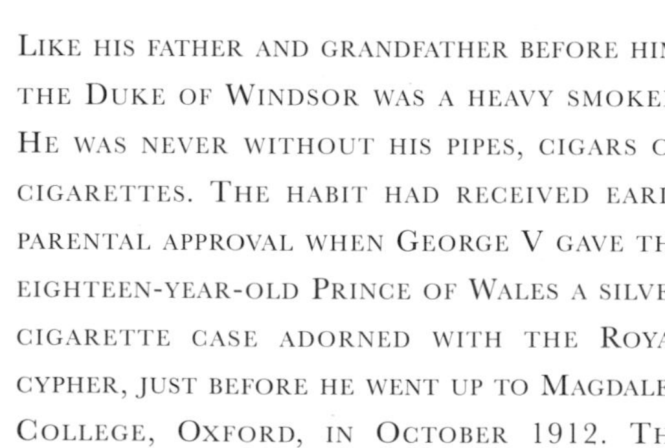

LIKE HIS FATHER AND GRANDFATHER BEFORE HIM, THE DUKE OF WINDSOR WAS A HEAVY SMOKER. HE WAS NEVER WITHOUT HIS PIPES, CIGARS OR CIGARETTES. THE HABIT HAD RECEIVED EARLY PARENTAL APPROVAL WHEN GEORGE V GAVE THE EIGHTEEN-YEAR-OLD PRINCE OF WALES A SILVER CIGARETTE CASE ADORNED WITH THE ROYAL CYPHER, JUST BEFORE HE WENT UP TO MAGDALEN COLLEGE, OXFORD, IN OCTOBER 1912. THE DUCHESS DISAPPROVED OF SMOKING, BUT THIS WAS ONE OF THE FEW AREAS IN WHICH HER ADVICE WENT UNHEEDED. THE DUKE CONTINUED TO USE THE CIGARETTE CASE THROUGHOUT HIS LIFE, IN LATER YEARS KEEPING IT IN THE POCKET OF THE TARTAN SUITS HE WORE AT THE MILL.

After four years of naval training, it was the natural ambition of all cadets to go to sea, but George V had other plans. Because of the impending Coronation the Prince had to forego the opportunity to train in North American waters and was plunged into his royal role as heir to the throne. Becoming Duke of Cornwall in 1910, he was swiftly created Prince of Wales. He was installed as a Knight of the Garter and took part in the his father's Coronation on 23 June 1911, wearing the Garter robes. The ancient Coronation ceremonial was followed a month later by the mock-medieval splendour of his Investiture as Prince of Wales in Caernarvon Castle. The Welsh politician David Lloyd George had recognised the merits of devising such a ceremony, particularly for the people of the Principality.

After this the Prince was given dispensation to serve for three months aboard the battleship *Hindustan*, around the South Coast ports, before being summoned to Sandringham, where his father outlined his future. He was to attend university with foreign excursions in the holidays. Lord Esher had the chance to have a long talk to him in September 1912, and found the Prince preoccupied with the Navy, to which he had become devoted. Esher told him that no Prince of Wales could have 'the advantage of his birthright without the disadvantages of a hampered youth.' To which the Prince replied: 'More of the latter than the former.'[32] That summer the Prince spent four months travelling in France where he learned French haphazardly, remaining reluctant to speak it in later life.

In October 1912, the Prince went up to Magdalen College, Oxford, somewhat unwillingly, still wishing that he could be back in the Navy. It was intended that he be treated as any other undergraduate, but he was assigned remote rooms, with his own bathroom, and was insulated from undergraduate life by the presence of Hansell and his equerry, William Cadogan, a gallant soldier, whose main job appeared to be to encourage the Prince to hunt.

A naval training was not in any case the best introduction to Oxford, where undergraduate life was shaped by cliques formed at public schools. Shyness was still a problem, but he did his best to circulate and made a life-long friend in Lord Ednam (later the Earl of Dudley). Academic life was largely secondary to sporting endeavours, which included riding, squash, runs, golf, football, and there were his excursions with the Officers' Training Corps. He enjoyed his tutorials on Constitutional Law with Sir William Anson, but was not a good attender of lectures, nor did he profit greatly from the many opportunities that Oxford presented.

ABOVE: *Life in the Highlands. Queen Mary with her children walking near Abergeldie, 1912.* BELOW: *A pipe-smoking Prince of Wales with his three brothers, wading in Loch Muick, 1913.*

OVERLEAF: *The undergraduates of Magdalen College, Oxford, June 1912. The Prince is unobtrusively positioned at the back, by the arch on the left.*

Throughout his college days there lurked the resentment that he was not serving in the Royal Navy.

Probably the most stimulating diversions in these years were his visits to Germany. The Prince stayed with one of his twelve godparents, the King of Württemberg, and with his cousin, Charles, Duke of Saxe-Coburg, who was also a godfather. He then went on to Berlin where he was given a taste of night-life by Godfrey Thomas, at that time an attaché at the British Embassy and later one of his Private Secretaries. From these visits the Prince acquired a love of the German language, which he spoke with pleasure in later life. However, his biographer, Philip Ziegler, finds no evidence that he developed any great attachment to the Germans as a race.[33]

LEFT: *The Prince of Wales's study at Buckingham Palace, 1914. On his desk are framed photographs of relatives and friends.* ABOVE: *With his brothers and sister, on horseback in Windsor Great Park, 1916.* BELOW: *A short spell with the Life Guards at Knightsbridge Barracks, London, in the summer of 1914 was intended to improve the Prince's horsemanship. The group includes Lord Althorp, the grandfather of Lady Diana Spencer.*

Because of the outbreak of war, the Prince did not return to Oxford for a third year, and came down from the University without a degree. In April he had managed to join Prince Albert on a ten-day cruise on HMS *Collingwood*, the battleship on which Bertie was serving. The pre-war summer was given over to balls, at which the Prince danced with fervour, combined with some training in horsemanship with the Life Guards. On 6 August, two days after war was declared, his father agreed to his eager request for a commission in the Grenadier Guards.

1914 was the year that changed him from boy to man. Photographs of the Prince in January 1914 show a strikingly youthful figure, but by December he had matured greatly, having endured many harrowing experiences, not least the loss of family and friends, killed in the Great War.

CHAPTER THREE

WORLD WAR ONE

PREVIOUS PAGES, LEFT: *Prince of Wales, Italy, 1918.* BACKGROUND: *His signature, 'Edward P'.* RIGHT: *On the Commander-in-Chief's houseboat, Suez Canal, 1916.* BELOW: *Leading his company of the 1st Battalion Grenadier Guards, 1914.* BOTTOM: *At Tramecourt, July 1917, when the King and Queen visited the front.* OPPOSITE: *A visit to the Italian Army, May 1916.* OVERLEAF: *The Prince watching the departure of King George on SS* Invicta, *Calais, 15 August 1916.*

The Prince of Wales underwent a two-week training course at Warley Barracks in Brentwood. Though he longed to go to the front, Lord Kitchener was unwilling to let him risk his life, thus his more public military duties were confined to the changing of the guard and leading his regiment through London as Ensign to the Colour. The Prince realised he was being held back and protected, and not being treated like any other officer of his generation. In a celebrated exchange with Kitchener, he asked: 'What does it matter if I am killed. I have four brothers.' To which the Field Marshal replied: 'If I were sure you would be killed, I do not know if I should be right to restrain you. But I cannot take the chance, which always exists until we have a settled line, of the enemy taking you prisoner.'[34]

From one point of view, the Prince's bravery in wanting to serve like any man of his generation was admirable. But equally it was quite unthinkable that his life should be put at risk. By putting pressure on the authorities, he was demonstrating the stubborn wilfulness that would become more evident with the passing of the years.

Casualties among British officers in the early months of the war were appalling. In October the Prince's cousin, Prince Maurice of Battenberg, had died of wounds acquired at Mons, and in November his Oxford equerry, Major Cadogan, was killed near Ypres serving with the 10th Hussars.

The Prince of Wales was at last allowed to cross to France in November to serve at the front as ADC to Field Marshal Sir John French, then commanding the British Expeditionary Force at St Omer.[35] Even so he rarely got near the action. Yet there was much he

ABOVE LEFT: *Primarily engaged in paperwork: the Prince at his desk at XIV Army Corps Headquarters, Poperinghe, France, in 1916.* ABOVE RIGHT: *The Prince with King Victor Emmanuel of Italy (second right) near Udine on a visit to the Italian front, May 1916.* BOTTOM RIGHT: *Enjoying a cigarette on top of the Great Pyramid at Giza, April 1916. The Prince visited Cairo on his way to the military headquarters at Ismailia.*

could do in the way of hospital visiting, where his genuine concern was deeply appreciated by the wounded. Indeed this was probably his most important contribution, as he did it so well. As a liaison officer, he also became a familiar figure speeding along the lanes on his bicycle.

Presently he succeeded in obtaining a posting to the staff of Major-General Lord Cavan, commanding the Guards Division, where he saw and photographed some of the activities on the Divisional front-line sector near Loos in the summer of 1915. At last he was able to observe at first hand the plans of attack and get some feel for what the men were going through.

Later the King came out to the Front and his son was naturally asked to be with him. He was shaken by the King's grave accident during a military inspection on this visit. When the cry for 'Three Cheers!' went up, Sir Douglas Haig's charger, on which the King was mounted, took fright and reared, falling on top of him. The King returned to England on a stretcher, while the Prince was quickly despatched home to break the news to the Queen. George V was left in a frail state and his health never fully recovered.

Returning to the front, the Prince found he had more freedom, since his particular safety was not the main priority of the high command. He later wrote: 'I saw a good deal more of the grim and sordid side of modern warfare than was generally known.'[36] He saw the dead bodies of men killed close to reaching their objectives. Once he returned to his car to learn that his driver had been killed by shrapnel. Alarmed by the risks the Prince was

THE PRINCE OF WALES COULD NOT WAIT TO GIVE HIS SERVICES TO HIS COUNTRY AT THE OUTBREAK OF THE FIRST WORLD WAR. IN AUGUST 1914, HE WAS APPOINTED 2ND LIEUTENANT IN THE 1ST BATTALION GRENADIER GUARDS. BY 1918 HE HAD BEEN PROMOTED TEMPORARY MAJOR. AT THE END OF THE WAR HE WAS MADE COLONEL OF THE RECENTLY FORMED WELSH GUARDS, BUT HE HAD MADE GOOD FRIENDS IN THE GRENADIERS AND RETAINED A GREAT AFFECTION FOR HIS OLD REGIMENT. THE DUKE TREASURED MANY EXAMPLES OF MILITARY MEMORABILIA AND AMONGST HIS COLLECTION IS THIS BRASS AND WHITE METAL BELT LOCKET OF A WARRANT OFFICER OF THE GRENADIER GUARDS FROM THE REIGN OF QUEEN VICTORIA.

running, Sir John French soon moved him further from the action.

Much of 1915 and 1916 was spent in a monotonous exercise of holding one muddy line. Often very little was happening, but it helped the Prince of Wales to meet a wide variety of different people, far wider than any of his predecessors, and he matured accordingly. He was a particularly unwilling recipient of the Military Cross, feeling that he had not earned it and that it further isolated him from his contemporaries.

In 1916 an expedition to Egypt was arranged for the Prince to inspect the Suez Canal defences. This was another way of keeping him out of direct enemy fire, as he was well aware. Lord Esher mollified him with the assurance that the Empire's future depended on him: 'This country . . . will require leadership from you, and if the Empire is to hold together, you, thanks to what you are, and what you have done and are doing, will provide a rallying point that no one else — not one of your brothers, for instance — can provide. . . . It is a big sacrifice, but a noble one! . . .'[37]

In Egypt the Prince encountered troops from Australia and New Zealand. As fighting was desultory, he was able to visit the Sudan, ride over the battlefield of Omdurman, and go down the Nile, taking in some sight-seeing on the way. After six weeks he went to serve under Lord Cavan once more, with the XIV Army Corps. As the Corps moved south to the Somme, he spent the winter months of 1916/17 living in a camp of canvas huts during what proved the

BELOW: *Viewing the temple of Karnak with his equerry, Captain Lord Claud Hamilton, a brother officer in the Grenadiers, April 1916.* ABOVE: *After visiting Egypt, Sudan and Italy, the Prince returned to the battles of the Western Front. Lunch in a dug-out ten metres below ground, with Brigadier-General Gathorne-Hardy (third right) and General Niessel (left), Guillemont, the Somme, July 1916.* LEFT: *'The grim and sordid side of war': dismembered bodies in a captured German trench photographed by the Prince in 1915.*

LEFT: *Visiting Indian Cavalry on the Suez Canal defences, April 1916.* ABOVE: *With the Belgian Royal Family at La Panne in 1916. Queen Elisabeth of the Belgians takes a photograph watched by her children, the Duke of Brabant (later King Leopold III), Princess Marie-José (later Queen of Italy) and Prince Charles Theodore.* BELOW: *On the terrace of the House of Commons in June 1919, at a reception for the crew of a US Navy flying boat after its trans-Atlantic flight.*

coldest winter of that bleak war. The Corps returned to the Ypres sector in May 1917 to prepare for the Passchendaele offensive. Here the Prince got his closest look at the horrors of war — loss of life and human exhaustion, not to mention the cynicism of the once enthusiastic men.

The summer was memorable for another reason. In July 1917, encouraged by his equerries, the Prince enjoyed the favours of his first *amourette*, who assisted the shy young man to dispose of his virginity.

In the autumn of 1917, Lord Cavan moved with his Corps to North Italy to reinforce the retreating Italian forces, and the Prince went too. Here they met King Victor Emmanuel III, who had joined his forces in the field. Another long winter was endured. The Prince had to return to London for a few weeks in 1918 to take his seat in the House of Lords, but was back in Italy for an uneventful summer. When Armistice Day came, he was in France, at Mons. He spent the following weeks visiting the occupation troops in Germany and did not return home until February 1919.

The Prince came back to England at a time of social discontent. He was much taken with a speech by Lloyd George, now Prime Minister: 'the strength and power of every land has been drained. . . . they have all bled at every vein, and this restlessness which you get everywhere is the fever of anaemia.'[38] The Prince saw at first hand the discontent that gripped Britain and realised for himself that this was by no means a 'land fit for heroes'.

The contact that the Prince enjoyed with servicemen during the war was of enormous

OPPOSITE: *The Prince in North Italy, 1918.* RIGHT: *Queen Mary with her daughter on her silver wedding day, 6 July 1918.* BELOW: *The Royal Family digging the potato plot in Frogmore Gardens, Windsor, spring 1917. With King George (third left) are his sons, Prince Henry (second left) and Prince Albert (centre).* BOTTOM: *In the months following the Armistice the Prince of Wales visited troops from the Empire and the United States. He was photographed here with officers at the Australian Corps Headquarters at Ham-sur-Heure, Belgium, 1918.*

importance to him, and he never forgot them. As Prince of Wales, he became their champion and continued to espouse their cause even during his brief reign. His championing of the 'working man' was outside the context of the workings and problems of government. With a few exceptions, he was somewhat isolated from politicians and political life in general. So while he was liked by the working people, he was less popular in Westminster and Whitehall. This imbalance would cause him trouble when the Abdication crisis loomed.

The Prince had the chance to comment about his war when he was given the Freedom of the City of London at a ceremony in the Guildhall in May 1919: 'The part I played was, I fear, a very insignificant one, but from one point of view I shall never regret my periods of service overseas. In those four years I mixed with men. In those four years I found my manhood. When I think of the future, and the heavy responsibilities which may fall to my lot, I feel that the experience gained since 1914 will stand me in good stead.'[39]

THE COLONEL WEARS THE UNIFORM OF HIS REGIMENT IN INDIA.
The King, who was appointed to the honorary colonelcy of a native regiment, wearing the turban of its officers on his tour of the East.

CHAPTER FOUR

THE PRINCE ON TOUR

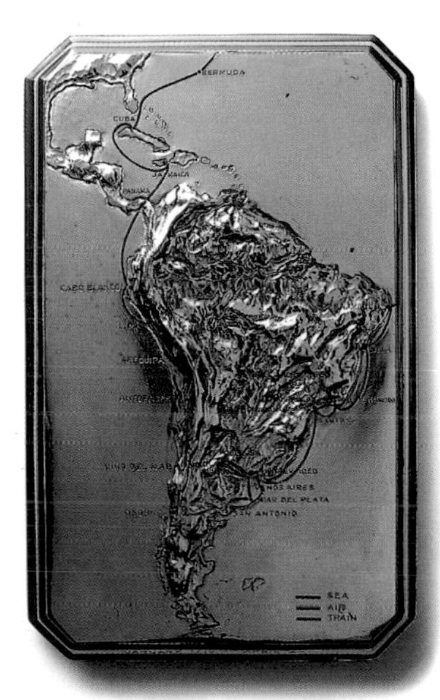

PREVIOUS PAGES, LEFT: *The Prince's tours took him all over the world, from India to South America.* RIGHT: *A silver plaque from his staff on the 1931 tour.* THIS PAGE, ABOVE: *With nurses, Halifax, Nova Scotia, August 1919.* RIGHT: *At the Studley Royal Quoit Club, Halifax: the Duchess of Windsor's favourite photograph.* BELOW: *Time off for golf, Montreal, September 1919.*

The Prince of Wales now entered a new phase of life, that long period of waiting to 'succeed' that has caused so many royal heirs to wonder what their role is. He was being prepared for the throne, yet he did not know how long the wait would be. In 1921 he read Max Beerbohm's essay on George IV and was particularly struck by one line, that he felt applied especially to him: 'He was indeed still a child, for royalties not being ever brought into contact with the realities of life, remain young far longer than other people'. The Prince wrote to his confidante, Mrs Freda Dudley Ward: 'No one realizes how desperately true that is in my case than I do.'[40] He was popular, but nervous, chain smoking and forever tugging at the knot of his tie, gestures which appeared charming but gave evidence of a certain inner tension.

Seen with the benefit of hindsight, the personal anxieties of the Prince in these years did not bode well. The Prince was popular in the eyes of the outside world, but discontented with his lot. His secretaries worried, and they worried more as the thirties approached. The outward veneer did not crack, the act held together, but not without much tension behind the scenes.

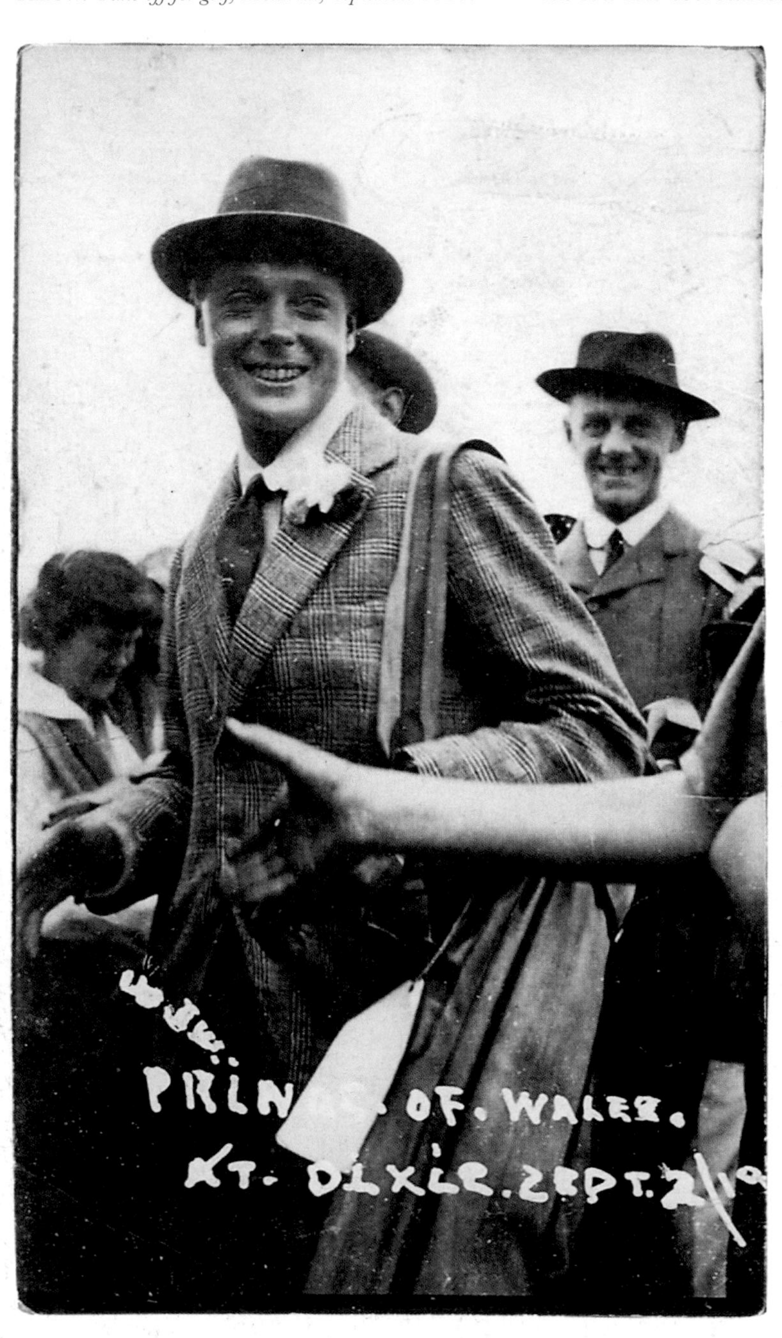

Captain Alan Lascelles, known as 'Tommy', accompanied the Prince as Assistant Private Secretary on many of his tours in the 1920s. On numerous occasions he found himself exasperated with his master as an individual and as future monarch:

'It is the impossibility of making him realise this side of his position that defeats me. All the work that his private secretaries have to do centres round that — the fact that he *is* the future king — and not round his individual personality; and as he makes no effort except in the direction of expressing that personality, in one form or another, and usually at the expense of the other thing, one is continually trying to carry water in a sieve. In fact, one is like a jockey trying to induce a race-horse to race, whose only idea is to stop in the middle of the course and perform circus tricks; or an actor-manager, whose Hamlet persists in interrupting the play by balancing the furniture on the end of his nose.'[41]

Yet Lascelles conceded: 'And, damn him, he is so affectionate to me, that I find it terribly hard to nourish vipers in my weak bosom.'[42]

Some of the Prince's private letters reveal just how much he felt oppressed by his role. As early as Christmas Day 1919, after the extraordinary success of his Canadian tour, he wrote to his Private Secretary and friend, Sir Godfrey Thomas: 'A sort of hopelessly lost feeling has come over me and I think I'm going kind of mad!! . . . [I] feel incapable of pulling myself together. Christ, how I loathe my job now and all the press "puffed" empty "succès". I feel I'm through with it and long and long to die. For God's sake don't breathe a word of this to a soul. No one else must know how I feel about my life and everything. You'll probably think from this that I ought to be in a mad house already . . .'[43]

For much of the 1920s the Prince was travelling. Of all his activities at this time his world tours stand out as glamorous and successful, fun as well as being useful. As seen on the newsreels, it was one adventure following closely upon another, the Prince travelling the Empire that would one day be his.

In July 1919 the Prince moved into York House, in St James's Palace, with his own establishment. This was to remain his London base until 1936. He had duties at home, but these tended to come in the general category of cutting ribbons and laying foundation stones. He hoped he could always make a good speech, and he took advice from one of the country's greatest orators, Winston Churchill.

A month later the Prince set off on the first of his world tours. It was the Prime Minister, Lloyd George, who had suggested that the Prince should travel to meet the Empire troops and thank their governments for their contribution to victory. More importantly, his father believed he should become acquainted with the Empire, so that he could get to know its peoples and they could get to know him. His future role was of crucial importance, since only the person of the King-Emperor held the disparate parts of the Empire together.

Between 1919 and 1930, there were many important trips. They were given extensive coverage in the world press at the time, and though they appeared successful to the outsider and the Prince was received with great enthusiasm, there exist a number of anxious contemporary accounts from those who accompanied him, which indicate that he often showed human frailty, lack of consideration to others, and selfishness. However, it is important to look at the positive side first.

The Prince's first great voyage was to Canada for a three-month tour, followed by a visit to President Wilson in the United States. He sailed from Portsmouth on HMS *Renown*, with a personal staff of ten, finally disembarking in Quebec.

His tour of the Dominion was extensive; he travelled to the far end of the country and back in a special train, taking in Toronto, Ottawa, Montreal, Winnipeg, Edmonton, Calgary, Banff, Vancouver on the westward journey, then returning by the southern route through the

THE PRINCE OF WALES WAS INSPIRED BY WHAT HE SAW OF RANCHING LIFE IN WESTERN CANADA ON HIS TOUR THERE IN 1919. HE IMMEDIATELY BOUGHT THE EP RANCH IN ALBERTA WITH 1,600 ACRES FOR £10,000. LIFE AT THE LOG-CABIN FARMHOUSE WAS COMFORTABLE BUT SIMPLE. THE STAFF CONSISTED OF A JAPANESE COOK, A GARDENER, A MECHANIC, A BUTTERMAKER AND A BUGLER. THE PRINCE'S AMBITION WAS TO CREATE A MODEL FARM AND RAISE HIGH QUALITY STOCK — CATTLE, SHEEP, DRAUGHT HORSES. ALTHOUGH THE DUKE ONLY MANAGED TO VISIT THE RANCH FOUR MORE TIMES IN HIS LIFE, HE TOOK A CLOSE INTEREST IN IT AND DID NOT RELINQUISH IT TILL 1962, WHEN HE KNEW HE WOULD NEVER VISIT AGAIN. IT SAYS SOMETHING ABOUT HIM THAT HE HELD ON TO THIS ROMANTIC VISION OF THE SIMPLE LIFE FOR SO LONG.

BELOW: *'I knew . . . this was the place for me': the Prince's first visit to the United States, November 1919. He was met in Washington by Vice-President Thomas R. Marshall. After visiting the ailing President Wilson, he went on to a tumultuous reception in New York. One purpose of the early tours was to thank the Empire and Britain's allies for their war effort, so the Prince was often in service uniform. Here he wears the khaki uniform of the Welsh Guards, whose Colonel he had recently become.*

Original photo of Prince of Wales
taken at Washington D.C. during
Red Cross Drive

ABOVE: *Photographs of the Prince's Canadian tour appeared in newspapers around the world. At Banff, Alberta, he was initiated as chief of the Stony tribe, under the name 'Chief Morning Star'.* BELOW: *At the controls of the engine of the Royal train that took him across the Dominion, Ottawa, November 1919.* RIGHT: *Many in the huge crowds that gathered to see him brought their cameras. This snapshot of the Prince with a Red Cross nurse taken during his Washington visit was later sent to him by an admirer.*

Rocky mountains.

The Canadian premier, W.L. Mackenzie King, dubbed him 'The Sir Galahad of the Royal House'. Everywhere he went he was greeted by wildly enthusiastic crowds. There were pageants, parades of war veterans, investiture ceremonies, and many official speeches (some made the more onerous for the Prince by the absence of any alcohol). He was invested with the head-gear of the Red Indian and he camped out in the wild. He travelled down rivers by rowing boat, fished at the Virgin Falls, attended a cow-pony stampede at Saskatoon. The photographs show him in military or naval uniform, or in grey suit and straw hat, a jaunty cigarette or cigar to hand, and a cane held at a debonair angle. The lasting memorial to this trip was the four thousand acre EP ranch that he bought forty miles south of Calgary.

It was early during the Canadian tour that he shook so many hands that within a week his right hand was 'blackened and swollen' and might have become permanently disabled had he gone on using it.[44]

The Prince caught the public imagination. This was the first opportunity for him to realise how much he was admired and loved for himself. Surrounded by adoring crowds he was genuinely surprised at the outpouring of such spontaneous affection. Nor did it stop there. When

his official duties were over, he did not rest, but went out to enjoy the night life.

He was in Canada for over two months before crossing to the United States, a late addition to his trip, to spend several days in Washington and New York. He had been determined to see something of America, that country being so close. There was a visit to President Woodrow Wilson, who was in ill health at the time, and photographs of the Prince's official engagements in the United States show the proceedings being taken rather more solemnly, formally and seriously than in Canada. However, by night he was being a wild success in New York, attending many parties and staying up late into the night, every night.

This visit to the United States took on a greater significance in the Duke of Windsor's mind in his later years. In the 1950s he went so far as to tell Lilli Palmer, then the wife of the actor Rex Harrison: 'My tragedy is that I couldn't stand England from the start. But the first time I set foot on American soil — I was still a very young man — there I knew at a stroke that this was the place for me. This was where I'd like to stay. And then I married an American and hoped we could live in America but destiny decided otherwise. My wife hates America and only wants to live in France. That's life.'[45]

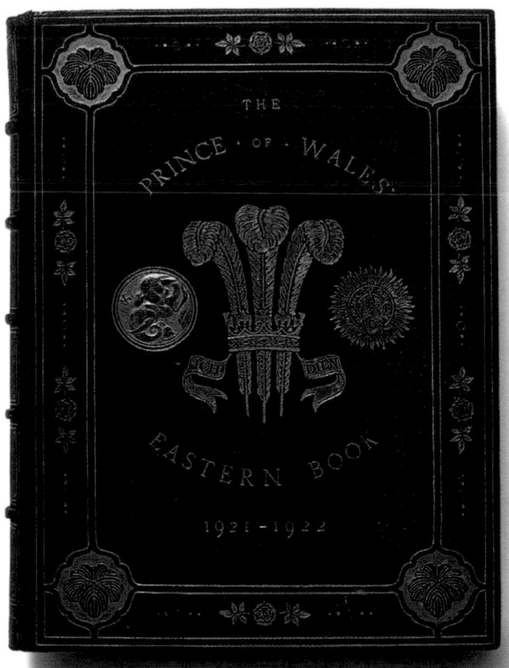

TOP LEFT: *His third Empire tour, to India and Japan in 1921-22, was 41,000 miles of pomp and pageantry. The Maharaja of Patiala, one of the Indian Princes in his suite.* BELOW: *At Government House, Rangoon, January 1922.* ABOVE: *The popular image of the Prince was enhanced by illustrated books tracing the progress of his tours. This specially bound copy of* The Prince's Eastern Tour *is from the Duke of Windsor's library.*

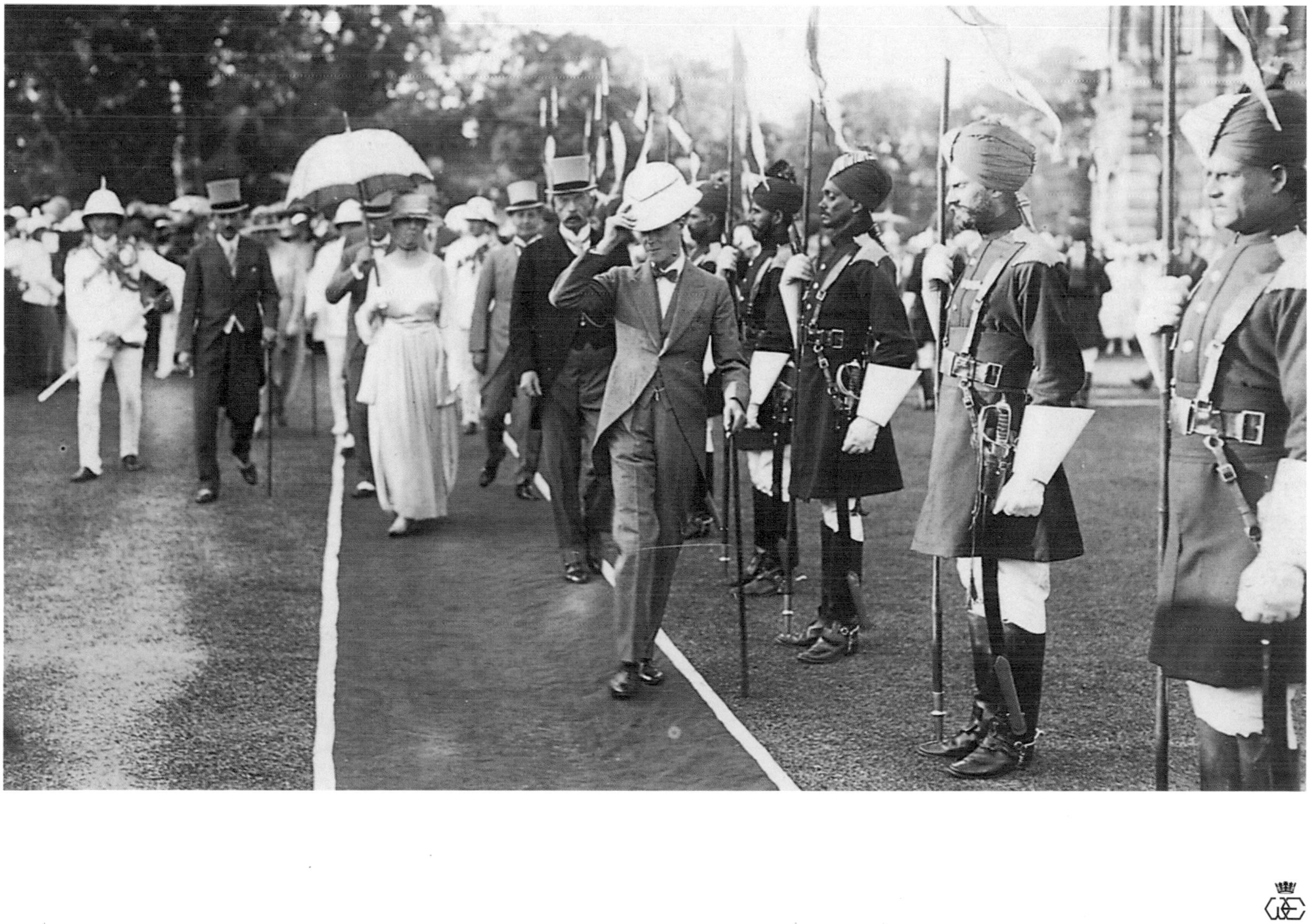

RIGHT: *The Prince's second Empire tour, March to September 1920, created immense enthusiasm in Australia and New Zealand. This postcard commemorates his visit to Queensland.* BELOW: *Japan, early summer, 1922. The Prince in naval uniform planting a tree at the Imperial Palace, Tokyo, with Crown Prince Hirohito (fourth right).* BOTTOM: *Shooting the rapids in Japan.* OPPOSITE: *In Japanese dress on HMS* Renown, *May 1922. The Crown Prince had ordered costumes for the Prince and his suite from Mitsukoshi, the Tokyo store.*

What this probably meant was that he had found the realities of his royal life in England difficult, and he had relished the contrast of the less constrained role he played abroad. In 1928, he had described England to Tommy Lascelles as 'a little cramped'.[46]

After a mere three and a half months at home, the Prince embarked on his second trip in 1920. This took him 46,000 miles round the world and lasted seven months. His entourage was increased by the addition of his distant cousin, the nineteen-year-old Lord Louis Mountbatten, who pulled every string possible to secure a place on board as a flag officer. He came to be the Prince's staunchest ally on this often wearing tour. Mountbatten had the chance to look at the letters that George V and Queen Mary wrote their son: 'I've seen all his letters from home. His father's might be the letters of a Director of some business to his Assistant Manager and even his mother seems so stiff and unnatural . . .'[47]

Such was the extent of the British Empire at that time that the Prince was either at sea or on British territory for almost the entire trip. After the West Indies, the *Renown* passed through the Panama Canal. The tour of New Zealand lasted a month, and was followed by a two-month tour of Australia, where he visited Melbourne and Sydney. New Zealand had been intensely pro-British, but Australians were harder to please. The wise Governor-General, Sir Ronald Munro-Ferguson, warned the Prince that the Australians expected informality, but added: 'You are in for a great experience, Sir; and you have nothing to fear for yourself!'[48] They called him 'Digger' at every turn, and at times he was literally pelted with bouquets.

During his round trip of the continent by train and ship, the Prince had the chance to

spend a week in the saddle, rounding up mobs of cattle, taking part in improvised races, and dismounting to shear a sheep. He made the acquaintance of at least one koala bear. Much of the trip was exhausting, the Prince being all too aware of the great efforts being made to entertain him, and the fear of disappointing his hosts. Often he stayed up too late, and he was forever afraid of the minefield of appearing ungrateful or of forgetting to meet some particularly deserving veteran. But there is evidence, too, of his lack of consideration. At times he was tired, discontented and bored, and found himself questioning the ever-present need to do his duty. The worst moment came when the Prince could not rouse himself from his bed to greet the crowds who gathered early in the morning at Gilgandra station. They expressed their disapproval by 'counting him out'. (On his return journey, the Prince emerged and made a speech. They 'counted him in' again.)

India was the next country on the list. After a year at home, the Prince made his famous visit in the autumn of 1921, going on to Japan and returning home towards the end of June 1922. This was a tour of 41,000 miles, deemed the most important to date and also the most varied and controversial. It came at a sensitive time, when British rule was being rejected by many Indians. King George V made it clear that while the informality of the Prince had gone down well in the Dominions, it would go down very badly in India. The King told the Prince that the Indians loved ceremonial and pomp, and advised him go along with all that the British and civil authorities planned for him.

The Prince sailed in the *Renown* once more via Gibraltar, this time visiting all the British possessions en route: Malta, Port Said, Suez and Aden. He arrived in Bombay on 17 November 1921. The four-month tour of the Indian Empire was divided into two parts, separated by a visit to Burma. In the first part he went north from Bombay through the native states of Rajputana to Nepal and on to Calcutta. In the second he travelled from Madras in the South to Delhi and Peshawar, and across the Sind desert to Karachi.

TOP: *Big game hunting: the Prince with a rhinoceros he shot from the back of an elephant in Nepal, where he was the guest of the Maharaja Sir Chandra Sumshere Jung, December 1921. On his later tours the Prince preferred the cine-camera to the gun.* BELOW: *Walking with King Fuad, the 'barking King', in the grounds of the Abdive Palace, Cairo, June 1922.* BOTTOM RIGHT: *Playing polo with members of the British team, at the Meadow Brook Club on Long Island, New York, during his second visit to the United States, September 1924.*

At all times he was accompanied by his staff of Indian Princes. He met ex-servicemen and pensioners, British and Indian troops, scouts and guides, police and civilians. He usually travelled by overnight train so as to begin each day in a new place. Security was strict: the line was guarded by troops who obeyed the order to look outwards and not at the passing train. Other modes of transport included elephants, a palanquin surrounded by torchbearers, and many camels. The Ruling Princes put on tremendous displays, exhibiting their fabulous collections of jewels, laying on cheetah hunts and the old sport of pig-sticking. There were sword dances and polo tournaments, processions and garden parties. When in uniform, the Prince invariably wore the sky blue riband of the Order of the Star of India, given to him by his father in honour of the visit.

Throughout the tour the Prince's energy was astounding, and in public he concealed his frequent bouts of depression (mainly due to his long enforced separation from his girlfriend, Freda Dudley Ward). He could not but be aware of the hostility of some Indians to his presence. The royal party occasionally arrived to find the streets deserted or a university ceremony boycotted by the students. At one point the Governor of Peshawar thought it wise to sneak the Prince in by a side door. The Prince wrote to his father saying he did not believe he was achieving a thing with his public work.

In Nepal he hunted tiger and rhinoceros in the jungle, though without much enthusiasm. To ensure good sport a number of buffaloes were tethered to trees at night. If these were eaten, the scouts could report that a gorged tiger must be nearby. The Prince and his party would then arrive by elephant and howdah. The tiger was 'ringed', and when it appeared it was shot. The bag at the end of the week was fourteen tigers, seven rhinos, two leopards and two bears. The Prince's indifference to big game shooting was made up for by Louis Mountbatten's eagerness to get credit for as many tigers as possible.

After Christmas in Calcutta, the Prince then spent nine days in Burma and set off on the second part of his Indian trip starting in Madras on 13 January, 1922. This was more the India of romantic literature, and a highlight was the *keddah* at Karapur, a rounding up of wild elephants for inspection by the distinguished visitor. He twice saw the Taj Mahal at Agra, once by day and once by moonlight. Then there was a week in Delhi with a heavy schedule of official engagements, during which the Prince made his first speech in Urdu. He finally sailed from India in March 1922.

The *Renown* took the Prince on to Ceylon, where he visited Kandy, to the Federated Malay states, the Straits Settlement, Hong Kong and thence to Japan.

Many British royal Princes had been to Japan before him, invariably on Garter missions, but the welcome given the Prince of Wales was magnificent. Japan had until lately greeted visiting royalty with deep silence as an appropriate mark of reverence. Freed from this custom, they cheered loudly. Four weeks of the most lavish hospitality followed.

The future Emperor Hirohito was then Crown Prince and acting as Prince Regent for his father. He was in charge of the visit. The Prince of Wales naturally called on the Empress and other members of the Imperial Family, but he never saw the Mikado, commenting later: 'He never appeared; it was said that he was mad and kept locked in a room at the palace.'[49] But

BELOW: *EP Ranch near Calgary was the only property the Prince owned, until he bought the Moulin de la Tuilerie near Paris in 1952. His second tour of Canada, in the autumn of 1924, was an opportunity to spend a fortnight there. He was photographed seated on his prize shorthorn bull.* BOTTOM: *Crossing from Vancouver to Vancouver Island on the SS* Princess Louise, *October 1924.*

TOP: *The Prince stayed at Government House, Pretoria in June 1925 with his aunt and uncle, Princess Alice, Countess of Athlone, and the Earl of Athlone ('Uncle Alge'). Princess Alice detected in him a resentment of parental authority.* BELOW: *On the way to an engagement in Buenos Aires with the city's Governor. After South Africa the Prince's exhausting itinerary took him to South America, where he visited Argentina and Chile in August and September. His presence was intended to boost British trade, but he could not disguise his fatigue and boredom, and his staff feared a nervous breakdown.*

he did meet the famous Admiral Togo, a member of the British Order of Merit and known as 'the Nelson of Japan'. Otherwise it was a round of operas, banquets, parades, inspections and garden parties. The Crown Prince often sported plus-fours, a habit he had adopted from his British guest. The two young heirs to the throne had met before in London. (They established sufficient rapport for the Emperor to take the trouble to visit the Duke of Windsor in Paris home during his European visit in October 1971.)

The Prince returned home by way of the South China Sea and Indian Ocean. He took the opportunity to visit Fuad, the recently proclaimed King of Egypt, in Cairo. This visit exacted the most strenuous courtesy from the Prince, for the unfortunate King spoke in a series of staccato barks, all wholly unintelligible, due to a throat wound acquired in early life. The *Renown* reached Plymouth on 20 June 1922.

1923 was a quiet year for the Prince with only two short overseas visits, one to Belgium, and the other a month's tour of Canada. The following year he made time for a private visit to the United States to play polo, to which sport he gave his attention after dutifully calling on President Calvin Coolidge. He took the opportunity to enjoy to the full the Americans' legendary hospitality, staying out dancing until the small hours, and acquiring a fondness for American slang, not to mention 'a taste for bathtub gin'.[50] He also packed in a visit to his ranch in Canada.

This American visit was the beginning of a fascination with the achievements of the great tycoons in Chicago and Detroit. The Prince noted that 'every Englishman in a position to do so should make a practice of visiting that great country at least once every two or three years.'[51] Unfortunately for him, the US newspaper reports sent back to Britain were so flippant and lacking in respect by the British standards of the day that King George V predictably came to disapprove of the United States and made it difficult for any of his sons to return there.

In 1925 there came the fourth and last of the Prince's big official tours, once more breaking new territory. The trip included a three-month visit to Gambia, Sierra Leone, the Gold Coast, Nigeria, South Africa, going on from there to South America. This time he travelled in the *Repulse* which conveyed him on a tranquil voyage down the west coast of Africa, calling in on colonies never before visited by a Prince of Wales. He enjoyed 'palavers' with local chiefs, but the highlight of his visit to Nigeria was the spectacle of 20,000 Moslem horsemen in chain armour, flowing capes and white turbans galloping past him in the desert.

In South Africa, the Prince stayed with his maternal uncle and aunt, the Earl and Countess of Athlone at Government House, and then embarked on a 10,000 mile tour of the Union, lasting thirteen weeks. He inspected much of the mining activity, met an ancient Zulu who had taken part in the Rorke's Drift siege of 1879, and became aware of the racial problems between so many differing communities.

From there he crossed to Argentina to return the state visit made by their President to Britain in 1924 and to boost trade in that country as well as Uruguay and Chile. Perhaps he had been travelling too often and too long but on this this trip he appeared markedly more bored and hung over than usual. It was certainly strenuous, with long days of official duties and the late nights of hospitality which seldom ended before 4 a.m. There was also the new irritation of press photographers firing their flashbulbs throughout his speeches. Before he left, however, he made his contribution to British exports with an important speech aimed at British manufacturers, urging them to explore the wants of markets overseas and to present their wares in attractive form.

ABOVE: *Argentina in 1925 was a daunting mixture of pomp and tedium, pretty girls and forbidding matrons. An evening reception in Buenos Aires, the Prince is between President Marcelo de Alvear (right) and the British Minister, Sir Bielby Alston, with their wives.* BOTTOM LEFT: *Yet another reception. As usual there were hordes of adoring fans eager to catch the Prince's eye.* BELOW: *After the round of engagements in Buenos Aires, the Prince and his staff were able to relax for a few days on a ranch.*

The Prince had become the 'Ambassador of Empire', and was one of the best travelled Englishmen of his day. Looking back on these official tours in later life, the Duke of Windsor believed that he had been fortunate to 'savour something of the atmosphere of hundreds of different communities.'[52] He had indeed seen a wide variety of life, not to mention planting enough official trees for a forest and laying enough foundation stones to build a small city. He saw the British Empire while it was still intact. Yet, in the end the impression was not strong enough to persuade him to put the Empire first, when tested in 1936. Despite having had the

LEFT: *Tiger-hunting was laid on for the Indian tour in 1921-22.* ABOVE: *A private visit to Spain in May 1922: shooting near Cadiz with his cousin Queen Ena and Alfonso XIII (left). Alfonso was rejected by his people in 1931, but refused to abdicate.* BELOW: *The Prince and Prince George (both looking hungover) in Canada to inaugurate the International Peace Bridge over the Niagara River, August 1927.* OVERLEAF: *Nairobi, Kenya, October 1928, Suk tribesmen contemplate the Prince's gift.*

chance to get to know many outposts in his father's Empire and many of its hospitable peoples, he was to put his own personal happiness before any sense of duty to them, when it came to deciding whether to respect their views on his intended marriage.

The Prince was able to confine his travelling to Europe in 1926 and 1927 and apart from a trip to Canada to attend the celebrations of the Diamond Jubilee of the Confederation and to make a five week tour. On this trip, as on a later one to South America, he was accompanied by his younger brother, Prince George. The Canadian trip gave the Prince the chance to study the Prime Minister, Stanley Baldwin, who accompanied him, with Mrs Baldwin. The Prince was impressed by his erudition and 'political sagacity' but detected 'traces of the arrogance that some Englishmen display when travelling abroad.'[53]

In 1928, accompanied by another brother, Prince Henry this time, he visited Uganda before undertaking a privately organised safari in Tanganyika. Tommy Lascelles was of the party. He explained to the Governor of the Kenya Colony that the Prince was at his best when things were spontaneous and 'informal'. Lascelles explained that to the Prince 'informal' was 'the most blessed word in the language', and continued: 'So long as he lives he will never, I am convinced, do one tenth as much good when there is a formal atmosphere as he will when there is only a barely-perceptible whiff of for-

mality.'[54] An important test of the Prince's enjoyment of any forthcoming engagement was whether or not he was required to bring a full dress-uniform.

The safari brought several adventures. In Uganda, the Prince was made to flee by a charging elephant, and on one unpleasant night his guide lost the way and he spent a night 'floundering through almost impenetrable elephant grass ten feet high, the hunting ground of lions and snakes.'[55] The safari was interrupted by news that King George was gravely ill. To the horror of Lascelles, the Prince appeared not to take this in and, unperturbed, continued with the seduction of the wife of a colonial official. Perhaps his apparent callousness masked the shock caused by the implication of the news. At any rate, a sense of duty soon re-established itself and he sped home. Thereafter his travels were curtailed because of the King's frail health, although in 1930 he managed to make a further safari trip to South Africa, Kenya, Uganda, the Sudan and Egypt.

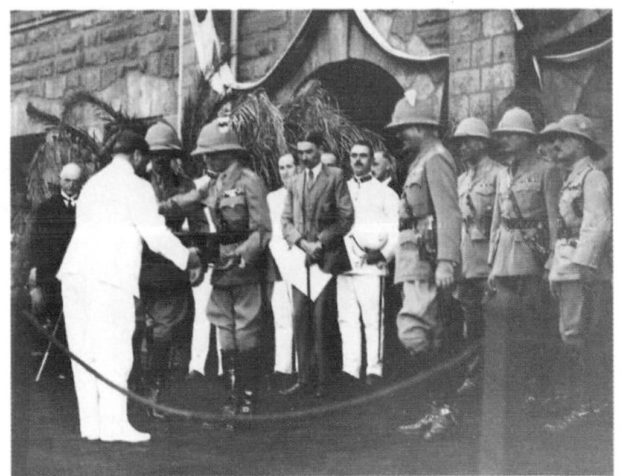

LEFT: *The Ugandan safari, 1928, the Prince relaxing with the ranger Captain Roy Salmon.* ABOVE: *Receiving an ivory casket from the Mayor of Nairobi.* BELOW: *With a crocodile shot on the banks of the Upper Nile, 19 October 1928. A month later, news of the King's serious illness forced the curtailment of the tour.* BOTTOM: *The Prince's team: Baron Blor Blixen (former husband of the writer Isak Dinesen), with Piers ('Joey') Legh (the Prince's equerry) and Alan ('Tommy') Lascelles.*

On this second safari, the Prince took to using a motion-picture camera rather than a gun. He relished this new hobby and was proud of the results of the filming. The only mishap was that he contracted malaria.

While each of these tours was reported in the press as being a success, and pictures of a smiling Prince circulated the globe, the problems encountered by his staff were considerable. He fell short of the high standards they expected of him on many counts. He was often depressed and homesick. He could be bored by the activities he was obliged to undertake, and showed it. He was unpunctual and temperamental and kept his staff up late. Tommy Lascelles wrote: 'Probably through sheer exhaustion he becomes fractious and unreasonable at times.'[56] During these years the courtiers and the politicians came to regard him with mixed feelings, and this was to serve him ill when the Abdication crisis arose.

There were good sides and bad. Alistair Cooke, a wise observer, was presented to him in 1932 and found the Prince approaching each introduction with an enthusiasm undimmed by endless repetition. Yet his later judgement was almost certainly right: the 'Prince Charming' had been 'a moody man and a defiant son who never did enough or never did it in the right way . . . to suit his father.'[57] Or, perhaps, the court. But as far as the world was concerned, seeing him distantly and judging him superficially, he was a bright hope and a refreshing contrast to the stiffer elements of the Royal Family in Britain.

Warner, Sheppard & Wade, Ltd.

Are favoured with instructions

TO SELL BY AUCTION,

At th ster,

SATUR rd, 1929,

H ES

The ENT exception

THE PROPERTY OF

H.R.H. the Prince of Wales,

who is not hunting any more, or riding in
any Point-to-Point races this season.

**They will stand in the Star Boxes
and be sold at about 1 o'clock.**

CHAPTER FIVE

PUBLIC LIFE AND PRIVATE WOES

The Prince of Wales was away from home for extended periods between 1919 and 1930, but when he was at home, he was much in the news. He succeeded in dividing his time between the official duties required of him and his more enjoyed social and sporting activities. These were also the years of his long affair with Mrs Freda Dudley Ward.

There were numerous photographs of the sporting Prince in his public role, teeing off as he opened the Richmond Golf Course in 1923, kicking off at a football match between Fulham and the Spurs at Sandhurst in 1921, or cheering the Welsh Guards at the Army Rugby Cup at Aldershot. His attire was closely monitored. He set new fashions with his ties, his pullovers and his boaters, and in 1927 by sporting a coat with an astrakhan collar in London. He planted many a tree, opened many a bridge, and laid yet more foundation stones and he attended many great ceremonies. In 1919 he had been initiated into Freemasonry, then a much more enclosed body than it is today.

These were the years when his siblings settled down into what he later called the 'matchless blessing' of domesticity. In 1922, his sister, Mary, had married Viscount Lascelles, later Earl of Harewood, and gave birth to two boys in the 1920s. And the Duke

PREVIOUS PAGES: *The Prince of Wales before a point-to-point race, 1923. He suffered quite a few falls, some serious, while riding, until his father insisted he give up this risky sport.* BACKGROUND: *The 1929 sale of all the Prince's horses.* RIGHT: *The race-going Prince.* THESE PAGES, TOP: *In Masonic regalia after his initiation, May 1919.* ABOVE: *The funeral procession of Field Marshal Earl Haig, London, February 1928. The Prince of Wales with the Duke of York (left) and Prince Arthur of Connaught.* RIGHT: *Tree planting made easy for the Prince, Birmingham, October 1934.* OPPOSITE: *A cutting sent by an American fan; it is marked 'our favorite'.* OVERLEAF: *The Prince speaking to the Captain of the Oxford University team at a charity match between Oxford and Tottenham Hotspur, February 1924.*

our favorite!

of York, a noticeably shy figure, pulled off a great coup when he finally persuaded Lady Elizabeth Bowes-Lyon to become his wife. In the early days of that marriage, the new Duchess of York was an understanding friend to the Prince of Wales and wrote him sympathetic letters. Later his different way of life, the endless travelling, and his continued bachelor status, served to isolate him from his family. He became a more restless cosmopolitan figure, an outsider in their domestic lives.

During these years the Prince took to flying between engagements, when his father allowed him to take to the air. He had made his first flight in 1916. In the late 1920s he started using planes for practical reasons to get to royal engagements. Presently the Prince began to have flying lessons and became the owner of a Gipsy Moth making two solo landings in December 1929. His personal pilot, Wing Commander Edward H. 'Mouse' Fielden, was to become Captain of the King's Flight, founded in 1936.

The Prince, unlike his father and grandfather, was an enthusiastic and fearless rider, and he had his share of falls which always attracted public attention. His riding career was finally to prove too hazardous. In March 1924, he suffered slight concussion when his horse fell with him at the Army point-to-point races at Arborfield Cross, and he had to be taken away in an ambulance. This necessitated a spell of recuperation in Biarritz. So in 1929, under pressure from his parents and the Prime Minister, he gave up riding and sold off his entire stable. Golf became his new passion and this he was able to play well into old age. To this end he rented a house at Sandwich

THE NAME CLOSELY ASSOCIATED WITH THE FEATHERS CLUB (REPRESENTED BY THIS BADGE) IS THAT OF FREDA DUDLEY WARD, MISTRESS AND LONG-TIME FRIEND OF THE PRINCE OF WALES. THE PRINCE'S SOCIAL CONSCIENCE WAS STIRRED BY THE HARDSHIP HE SAW DURING HIS TOURS OF AREAS HARD HIT BY UNEMPLOYMENT IN THE TWENTIES. FREDA DUDLEY WARD SPURRED HIM ON TO TAKE PRACTICAL ACTION AND TOGETHER THEY FOUNDED THE FEATHERS CLUBS. THESE WERE SOCIAL CLUBS FOR THE UNEMPLOYED AND THE FIRST WAS AT LADBROKE GROVE, LONDON. FREDA WAS CHAIRMAN AND REMAINED SO UNTIL 1964, CALLING IN AT HER OFFICE EVERY DAY OF THAT TIME. THE PRINCE GAVE HER A BRACELET WITH A CHARM OF PRECIOUS STONES IN THE FORM OF THIS BADGE FOR EACH CLUB OPENED. THE PRINCE GAVE ANOTHER SUCH CHARM BRACELET TO WALLIS SIMPSON WHICH ALSO COMMEMORATED SIGNIFICANT EVENTS.

OPPOSITE: *The Prince of Wales and his favourite brother, Prince George, with the Quorn Hunt, 1932.*
BELOW: *The Prince concussed after falling at an Army point-to-point, Arborfield Cross, early 1924. He was laid up for four weeks and questions were asked in Parliament.*

From 1919, the Prince of Wales's London address was York House, part of St James's Palace. Freda Dudley Ward helped him to convert the 'rabbit warren' into spacious and elegant apartments. ABOVE: *The arcade entrance to York House from Ambassador's Court.* LEFT: *The Chinese Room.* BELOW: *The Prince's first-floor Sitting Room. A door in the corner led directly into his Dressing Room where he normally slept. Over the fireplace hung the Llewellyn portrait of Queen Mary now in the Salon at the Windsor Villa. The map of the world shows the Prince's extensive tours.*

Bay in Kent, which not only enabled him to play, but was also conveniently near the holiday home of Freda Dudley Ward.

Mrs Freda Dudley Ward was his most important girlfriend until Mrs Simpson. The Prince was very susceptible to women; there had been the occasional physical entanglement during the late years of the Great War, and thereafter the Prince juggled sentimental and romantic love with bouts of casual sex, never finding it difficult to justify his right to both. He fell in love with Viscountess Coke and with Lady Portia Cadogan, and he was more publicly linked with Lady Rosemary Leveson-Gower, though with less evidence of any real interest on his part.

In February 1918 the Prince met Freda Dudley Ward, the diminutive, slim and attractive wife of a Liberal MP. It was a romantic chance encounter in a doorway in Belgrave Square, where the Prince, Freda and her companion happened to shelter from an air raid warning. They were going to a party and they invited him too. He spent the rest of the evening dancing with Freda. The relationship became more intense and dominated his next years, including his travels, during which he missed her desperately and constantly moped to her and to his companions about his separation from her.

As with his later relationship with Wallis Simpson, the Prince was completely besotted, seeing Mrs Dudley Ward as the only possible source of happiness. At the same time he frequently bemoaned to her the fate of being the Prince of Wales. She was not free, nor did she hope to alter her situation, and she accepted (as did he) that there was ultimately no future in the relationship, but while she held sway she was a sensible and comforting influence on the Prince. Freda Dudley Ward was an unusual woman. She was married with two daughters and conducted her life with some independence of mind and without regard to the conventions of

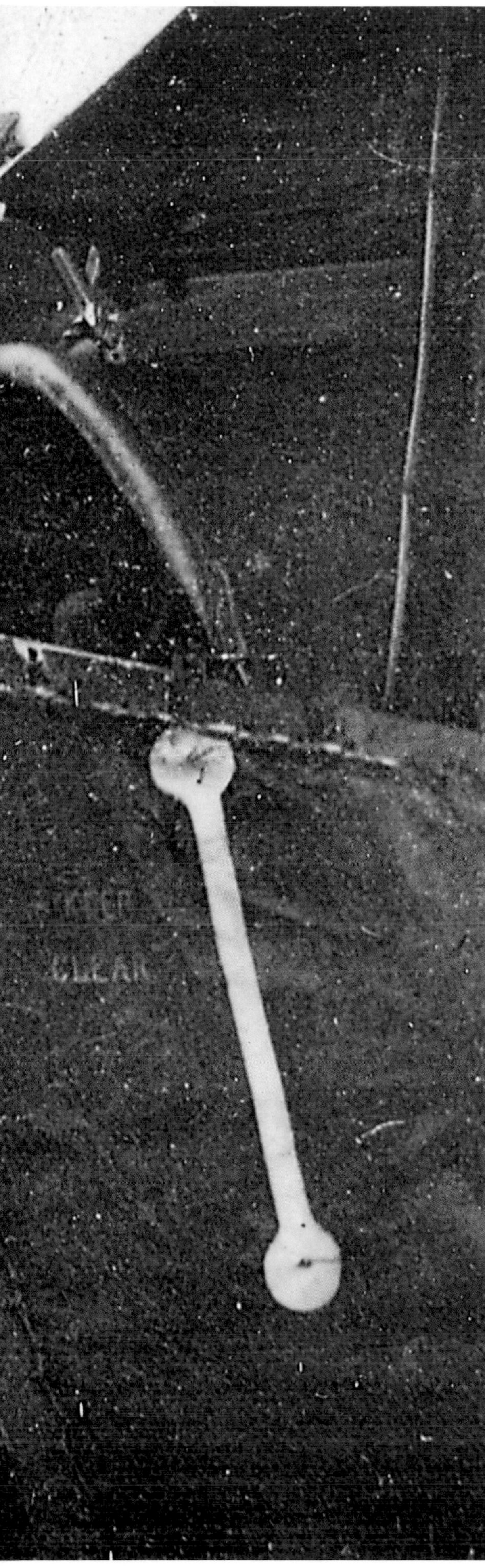

her class. She did not banish her children to the nursery, and she did not banish the disadvantaged from her thoughts. She shared the Prince's interest in less fortunate members of society, awakening his incipient social conscience in practical ways. Bruce Ogilvy, his equerry, described her as 'one of the best friends he ever had in his life'.[58]

When the affair went wrong for a while in 1923, the Prince, in the words of Philip Ziegler, sought 'solace in drink, night clubs and the ostentatious pursuit of other women.'[59] Despite the threatening presence of a variety of suitors on both sides, the Prince and Mrs Dudley Ward remained in a loving relationship until some time in 1931. Her influence was to leave its mark in the decoration of his apartment at York House, St James's Palace, and later Fort Belvedere, in the refurbishment of which she had more than a hand.

During the 1920s the Prince continued to interest himself in the welfare of former servicemen, particularly those who were unemployed. He was very aware of housing problems and made a point of visiting slum areas. Great improvements were made on his Duchy of Cornwall estates, which included impoverished districts of South London. His genuine concern and interest in people made him popular on his regional tours.

In the course of the decade, although outwardly the Prince continued to be the youthful, attractive man with the world at his feet, to his family and staff he became a worry and even a cause of despair. In a remarkable exchange during the 1927 Canadian tour, Tommy Lascelles and the Prime Minister, Stanley Baldwin, admitted they had both contemplated the benefits to the country should he break his neck when steeple-chasing.[60]

Certainly, the Prince felt considerably constrained by being 'The Prince of Wales'; he hated many aspects of being heir to the throne, particularly the police protection that surrounded him, and the newspaper intrusion into his private life as opposed to his public duties. He barely tolerated the Establishment (a word which was to become fashionable in the thirties) and he longed to make his role more informal. The gulf between him and King George widened accordingly.

The Prince yearned after quite a few of his youthful dancing partners. TOP: *Lady Sybil 'Portia' Cadogan who flirted with both the Prince and his brother, Bertie.* ABOVE: *Lady Rosemary Leveson-Gower with the Prince (right), France, 1915, when she was a voluntary nurse. She later married his great friend, Lord Dudley.* BELOW LEFT: *Freda Dudley Ward, mistress and valuable friend to the Prince during the 1920s.* LEFT: *The Prince of Wales in a Sopwith Camel aeroplane with Canadian pilot, Captain Syd Dalrymple Barker, Italy, September 1918, possibly his first flight.*

In 1927, in Canada, Lascelles had become exasperated with the constant last minute changes of plan. He voiced his fears to his wife, who wrote back commiserating about 'the disappointment as regards his [the Prince's] character.'[61] As the decade drew to a close, his secretaries conferred amongst themselves. They were not optimistic. In January 1929, Godfrey Thomas told Tommy Lascelles that the Prince would go on believing that all he had to do was to carry out his public duties to the satisfaction of the press and the man in the street, and that his private life was entirely his own concern. 'I'm terribly sorry for him,' wrote Thomas, 'but unless someone can succeed in disabusing him of this *idée fixe*, I can see nothing but disaster ahead.'[62] By the end of 1928, Admiral Sir Lionel Halsey, Sir Godfrey Thomas and Lascelles were all on the point of resignation.

Lascelles was the one to escape. He left the Prince's staff in February 1929 (though he returned to work for King George V in 1935, and found himself serving Edward VIII in 1936). On departing he told the young man exactly what he thought of him and his way of life, and prophesied his doom. The Prince listened patiently and then said: 'Well, goodnight Tommy,

OPPOSITE AND BELOW: *Glamis Castle, the family home of Lady Elizabeth Bowes-Lyon, autumn 1922. Her hopeful suitor, the Duke of York (later George VI), visited her with his elder brother, the Prince of Wales.*
TOP LEFT: *The Duchess of York gave the Prince this portrait in 1926 soon after the birth of her daughter (the future Queen Elizabeth II). The Duchess, his first sister-in-law, was an understanding friend to him till constant travelling drew him away from his family.*

Fort Belvedere was the beloved home of the Prince from 1929 until his Abdication. He lived exactly as he wished there – informally and in company with undemanding friends. ABOVE RIGHT: *Aerial view of the Fort. The core built around 1750 had many later additions. The rampart with its 31 guns can be seen in the foreground.* ABOVE: *The octagonal Drawing Room with its* trompe l'oeil *pine panelling.* RIGHT: *The Prince of Wales's bedroom was adapted from a former hall. His later bedroom in Paris is very similar with the same armorial wall hanging and footstool.*

and thank you for the talk. I suppose the fact of the matter is that I'm quite the wrong sort of person to be Prince of Wales.'[63] The Prince had taken the criticism on the nose as usual, nor had he even seemed surprised.

Many of the forebodings of the courtiers about the future King's lack of a sense of duty were to crystallise during the reign itself. With hindsight, their earlier complaints took on a deeper significance, and some came to feel that the reign had been doomed even before it began.

One preoccupation that brought out the Prince's best side, and earned his mother's lasting gratitude, was his concern for Prince George, his younger brother. On leaving the Navy in 1929, George came to live at York House, but fell into the clutches of the notorious 'Kiki' Preston, dubbed 'the lady with the silver syringe', an American divorcee in the Kenyan 'Happy Valley' set.[64] The Prince of Wales, aided by Freda Dudley Ward, took charge of the matter, and with considerable effort, rescued his brother from his trouble. This was only achieved by dint of close personal involvement, since Prince George used all the wiles of an addict.

Late in 1929 the Prince had found the home he loved best, Fort Belvedere, at Shrubs Hill near Virginia Water, not far from Windsor, and had set about restoring it with a

passion. The ornamental fort had originally been built for William, Duke of Cumberland between 1746 and 1757, and then considerably altered by Wyatville in the reign of George IV. The effect was well described by Lady Diana Cooper in 1935: 'The house is an enchanting folly and only needs fifty red soldiers stood between the battlements to make it into a Walt Disney coloured symphony toy.'[65] The Prince did not change the structure of the building but, assisted by Mrs Dudley Ward, he modernised the interior, turning it into a haven of informality. He created a Turkish bath and shower in the basement, built an outdoor swimming pool, and added a battlement walk.

Above all the Prince worked in the garden, carving vistas through the rhododendrons and scrub. During every spare hour he cheerfully toiled away in the undergrowth, often obliging his guests to join him. At Fort Belvedere, the Prince was at his happiest, and when in the later years he looked back, it was to the Fort that his heart went, to the informal retreat which he had created for himself, where he entertained his friends, played the bagpipes and the ukulele, where, in due course, his friendship with Mrs Simpson blossomed, and where, in the fullness of time, the drama of the Abdication was to be played out.

By the end of the 1920s the Prince was a deeply frustrated man. His world travels were behind him and a repetitive mode of life stretched ahead. The early 1930s brought the first encounter with Mrs Wallis Warfield Simpson, who was to be the cause of his departure from the royal scene he found so constraining.

ABOVE: *The Duke of York and Detective Storrier battle with the rhododendrons at the Fort. The Prince dragooned all his guests into helping with clearance of the garden.* LEFT: *The Duke and Duchess of York clowning for the camera not long after their marriage, autumn 1923.* BELOW: *The Prince of Wales with the Duchess of York and Mrs Arthur Crichton at Small Downs House, Sandwich Bay, rented by the Prince for the local golf, early 1924.*

Wallis Warfield Spencer

Warrenton

Va

U.S.A.

CHAPTER SIX

WALLIS

Wallis Simpson was born at Blue Ridge Summit, Monterey, Pennsylvania on 19 June 1896. She was the only child of Teackle Wallis Warfield, of Baltimore, and his wife, Alice Montague, from Virginia. Her father died when she was five months old. The Warfields were a more than respectable Southern family, who could trace their ancestry back to the earliest colonial times. But, following the death of Mr Warfield, his widow was forced to survive on the kindness and charity of her relations. Thus young Wallis was brought up as a poor relation suffering from the problems and calculations that such a situation invariably entails. Mrs Warfield was to marry again twice and led an adventurous, cheerful life, dying in 1929, somewhat before her daughter's involvement with the Prince of Wales. It was Aunt Bessie Merryman, her mother's sister, who was destined to be the strong influence in Wallis's life, giving her niece stability, and wise counsel, not to mention financial assistance, over the years. At the time of the Abdication, she was the only member of her family whom Wallis could turn to for support.

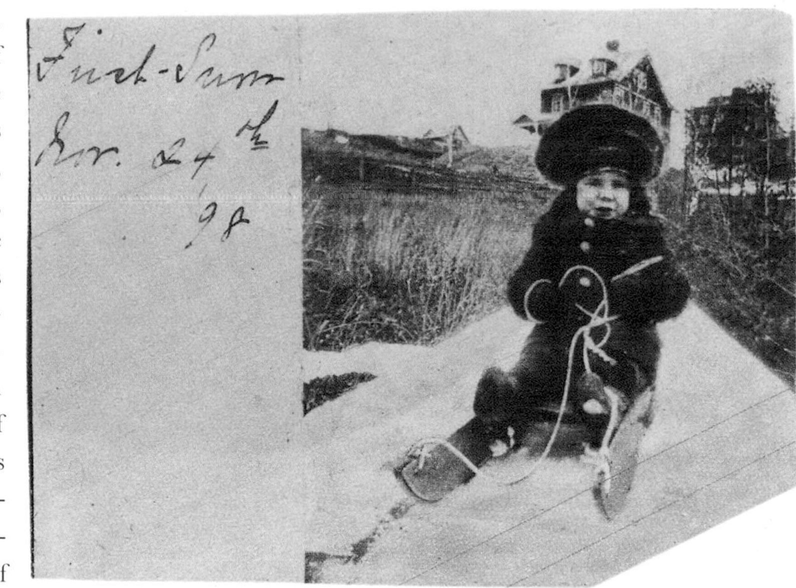

By her own admission the Duchess of Windsor was neither an intellectual nor a beauty. She lacked an ear for music or aptitude for mathematics. All her life she suffered from many haunting fears: she disliked the dark, feared thunder and dreaded flying. But she had a facility for attracting people to her, and with limited resources, made an impression. As she travelled further into the world, this art became

PREVIOUS PAGES, LEFT: *Wallis Spencer with her first husband, at the Mexican border, 1918.* BACKGROUND: *Inscription in Wallis's Baedeker to France.* RIGHT: *Wallis Warfield, aged about nine.* OPPOSITE: *Wallis's grandmother, Mrs Anna Warfield, with members of her family; clockwise: Elizabeth, her daughter-in-law; her grandsons, Douglas and Henry, and Sol, her son,* c. *1907.* ABOVE LEFT: *Teackle Wallis Warfield, Wallis's father who died five months after she was born.* TOP RIGHT: *Wallis, aged two, on a sledge.* ABOVE: *The baby Wallis with her nurse, 1896.* LEFT: *Wallis is at the far end of the table at Wakefield Manor, her cousin Lelia Barnett's house in Virginia,* c. *1906.*

OPPOSITE: *Young Wallis's own album of her family and friends; top right: a chained bear with farm children; central row: Wallis with her favourite cousin, Anita, both dressed as boys; bottom left: Wallis in Mount Vernon Place, Baltimore.* ABOVE LEFT: *Anita Warfield (centre), with Wallis and Uncle Sol Warfield, 1907. The Duchess of Windsor's Uncle Sol was the dominant male influence in her early life: 'I was always a little afraid of Uncle Sol.' Although stern, he supported the widowed Alice Warfield and Wallis for many years.* BELOW LEFT: *Uncle Sol's house, Manor Glen, Maryland, 1920.* ABOVE: *Mrs Bessie Merryman, Wallis's aunt, her trusted confidante and advisor, 1900.* BELOW: *Wallis Warfield in her débutante year, 1915.*

more polished. But looking back, the Duchess of Windsor professed: 'Mine is a simple story — or so I like to think. It is the story of an ordinary life that became extraordinary.'[66]

In their penurious state, Wallis and her mother were helped many times by Mrs Merryman. In time mother and daughter set up their own home in Baltimore. Aunt Bessie paid for Wallis's education at good schools. Oldfields, a boarding school in Glencoe, she much enjoyed. After that, to her great excitement, and on a restricted budget, Wallis came out, taking part in a cotillion at the Lyric Theatre. Local papers described her as 'one of the most attractive of the season's débutantes'.[67] She was restless and keen to escape from home. Not long afterwards the opportunity arrived when Wallis went to Florida to stay with a cousin. There she was introduced to a naval officer from Chicago called Lieutenant Earl Winfield Spencer, Junior.

OPPOSITE: *Wallis made her own blue lace gown for the Princeton Prom, 1916.* ABOVE: *Wallis Warfield and her mother, Alice Raisin, 1916. Alice was then married to her second husband, John Freeman Raisin.* ABOVE RIGHT: *Portrait of Wallis Warfield in her wedding dress. She married Lieutenant Earl Winfield Spencer on 8 November 1916.* BELOW: *Win Spencer, San Diego, California, flying instructor in the Navy.* RIGHT: *Wallis Spencer, San Diego.* BELOW RIGHT: *Wallis Spencer with Aunt Bessie Merryman outside her home, Coronado, California, 1917.*

Wallis detected flaws in Win Spencer's character from early on: 'Deeply imbedded in his nature, under the surface layer of jauntiness and gaiety, was a strange brooding quality that verged on bitterness and even cynicism; a word or gesture could change his manner in a flash.'[68] Nevertheless, on 8 November 1916 Wallis became his wife in a fashionable wedding. In her memoirs, she was to relate many grim stories of his cruelty to her. Spencer was a heavy drinker, and the bottle of gin he produced on their honeymoon was the first of many. While he was invariably extrovert and friendly in public, he played cruel practical jokes in private. Within a year Wallis knew they were incompatible.

Spencer was a flying instructor in charge of the naval aeronautical school at Rockwell Field, California. He hoped for an overseas posting, but found himself moved to San Diego. Feeling passed over, the suspicion of his own failure turned him in on himself. His practical joking became more cruel. He often locked Wallis in her room all day. Separation became inevitable, but at first divorce was unthinkable.

Wallis headed for Washington, 'a castaway upon an emotional sea'.[69] After a period of travel and freedom, during which she travelled to Paris with her cousin and had an affair with Felipe Espil, the First Secretary at the Argentine Embassy in Washington, Wallis decided to give her marriage another try. She set off for Hong Kong where Win was now stationed, in 1924. Their reunion was not a success. Wallis

withdrew from this unsatisfactory situation and, in the company of other naval wives, visited several Chinese cities, and enjoyed what she called her 'lotus year' in Peking. Here she was much in the company of an old friend, Katherine Bigelow, a war widow who was now married to the wealthy Herman Rogers. Living for the moment in China, the couple's only aim in life was their quest for the most beautiful house in the world. Both were to be life-long friends and supporters of Wallis.

The Spencers' marriage lasted officially until 1927, when Wallis obtained a divorce in Virginia. Win Spencer went on to marry three more times, he had several children and died in San Diego on 29 May 1950.

Wallis's second husband was Ernest Simpson, whom she met in New York at the home of her friends Jacques and Mary Kirk Raffray. As she recalled in her memoirs, Ernest was still married, though unhappily, to his first wife, Dorothea. Thus, at this time, he was in the close company of three of the four women he was to marry (Mary Raffray was to become his third wife after the Abdication drama). Simpson was the son of an American father and an English mother. He was a partner in a shipping firm with interests in both countries and had served in the Coldstream Guards during the First World War. He and Wallis saw more and more of each other. Eventually he decided to seek a divorce and asked her to marry him when he was free. Their wedding took place at Chelsea Registry Office on 21 July 1928, and they settled in London, first at 12 Upper Berkeley Street and later at 5 Bryanston Court.

Ernest Simpson represented something of a port in a storm. He was conventional and respectable, a well-read and well-travelled man, if not particularly interesting. But he was kind and reliable. With him Wallis felt safe and must surely have believed that at last she had settled down. Even if this was not going to be a love-match of deep intensity, it was certainly never dull. Gradually they became well-known in Anglo-American circles.

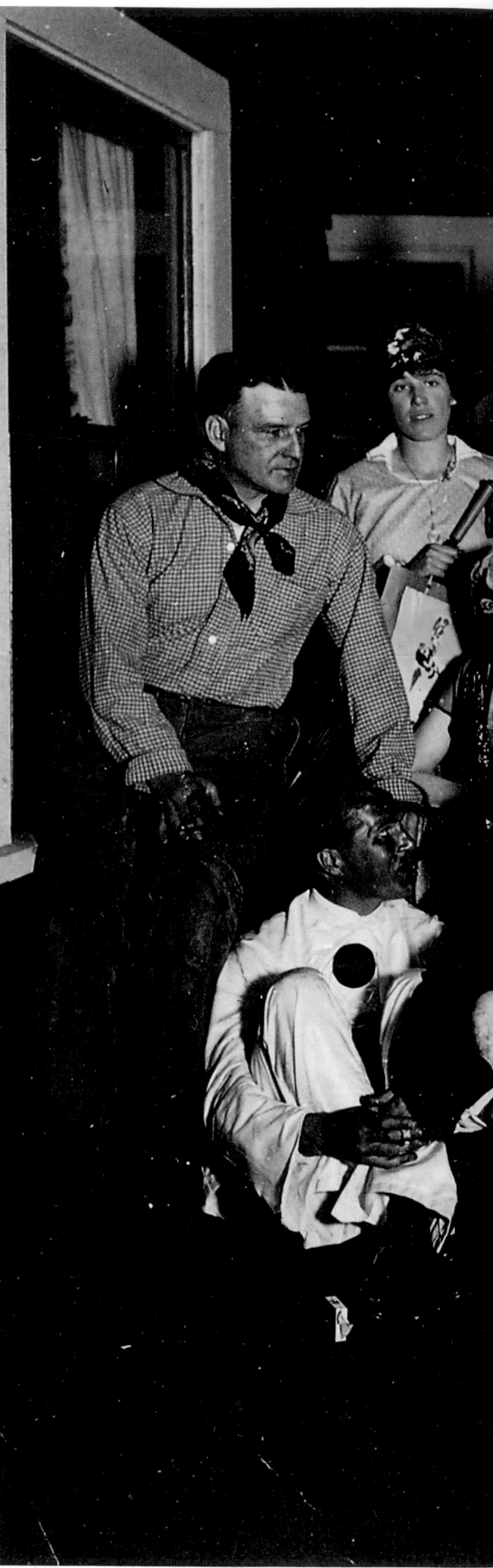

RIGHT: *Win Spencer, Grand Canyon, 1917. Wallis's marriage to him was already unhappy. Win behaved badly and drank too much, embittered by his lack of promotion.* ABOVE: *Wallis on the beach with her husband and her lifelong friend, Katherine Bigelow (later Rogers), California, 1918.* FAR RIGHT: *A fancy dress party with naval friends, Coronado, California, 1919. Wallis is in Chinese dress (front row, centre).* OVERLEAF: *Charlie Chaplin arm-in-arm with elegant Wallis and Rhoda Fullam, with Marianna Sands (left). The friends met him at the Hotel del Coronado, 1919.*

9021.

MAKE
RAISIN BREAD

Having been an attractive but never a beautiful woman, Mrs Simpson gradually acquired a certain chic as she conquered London's café society with the help and blessing of the famous hostesses, Lady Cunard and Lady Colefax.

Cecil Beaton, who photographed her often, recorded her gradual transformation. In his diary he described his first impression of her in the early 1930s: 'To hear her speak was enough. Her voice was raucous and appalling. I thought her awful, common, vulgar, strident, a second-rate American with no charm.' By 1936 he had revised his opinion: 'Now she is all that is elegant. The whole of London flocks after her as the mistress and possible wife of the King. . . . I am certain she has more glamour and is of more interest than any public figure.'[70]

It was her chance meeting with the Prince of Wales that had altered everything. In her memoirs, the Duchess of Windsor wrote of the awe that had seemed to accompany every royal happening or reported royal remark. She had followed the doings of the court through the Court Circular, and like the British people, she had been worried by the serious illness of the King in 1928. She wrote of how, at that time, almost as in a novel, she had once glimpsed through a car window 'a delicate boyish face staring straight ahead, the whole expression suggesting the gravity of a deep inward concern.'[71] She had therefore expected much from her first encounter with the Prince. The exact date of their meeting would now appear to have been established as 10 January 1931.

Her friend Connie Thaw was unable to accompany her husband, Benjamin, First Secretary at the American Embassy, to a shooting weekend in Melton Mowbray with Connie's sister, Thelma, Viscountess Furness, at which the Prince of Wales would be present. (Lady Furness was then enjoying a romance with the Prince.) Connie asked the Simpsons to go with her husband instead. Wallis was so unused to such society she had to be taught to curtsey by Benjamin Thaw and practised in the train on the way to

LEFT: *Wallis and her cousin, Corinne Mustin, both immaculately turned out, at a riding stable, Del Monte, California, 1920.* RIGHT: *12 Upper Berkeley Steet was Wallis's London address when she moved to England, after her second marriage to Ernest Simpson. Wallis on the balcony of her new home with sister-in-law Maud Kerr-Smiley and Maud's son, Peter, 1928. The house, described by Wallis as small, was rented furnished from Lady Chesham.* TOP RIGHT: *Ernest, Wallis and Aunt Bessie Merryman at Baden-Baden during a motoring holiday in Germany, 1930.*

At the final break-down of her first marriage Wallis was stranded in China. There followed her 'lotus year' in Peking. BELOW: *Outside the walls of the Forbidden City.* BOTTOM LEFT: *At the races with Aldo da Zara, an ardent admirer, 1925.* RIGHT: *A day in the Western Hills.* BOTTOM RIGHT: *At Katherine Rogers's house, the Black Dragon Temple outside Peking, with their old friend, Colonel Louis Little.* OPPOSITE: *With Herman Rogers by the pool.*

Melton Mowbray.

When they were introduced, as the Duke of Windsor later recalled, he ventured the idea that she must be missing the central heating for which America was famed. 'I am sorry, Sir, but you have disappointed me,' she said. 'In what way?' he asked. 'Every American woman who comes to your country is always asked that same question. I had hoped for something more original from the Prince of Wales.'[72]

Mrs Simpson did not try to please in a conventional way. At their next meeting, following her presentation at court, Mrs Simpson revealed that she had overheard him saying to the Duke of Connaught that the lighting at the Palace was so bright that all the women looked ghastly. From these small beginnings, combined with a few more chance encounters, came an invitation to the Fort.

Gradually, slowly and imperceptibly, the American who a few years earlier had seen the lonely Prince of Wales drive by, became a regular guest at the Fort, while the once distant Prince seemed more than happy to accept invitations to Bryanston Court. Thelma Furness's hold on him proved transitory, Freda Dudley Ward found her calls were no longer put through. Before any of them realised it the Prince had fallen under Wallis Simpson's spell.

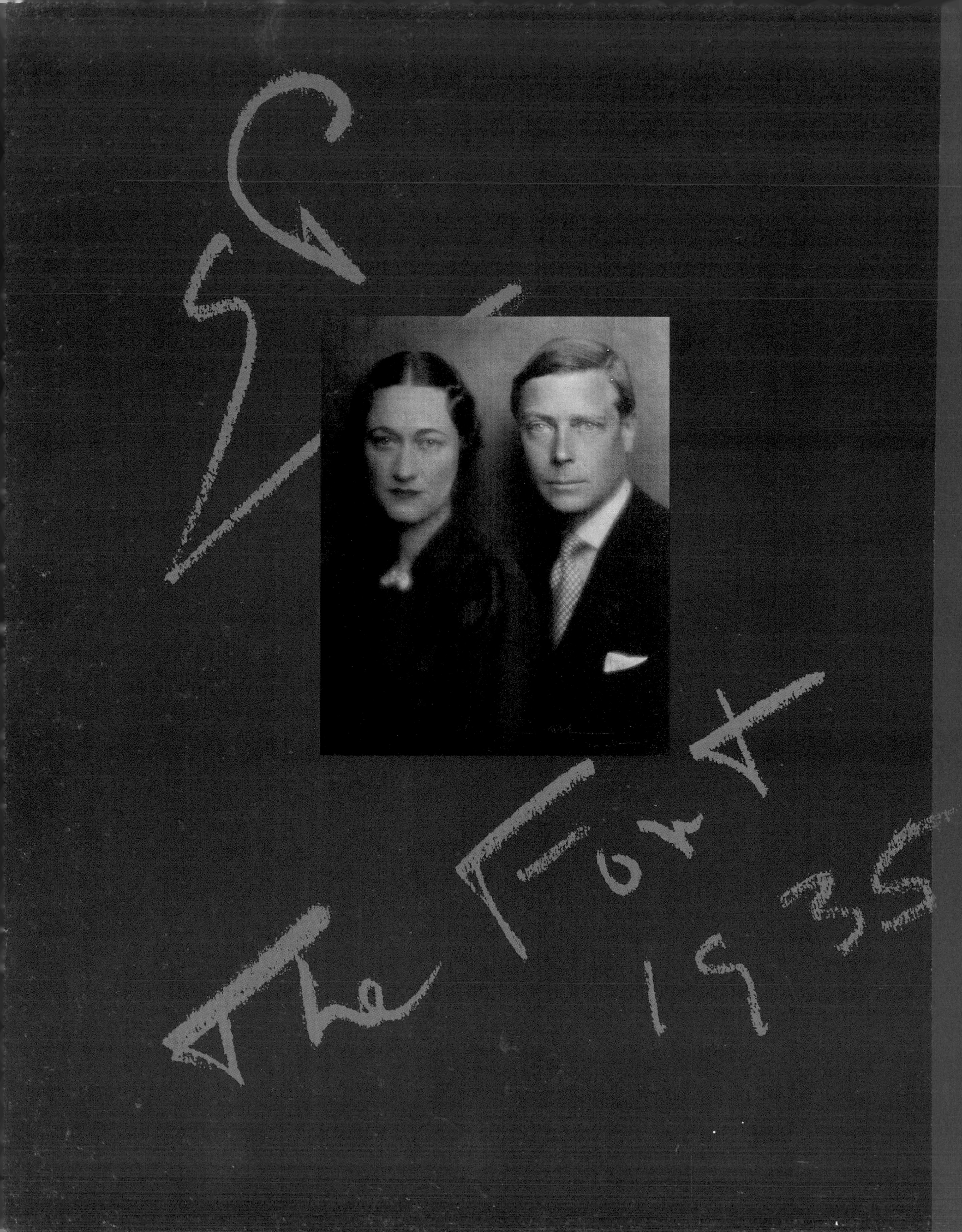
The Fort
1935

CHAPTER SEVEN

THE PRINCE OUT OF STEP

PREVIOUS PAGES, LEFT: *The Prince and Mrs Simpson, portrait by Hugh Cecil, June 1935.* BACKGROUND: *Inscription in a book from Fort Belvedere.* RIGHT: *A signed and framed photograph from the Kitzbühel skiing holiday, February 1935.*
BOTTOM: *There were fewer overseas tours, but still public engagements at home. Opening Twickenham Bridge, July 1933.* RIGHT AND BELOW: *Holiday snapshots in Central Europe, February 1935: the Prince in Budapest, Mrs Simpson in Vienna.* OPPOSITE: *Wallis with Slipper at Villa Le Roc, August 1935.*

By the beginning of 1930, the Prince of Wales was out on a limb as far as the court was concerned, and relations with his father were distant if not actually strained. He appeared at court functions when he was required, but otherwise he went his own way, generally abiding by court conventions but setting occasional new trends.

During these years the Prince liked to believe he was a man in touch with his people, even a step ahead of his time in matters of fashion and social behaviour. In old age the Duke of Windsor explained this to Kenneth Harris: 'The Duchess and I were so much "with it" in our day that that was one of the accusations levelled against us.'[73]

The Prince's popularity had been earned by his courageous efforts in the Great War and the well-established images of him travelling the world with his winning smile. His concern with the underprivileged had also gained him many loyal supporters throughout Britain.

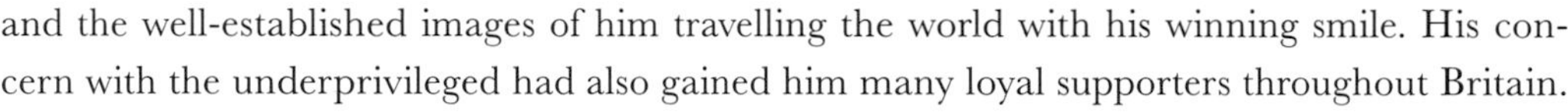

Even beyond the British Empire the Prince made a huge impression. The distinguished American columnist Adela Rogers St Johns was one who observed him from overseas. To girls of her generation he was an icon: 'We didn't have movie heroes or aviators in uniform to worship. Most of us concentrated on the Prince of Wales. I had his picture in a silver frame on my

B

dressing table. The dream of every American girl was to dance with him.'[74]

In this respect the Prince enjoyed a glamorous role in the public eye somewhat akin to that of Diana, Princess of Wales, today. His popularity almost certainly gave him the impression that there was much that his people would allow him to get away with, that his personal wishes would be accepted because they liked him. In his confrontation with the Establishment later on, he was to find that his personal popularity counted for rather less than he imagined.

To the disappointment and concern of King George V, the Prince had remained resolutely unmarried. The pattern of sharing his private life with safely married ladies had been long established. That he was again deeply enthralled with such a lady gave no special cause for concern. Members of the Royal Family have often been in love with married people, partly because of the element of forbidden fruit, partly because of the greater sophistication of married people and partly out of safety.

The Prince's main obsession during the early 1930s was Mrs Simpson. He dined often with Ernest and Wallis Simpson at their flat and appeared happier there than at other functions. They went to nightclubs together, and there were many weekend parties at the Fort, but Mrs Simpson's reign truly began when Thelma Furness left for the United States in January 1934, urging Wallis to look after the Prince in her absence. This she did so well that there was no room for Thelma on her return in March. Ernest Simpson did not appear to mind much, and as he and his wife drifted apart, so his attention turned to their friend, Mary Kirk Raffray, whom he married quietly some years later. But in the early days, he was always of the party.

LEFT: *Wallis Simpson, with Lord Louis Mountbatten, and Herman and Katherine Rogers, photographed by the Prince of Wales on the Rogers' yacht,* Angelique, *August 1935.* RIGHT: *The Prince with guests in Corsica, September 1935; left to right: Katherine Rogers, Mrs Simpson, John Aird, Gladys Buist, Helen Fitzgerald, Lord Sefton and the Prince.* ABOVE: *The Prince wore an eye-catching, yellow, double-breasted suit during the winter sports holiday at Kitzbühel, Austria, February 1935.*

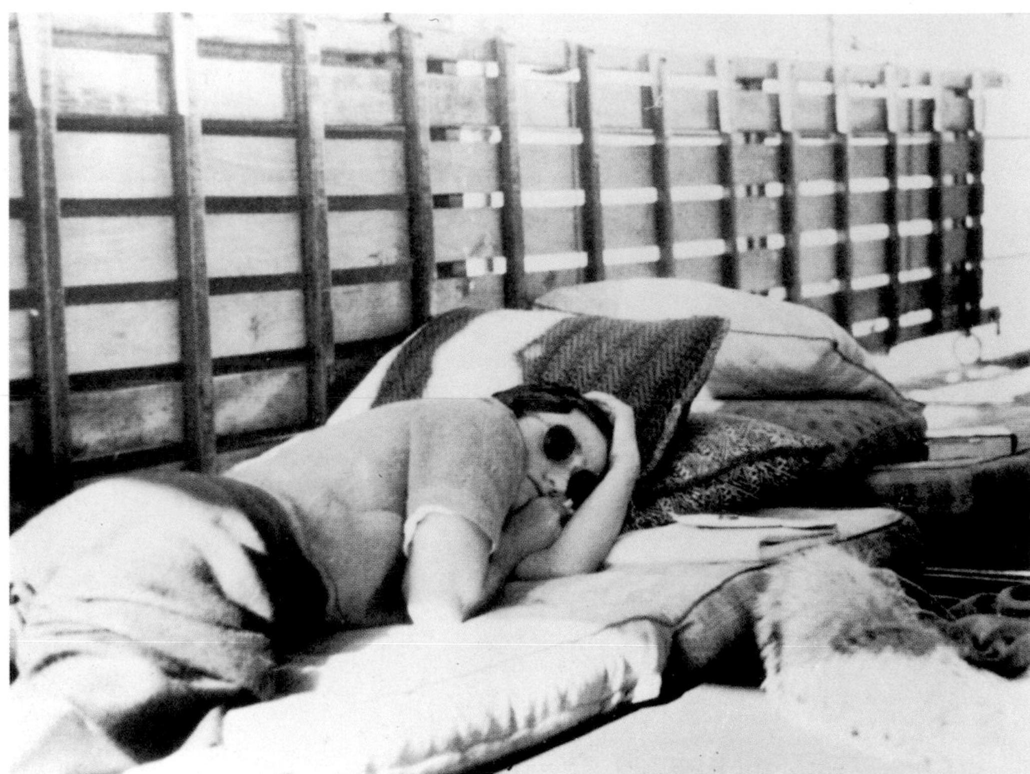

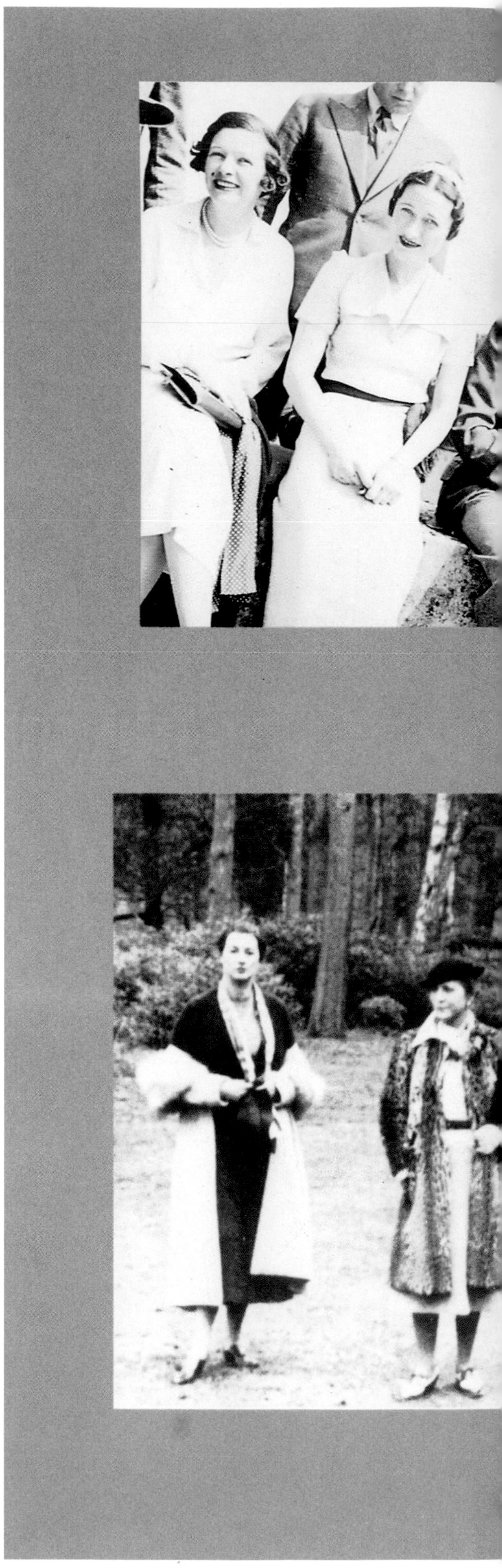

Mrs Simpson was obviously a figure of increasing fascination to those who saw her at this time. By April 1935, the politician and diarist Chips Channon noted: 'she has already the air of a personage who walks into a room as though she expects to be curtsied to. At least, she wouldn't be too surprised'[75]. Chips thought that Mrs Simpson was trying to storm society during what might prove to be a brief reign in the King's affections. At other times he was generous in her praise: 'a woman of charm, sense, balance and great wit, with dignity and taste' and later 'an excellent influence on the King [Edward VIII]'[76]. The journalist Robert Bruce Lockhart was another who noted that the Prince had gained confidence since Mrs Simpson took him on.[77] Of course, judgements by contemporaries were not always impartial. The favourite of the Heir to the Throne inevitably became endowed with added charm in the eyes of those who saw her as a way of gaining access to the future King.

There was a certain amount of official travel for the Prince in the 1930s, but none of the lengthy Empire tours of the previous decade. Again in the company of Prince George, he went to South America on a trade mission, and then opened the British Empire Exhibition in Buenos Aires in 1931. In 1932,

ABOVE: *The Prince photographed Wallis constantly — here during a siesta on the 1935 cruise.* LEFT: *The engagement of Prince Henry to Lady Alice Montagu-Douglas-Scott, November 1935.* RIGHT: *Country weekends; above: Wallis and the Prince as guests at Mereworth Castle, summer 1935; right: the Prince with their host, Esmond Harmsworth (standing, second left), the tennis champion Helen Wills (left), Sir Samuel Hoare (behind her), Lady Cunard (with hat) and others; below: snapshots near Virginia Water, when Wallis's old friend Mary Raffray (left), future wife of Ernest Simpson (right), visited the Fort, March 1936.*

A
B

PREVIOUS PAGES: *The Prince photographing Wallis and Slipper, Porquerolles, August 1935.*
ABOVE: *Wallis, portrait by Fayer of Vienna, February 1935.* ABOVE LEFT: *Duff Cooper, Secretary of State for War (left), and Anthony Eden, Foreign Secretary, Fort Belvedere, 1935.* BELOW: *The* Rosaura *cruise, September 1934. The Prince and Wallis walking hand in hand; foreground John Aird (centre) and Lord Moyne (right).*

he and Prince George also went to Corfu to pay a morale-boosting visit to the Mediterranean Fleet in Malta. Following the King's serious illness in 1928, the Prince of Wales generally confined himself to short public and private visits to Europe.

The Prince's bachelor state was made even more conspicuous when his two younger brothers married, Prince George (Duke of Kent) to the beautiful Princess Marina of Greece in 1934, and Prince Henry (Duke of Gloucester) to Lady Alice Montagu-Douglas-Scott in 1935.

In 1934, the Prince and Mrs Simpson took the first of their long Mediterranean cruise holidays together. When they went to Biarritz with a party of people, Mrs Simpson was chap-

LEFT: *The Prince in full evening dress leaving the informality of Fort Belvedere to attend a court function at Windsor Castle, 1935. Below his left knee he wears the Garter.* BELOW: *The old King's reign was drawing to a close. George V photographed at Sandringham in 1934 with his favourite shooting pony, Jock, who followed his master's coffin in the funeral procession in January 1936.*

eroned by her aunt, Mrs Merryman. For the first time she was without her husband. While in Biarritz they went on board Lord Moyne's converted Channel steamer, *Rosaura*, for a three-week cruise. This was followed by an eleven-day voyage along the Spanish, Portuguese, Corsican and Italian coasts, with a week on Lake Como.

The pleasures and privacy of the sea cruise must have impressed the Prince, and 1934 was to set the pattern for the following three summers. In August 1935 the Prince rented Villa Le Roc, the Golfe Juan home of the Marquess and Marchioness of Cholmondeley, where he and Mrs Simpson entertained a number of house guests, and were visited by such distinguished figures as Mr and Mrs Winston Churchill and Lloyd George. Early in September they took a cruise on the *Cutty Sark*, the Duke of Westminster's yacht, later borrowing the *Sister Anne* from their friend Daisy Fellowes for a two-day cruise to the island of Porquerolles. They then extended the holiday by travelling to Hungary, spending a week on a lake near Budapest, progressing to Linz for golf, and then making an overland trip through the Austrian Tyrol, before finally arriving at Munich. The visit caused anguish to the Prince's staff since he cancelled some official engagements at home in order to prolong his idyll. During the trip the Prince took huge numbers of photographs of Mrs Simpson. They are evidence of his fascination with her and of her response to it.

The trip came towards the end of the year of King George V's Silver Jubilee, which was also the last year of his reign. He processed with Queen Mary through the streets of London, marvelling at the reception he received. But he was tired and the celebrations wearied him further. In December he was due to open Parliament, but then the sister closest to him, Princess Victoria, died at Coppins. The King retreated to Sandringham for Christmas, destined to outlive her by only a matter of weeks.

This silver pepper pot was presented to the Prince of Wales by the Great Western Railway in gratitude for his support during the General Strike in 1926. He had lent a vehicle to deliver the anti-strike government newspaper to Wales. Such an action may surprise those who remember his 'Something must be done' comment after visiting the poverty stricken provinces. The Prince's sympathy after the 1914-18 war was very much with the working poor, many of whom were his old comrades-in-arms. But he was instinctively to the right in politics and he saw the General Strike as a threat from communist agitators. At the end of the strike, however, he was anxious that there should be no punishment for the ringleaders.

I, Edward the Eighth, of Great Britain, Ireland, and the British Dominions beyond the S

f India, do hereby decla termination to renounce f and for My descendan at effect should be gi nt of Abdication i

In e hereunto set My hand this er, nineteen hundred and thirty six, in the presence of the witnesses whose signatures are subscribed.

SIGNED AT
FORT BELVEDERE
IN THE PRESENCE
OF

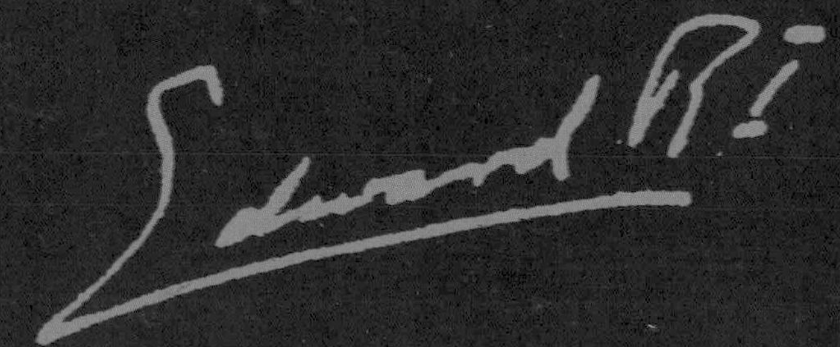

CHAPTER EIGHT

REIGN AND ABDICATION

DAILY SKETCH, WEDNESDAY, JANUARY 22, 1936

PROCLAMATION NUMBER—PAGES OF PICTURES

DAILY SKETCH

ROYAL FUNERAL PLANS

No. 8,341 WEDNESDAY, JANUARY 22, 1936 ONE PENNY

OUR NEW KING BEGINS HIS WORK

From House Of Sorrow To State Council

'Plane Flight To Make His First Speech As Monarch

WHILE THE Empire and the world mourned the death of King George, the new King, his sorrow still heavy on him, yesterday took up the reins of monarchy.

Edward the Eighth, King-Emperor, flew from Sandringham to London—the first reigning King of England to fly—and at St. James's Palace held his first Privy Council and made his first speech as King.

With the King on his flight was the Duke of York, the heir-presumptive.

The King's first signature as sovereign—"Edward R.I."—was attached to a message sent to the Army last night. The message, dated "Buckingham Palace," said:

"I desire on my accession to the Throne to express my thanks to the Army for its devoted services to my beloved father. I recall with gratitude the noble response which the Army made during the Great War to his proud confidence in its loyalty, valour and steadfastness.

"I look back to my service as a young officer in the Great War as one of the most valuable experiences of my life. It gave me the privileges of comradeship with soldiers drawn from the United Kingdom, from the Dominions, from India and from the Colonies.

TO THE NAVY—

"I learned to understand and to appreciate those essential characteristics which united them in the sternest crisis of our history—the same fervent attachment to the Crown, the same good humour and endurance in adversity and the same determination to uphold the traditions of chivalry and courage which are our common inheritance."

The King's message to the Navy was: "I desire that the Royal Navy and all my other Naval forces throughout the Empire should know with what gratitude I recall the distinguished services rendered by them during the reign of the King, my beloved Father, and how much I cherish the recollection of the intimate personal association so long existing between my family and that profession to which my Father devoted his youth and early manhood, and in which I and two of my brothers received our early training."

FUNERAL PLANS

In a message to the Royal Air Force the King says: "If the air forces of the Empire are young, they have all the vigour of youth; and, in the space of a few years, they have already achieved a high tradition. I shall watch their further progress with a keen personal solicitude."

At noon to-morrow a train will leave Wolferton Station, bringing the body of King George to London, where it is to lie in State. The funeral will be at Windsor on Tuesday (see page 3). How the new King will be proclaimed in London to-day is told on page 2.

Meanwhile, yesterday the world paid lavish tribute to King George, who, more than any man, influenced its destiny in the troublous days that followed the Great War.

Mussolini, Hitler and Kalinin all sent expressions of regret for the passing of a great man.

'THE EMPIRE—HOW IS IT?'

Sandringham . . . the King, his last moment near, returned to consciousness. He spoke . . . to his secretary: "How is it with the Empire?"

"All is well, sire," came the answer. The King smiled . . . and sank again into unconsciousness. . . .

—Mr. Baldwin, broadcasting last night.

A hitherto unpublished portrait of the new King in the full-dress uniform of an Admiral. —(Hugh Cecil.)

King George V died at Sandringham at 11.55 p.m. on 20 January 1936, helped into his peaceful sleep by the guiding hand of his doctor, Lord Dawson of Penn. The new King came to the throne with the customary good wishes of the press. There was a genuine feeling that this youthful monarch with his winning looks and nervous charm had earned the affection of the nation. *The Times* welcomed his accession: 'As a King the nation and Empire will be able to look up to him as one who has a statesman-like knowledge and sympathetic understanding of the wants and interests of all creeds and races over whom he has been called to reign and a worthy successor of the beloved Sovereign whose loss they now deeply deplore.'[78]

On St David's Day, the King himself spoke directly to his people, using the radio, the medium his father had made so popular. He concluded with some personal words:

'I am better known to you as as the Prince of Wales — as a man who, during the war and since, has had the opportunity of getting to know the people of nearly every country of the world, under all conditions and circumstances. And, although I now speak to you as King, I am still that same man who has had that experience and whose constant effort it will be to continue to promote the well-being of his fellow men . . .'[79]

Something in these words suggests that Edward VIII feared he might lose the identity he had established as the golden boy 'Prince of Wales', and indeed when he became King he underwent a transformation. While the Prince had appeared, at least in the popular imagination, as an eternally boyish figure, full of energy, fun and laughter, a man for whom nothing was too much trouble, the new King looked worn and troubled from the outset of his reign. He looked glum as he arrived at Buckingham Palace for a levée or to receive loyal addresses, and the homage that was paid to him seemed to isolate him further, acting as a stark reminder of the responsibilities that were now his, and with which he was miserably ill at ease.

In part, these were symptoms of the traditional problems faced by any new king as he

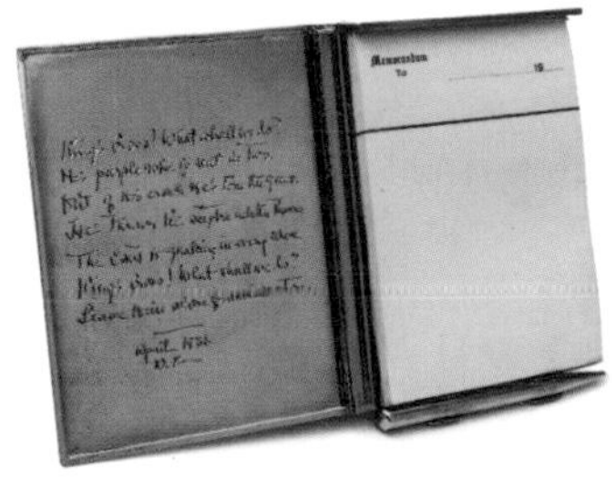

As a hostess, the Duchess of Windsor was a perfectionist. By her side during dinner parties she kept what the servants came to know as the 'complaint pad', in which she would jot down any failings in the food or service. The gold Van Cleef & Arpels memorandum case which held the notepad was a present she had given the Duke when he was King, in April 1936. The Imperial cypher ERI that adorns the cover is the modern design the new King had adopted. Inside, engraved in facsimile of Mrs Simpson's handwriting, is a poem by Eleanor Farjeon beginning: 'King's Cross! What shall we do? His purple robe is rent in two. . .' The King was anxious and irritable in the first months of his reign, and the pun on the name of the London railway terminus appealed to Wallis's sense of humour.

PREVIOUS PAGES, LEFT: *Official portrait in Welsh Guards uniform, by Hugh Cecil, 1935.* BACKGROUND: *The Instrument of Abdication.* LEFT: *Label of an American record of the Farewell Broadcast (see page 157).* OPPOSITE: *The new King caused a stir by arriving in London by air.* BELOW LEFT: *The last weeks as King. At the review of the Home Fleet, Portland, 12 November.* BELOW: *His visit to depressed industrial areas of South Wales the following week received much press coverage. The public was still unaware of the impending crisis.*

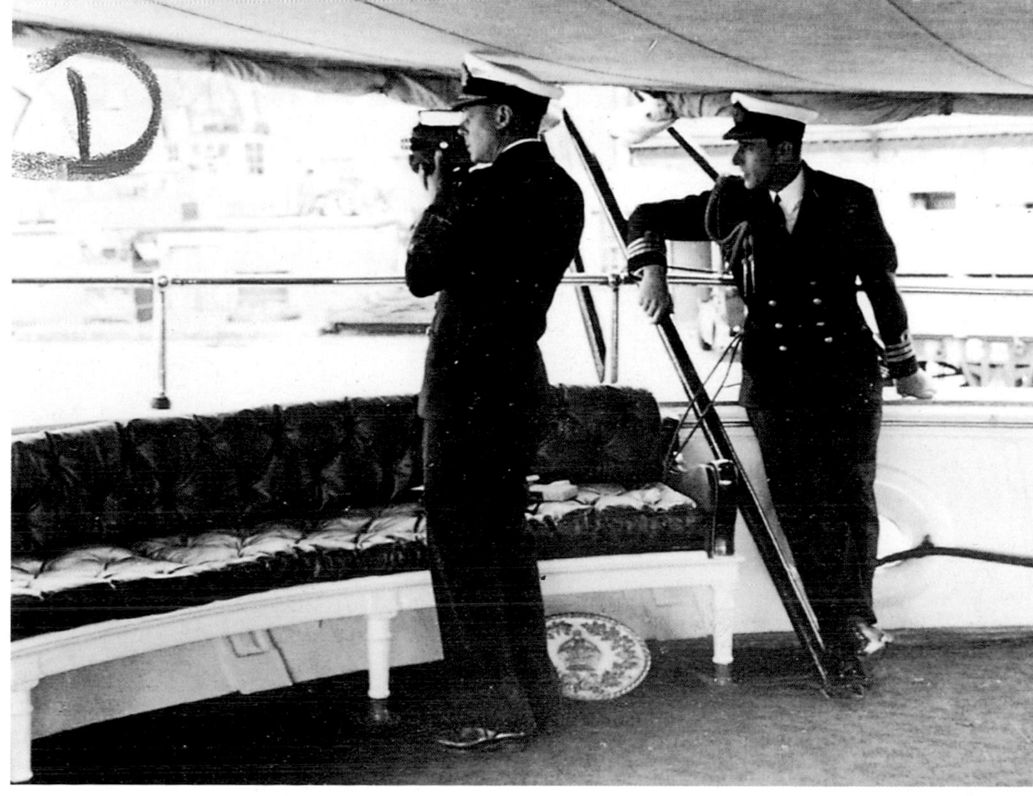

turns himself from heir into monarch. The years as Prince of Wales had been a kind of apprenticeship for the job, but at his accession he felt stunned, just as his father had been been before him, and inadequate, as if he were not capable of taking his father's place.

Yet this was not all. Edward VIII was already a troubled man when he came to the throne, weighed down by an additional burden. He was worrying how he could retain his private life whilst fulfilling his public duties. He wanted to marry Wallis Simpson, hoping, and sometimes believing, that he could make her his Queen. The threat of the looming Coronation (set for May 1937) hung over him, and he believed that he must resolve his problems before then.

His short reign had its splendid moments and its dramatic ones. On 16 July 1936, at a ceremony in Hyde Park, the King presented new colours to two battalions of Grenadier Guards, all three battalions of Coldstream Guards and the 2nd battalion, Scots Guards. The Royal Family was there in force for this grand occasion. The King spoke to his soldiers, recalling the horrors of the Great War at a time when international tension in Europe was increasing:

'With all my heart I hope, and indeed I pray, that never again will our age and generation be called upon to face such stern and terrible days. Humanity cries out for peace and the assurance of peace, and you will find in peace opportunities of duty and service as noble as any that bygone battlefields can show . . .'[80]

The King departed from Hyde Park on horseback, accompanied by the Duke of York. As he rode down Constitution Hill, a man pushed through the crowd and aimed a loaded revolver at him. The revolver was knocked from his hand, landing at the King's feet. How serious the man's intention was as unclear then as now, but the King's courage in this terrifying moment was manifest to all who saw it.

A few days later the World War was again remembered. On 26 July the King flew to France to inaugurate the Canadian War Memorial at Vimy Ridge in the presence of 3,500 war veterans.

ABOVE: *Royal duties. Riding back from the Guards Colours ceremony at Hyde Park, 16 July. The King showed admirable pluck when a gun was hurled at him in Constitution Hill by a would-be assassin.* TOP: *Protocol required the King to call on the heads of state of countries he visited on his Continental holiday, August-September 1936. He is here leaving the residence of the Austrian President, Vienna.* BELOW: *With Atatürk, during the semi-official visit to Istanbul, 4 September.* RIGHT: *With King Boris of Bulgaria (centre) and Prince Cyril, Sofia, 7 September.*

While the King's public appearances were always popular, his office at the Palace did not always find it easy to handle the King's business, the everyday work of a constitutional monarch. The late King's Private Secretary, Lord Wigram, stayed on for the first months, as is customary, before being succeeded by one of the Assistant Private Secretaries, Major Alec Hardinge. Hardinge's relationship with his Royal master was to prove an uneasy one. The King never took his Private Secretary into his confidence about his relationship with Mrs Simpson, nor at any stage did he discuss the crisis with him. Hardinge was, of course, aware of the existence of Mrs Simpson and of the distress the liaison had caused the late King. But he did not consider the matter particularly serious while she remained married to Mr Simpson. Hardinge's view of his new master was not

entirely negative: he liked the new King's forthright approach to his job, if not his irregular hours. But the lack of sympathy between the King and the man who should have been his closest adviser was to play an important part when the Abdication crisis broke.

The crisis was to focus entirely on the marriage issue, but the King's marriage plans were not the first cause for official anxiety. What concerned Hardinge and government officials was the King's neglect of his red boxes. He would leave state papers unread at Fort Belvedere, often for weeks on end, thus delaying government business.

There were also disturbing rumours concerning national security. As was normal in London society, the King and his friends mixed freely with foreign diplomats. Joachim von Ribbentrop, the new German Ambassador, was something of a favourite with Emerald Cunard, the celebrated hostess, who was also a friend of the King and Mrs Simpson and a regular visitor at the Fort. 'Chips' Channon had heard gossip about the King's 'Nazi leanings' as early as June 1935 and commented lightheartedly in his diary: '. . . he is alleged to have been influenced by Emerald (who is rather *éprise* with Herr Ribbentrop) through Mrs Simpson.'[81] It was no secret that the King believed war should be avoided at all costs, and he was less fearful of the threat of Germany than he was of the spread of communism. The King's advisers were not convinced by stories of his Nazi sympathies; for them the most worrying aspect was that the King was not taking affairs of state sufficiently seriously, nor did he seem to care what they thought.

BY TRADITION THE OFFICIAL PORTRAITS OF SUCCESSIVE MONARCHS ON COINS AND STAMPS FACE ALTERNATE WAYS. EDWARD VIII BROKE WITH THIS CONVENTION; HE THOUGHT HIS LEFT PROFILE WAS HIS BEST SIDE AND INSISTED THAT HE SHOULD BE DEPICTED ACCORDINGLY, FACING THE SAME WAY AS HIS FATHER. HUGH CECIL WAS COMMISSIONED TO TAKE THE PORTRAIT PHOTOGRAPH TO BE USED FOR THE DESIGN OF THE STAMPS. IT WAS PROBABLY THE OPEN-NECKED INFORMALITY OF THIS PHOTOGRAPH THAT APPEALED TO THE KING. HE INSCRIBED TWO PRINTS OF THE PICTURE FOR WALLIS SIMPSON AND HAD THEM SET IN A DOUBLE-FRONTED GOLD CARTIER FRAME. THE NEW STAMPS LOOKED VERY MODERN COMPARED TO THOSE OF HIS OF HIS FATHER'S REIGN. GEORGE VI REVERTED TO THE OLDER STYLE.

Then came the famous Mediterranean summer cruise on the steam-yacht *Nahlin*. Foreign press coverage of the cruise made the King's involvement with Mrs Simpson public (at least to people outside Britain), but of immediate importance to the Government was the potential value of the cruise in international diplomacy, as the holidaying King mixed work with pleasure, paying visits to the heads of state the countries he passed through.

The *Nahlin* cruise kept the King out of England for a month between mid-August and mid-September. The main party consisted of the King and Mrs Simpson, and regular cronies special friends such as the Duff Coopers, Lord Sefton, Helen Fitzgerald, as well as various

LEFT: *During his reign, Edward VIII continued to live at Fort Belvedere, his haven of informality as Prince of Wales. Mrs Simpson usually acted as hostess, but guests could find themselves served with drinks by the King himself, who would then entertain them with bagpipe music.* ABOVE: *With Slipper by the pool.* TOP: *Luncheon at Blenheim, with Winston and Clementine Churchill, Emerald Cunard (second left) and Diana Cooper (right), May 1936.*

members of the Royal staff. This was an extensive Mediterranean tour, though for political reasons Italy was not on the itinerary. It began at Sibenik in Yugoslavia, and made its way along the Dalmatian coast to Corfu, where the party dined with the deposed King George II of Greece, who was spending the summer there with his English mistress, Mrs Butter-Jones.

They then passed through the Corinth Canal to Piraeus and Athens, and on across the Aegean to Gallipoli. Here the King visited the battlefields and then moved on to Istanbul, where at the instigation of the Foreign Office, which was anxious to improve Anglo-Turkish relations, the King paid a semi-official visit to the President, Mustafa Kemâl Atatürk. This was the most important diplomatic engagement on the cruise and the most successful. It left a strong impression on all the party. Tommy Lascelles remembered it as the most interesting day of his life as a courtier. He observed a charming host with penetrating sapphire eyes, but was aware of the President's reputation of having committed every crime known to the most expert criminologists.[82]

ABOVE: *The* Nahlin *cruise, August-September 1936. Wallis Simpson with Duff Cooper sightseeing in Kotor on the Dalmatian coast.* TOP: *Relaxing on board: the King (standing) with guests, Lord Sefton (right), John Aird (left), Katherine Rogers (second left). In the foreground are some of the jigsaw puzzles brought for their entertainment.* RIGHT: *Wallis Simpson relaxing on the* Nahlin.

The party then sailed along the Bosporus, after which the King and Mrs Simpson left the *Nahlin* and travelled with their party to Budapest, first in Atatürk's private train, then in King Boris of Bulgaria's train (gamely driven by King Boris himself), and then in Prince Paul of Yugoslavia's train.

Later in the summer, after the publicity of the cruise, the King aggravated the fears of his family and courtiers by taking Mrs Simpson on his first visit to Balmoral as King. Local people were offended when he did not attend a public engagement: while the Duke of York opened a new hospital in Aberdeen in his place, the King was photographed driving informally to the station to pick Mrs Simpson up.

The British press remained silent on the subject of Mrs Simpson, keeping the majority of the public in ignorance. But the foreign press were far from silent. Soon concerned letters began to arrive at Buckingham Palace from British citizens living overseas. Hardinge used to send a selection of these to the Fort, including the famous 'Britannicus' letter from an expatriate living in New Jersey.[83]

It was only when the Simpson divorce proceedings opened in Ipswich in October that official concern became urgent. As Hardinge put it: 'This piece of news seemed to me to be very serious, for if Mrs Simpson obtained her divorce, the sword of Damocles would, after the necessary six months, be hanging over the people of the British Empire.'[84] Hardinge therefore contacted the Prime Minister, Stanley Baldwin, thus establishing the interests of the Crown above those of the King as an individual. He also contacted Lord Tweedsmuir, the Governor-General of Canada, asking him to give an assessment of possible Canadian reaction in a letter that could at some point be shown to the King.

In mid-October, Baldwin first raised the question with the King. Meanwhile Mrs Simpson was warned of the full implications of the impending crisis. Under English law the King could marry whomsoever he chose, but constitutionally his choice of wife required the approval of Parliament. Such approval was all the more important, if the bride he chose was a twice-

divorced foreign commoner. Nevertheless, the divorce proceeded and the decree *nisi* was granted on 27 October.

There were many in London Society who thought that, in the existing circumstances, Mrs Simpson's influence on the King was for the good. The MP Victor Cazalet, for instance, observed her in November 1936 and wrote in his diary: 'She is the one real friend he has ever had. She does have a wonderful influence over him, but she knows how stubborn he is, and how difficult to influence.'[85]

By now the King's utter infatuation was making it practically impossible for Mrs Simpson to extricate herself from the situation, though there is strong evidence that by September 1936 she was making attempts to do so. Her lawyer, Theodore Goddard, the man assigned to handle her divorce, produced a long written account of the days before the Abdication and the conversations he had with the King and Mrs Simpson. At the end, he came to two categorical conclusions: that Mrs Simpson was prepared to give up the King; but that the King was definite in his decision that he would not give her up: he intended to abdicate and eventually to marry her.[86]

LEFT: *The Nahlin party at Aegina near Athens.* ABOVE: *In Greece; left to right, back row: Herman Rogers, Sir John Aird, Alan Lascelles; front row: Katherine Rogers, Helen Fitzgerald, Wallis Simpson and Sir Sydney Waterlow, the British Minister at Athens, with his wife and daughter.* BELOW: *Mrs Simpson bathing in the sea off an Aegean island, September 1936.* OVERLEAF: *Extending his holiday (to the annoyance of his staff), the King stopped off at Vienna, and found time to go shooting near Schloss Enzesfeld, with Lord Sefton (second right) and Sir Walford Selby, the British Minister in Vienna (right).*

Alec Hardinge later concluded that the King had known, deep down, that he would never be allowed to marry Mrs Simpson, as Queen or as morganatic wife. Hardinge was less convinced that she realised this, wondering if she did not taunt the King that he could achieve his way because of his personal popularity. Those around her tried to get her to encourage the King to back down, temporarily at least, in order to gain time and to allow the Coronation to take place and give him a stronger position. But the King was adamant: the matter had to be

CD
182

D

resolved before the Coronation.

In the meantime the King continued his public duties. His speech at the State Opening of Parliament passed off well. On Armistice Day, accompanied by Queen Mary, he led the nation's remembrance of the war dead at the Cenotaph.

Nothing changed until mid-November, when it became increasingly clear that the British press would soon break its silence about Mrs Simpson. On 13 November, Hardinge wrote his letter of warning to the King. He pointed out that the press silence would soon be broken, and that the effect of this would be calamitous. He reported that the Prime Minister was to meet senior members of the Government to discuss the crisis, which might result in resignation or a request for dissolution, and urged that Mrs Simpson should go abroad without delay.

The King did not respond directly to Hardinge's letter, but he asked to see Mr Baldwin. As soon as Baldwin consulted the Cabinet the constitutional implications became clear: once the Cabinet had expressed its disapproval of the proposed marriage, political controversy hovered over the issue, and there was a possibility that the country would split between supporters of the King and those of the government. To his credit, the King understood this and was anxious to avoid political upset throughout the crisis. Thereafter the end result was never really in doubt. For the last weeks of his reign, he kept away from London and never attempted to exploit his personal popularity to win support, though at one point before his Abdication he hoped that he might be allowed to explain himself to the nation in a radio broadcast.

In the weeks following Hardinge's letter and Baldwin's audience with the King, a number of red herrings were set up in the political arena, including the possibility that the King might enter a morganatic marriage (to which idea he listened with interest, according to Lord Beaverbrook, although eventually he dismissed it as 'inhuman').

The King had put himself in an impossible situation. Another man might have resolved the dilemma by marrying for convenience and keeping Mrs Simpson as his mistress. But that was a possibility that he never entertained; from the moment he met Mrs Simpson he never looked at another woman. On the other hand, Mrs Simpson's existence was about to become

OPPOSITE: *Mrs Simpson at the Wien-Lainz International Country Club, Vienna, September 1936.* ABOVE: *The Royal Family's annual holiday at Balmoral was an established tradition. The presence there for the first time of Wallis Simpson caused some alarm among courtiers; other friends, such as Herman and Katherine Rogers, were also guests. Wallis Simpson walking near Balmoral with the King and Mrs Rogers, September 1936.* BELOW: *The King and Mrs Simpson on the Castle terrace.*

public knowledge. He could have renounced her in order to keep his throne, but again he never considered that option.

There is enough evidence of his intolerance of his official role in his years as Prince of Wales to suggest that he was not unhappy to give up his throne, and that there was never any doubt that he would stand by Mrs Simpson. Just as he had always been drawn to the newness of America, so in her he saw not only the woman who attracted him but also a refreshing contrast to the stuffy life of the British court, which he loathed. It was inevitable that sooner or later he would choose to go rather than stay on the throne without Mrs Simpson. This was clear as early as 20 or 23 November. By the time the crisis became common knowledge, its outcome was already decided.

The crisis duly broke. Mrs Simpson made her dramatic flight to Cannes in the company of Lord Brownlow on 6 December.

Two years after the Abdication, Queen Elizabeth, formerly the Duchess of York and now the new Queen Consort, was correct when she wrote of the ex King: 'The melancholy fact remains still at the present moment, that he for whom we agonised is the one person it did not touch.'[87] He went through the whole crisis in a trance, in which his resolution was unswerving. Robert Bruce Lockhart wrote: 'He is not a strong man. To have resisted the pressure which has been brought to bear on him must have meant that he was completely obsessed by one thought.'[88]

OPPOSITE: *The King with his nieces, Princess Elizabeth (the future Queen Elizabeth II, left) and Princess Margaret Rose, with their father, the Duke of York, and corgis, Balmoral, September 1936.* TOP: *Shooting party at Sandringham, October; his brother-in-law, Lord Harewood (hidden, right), was a guest.* ABOVE: *On the way to Sandringham on 18 October, the King called at Beech House, Felixstowe, where Wallis Simpson was staying; she probably took this snapshot. Had this visit become known, collusion would have been suspected, and the divorce proceedings jeopardised.*

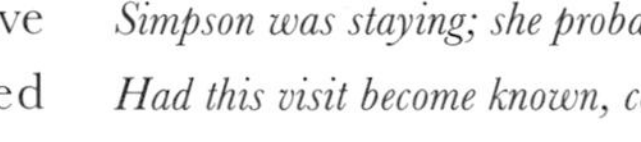

Despite the efforts and advice of Queen Mary, the Prime Minister, Walter Monckton and others, the King headed towards abdication. While he appeared to suffer no agony over the decision, others were more obviously distressed. Queen Mary spoke to him of the sacrifices made by so many soldiers who laid down their lives in the Great War. The King replied: 'All that matters is our happiness.' On this point he proved inflexible. In 1938, Queen Mary returned to the subject: 'I do not think you have ever realised the shock, which the attitude you took up caused your family and the whole Nation. It seemed inconceivable to those who had made such sacrifices during the war that you, as their King, refused a lesser sacrifice. . .'[89]

Hardinge thought the King's attitude to his own mother in the crisis was as good an example as anything that 'his mind was at least temporarily unbalanced.'[90] Queen Mary went further, describing him as 'absolutely unhinged'.[91]

The King's decision would not have been affected by any amount of public demonstrations or newspaper debate. The instrument of Abdication was signed on 11 December 1936. Only then was the former King allowed to say some words to his people, broadcasting his famous speech from a room in Windsor Castle.

Edward Addresses His People Today

London, Feb. 29.—King Edward VIII will speak to the people of the British Empire tomorrow in a radio address beginning at 4 P. M. (11 A. M., Eastern standard time.)

His speech will be carried by all British transmitters and is to last about ten minutes.

Edward's broadcast to Boy Scouts in 1922 was the first speech any member of the English royal family ever made into a microphone. Since that time King Edward's speeches have been in great demand whenever they are put on the air. Every time announcement is made of a forthcoming broadcast requests pour in for their relay to the United States.

His 1928 radio appeal for gifts for relief of distress among miners brought a contribution of almost $100,000 from a New Yorker.

Among Edward's famous broadcasts was that at the inauguration of the "Buy British" campaign in 1931, when he made a plea for "good, honest teamwork in industry."

The King's voice comes over the radio with unusual clarity.

King Edward
Empire will tune in on his address

Many phrases in the broadcast have become well known. 'At long last', he began, ' I am able say a few words of my own'. He had found it impossible to carry out his duties 'without the help and support of the woman I love'. The decision to abdicate had been 'mine and mine alone'. Warmly commending his brother as his successor, he expressed envy of the 'one matchless blessing, enjoyed by so many of you and not bestowed on me — a happy home with his wife and children.' He thanked his family and his ministers and stressed that there had never been any constitutional disagreement. He was grateful for the kindness that had always been shown him by all classes thoughout the Empire. In his closing words he looked to the future:

'I now quit altogether public affairs, and I lay down my burden. It may be some time before I return to my native land, but I shall always follow the fortunes of the British race and Empire with profound interest, and if at any time in the future I can be found of service to His Majesty in a private station I shall not fail. And now we all have a new King. I wish him, and you, his people, happiness and prosperity with all my heart. God bless you all. God Save the King.'[92]

That very night, having bidden farewell to his family, the ex-King was driven to Portsmouth and embarked for France. There can have been few departures so poignant in the course of Britain's long history: the ex-monarch and his small retinue waiting on the deserted quayside in the cold of a December night, the ex-monarch crossing the gangway of HMS *Fury*, with his beloved dog, Slipper, under his arm, and granting the Captain leave to cast off, heading to an uncertain future. 'I knew now that I was irretrievably on my own' wrote the Duke of Windsor in his memoirs. 'The draw-bridges were going up behind me.'[93] He had not, perhaps, found it so hard to give up his throne, but he felt a deep sorrow at leaving his country, though he did not have the remotest idea how long his exile was to last. He watched as the lights of England receded in the dark mists of night.

OPPOSITE: *At Fort Belvedere, November 1936, after Wallis had been granted a decree nisi; left to right: Mrs Simpson, the King, Sybil Colefax, Charles Lambe (an equerry), Paul Bonner (an American guest).* TOP RIGHT: *One of the last public engagements as King: attending the Cenotaph Service with Queen Mary on Armistice Day.* ABOVE: *On 11 December, after his Abdication, Prince Edward (as the ex-King was now styled) was allowed to make his farewell radio broadcast.* TOP LEFT: *The broadcast was relayed by American radio stations. This recording, in the Duke of Windsor's collection, was made by WJZ station, New York; such recordings were forbidden in Britain.*

Earum Pig

to

Just a Pig

CHAPTER NINE

CAST ADRIFT

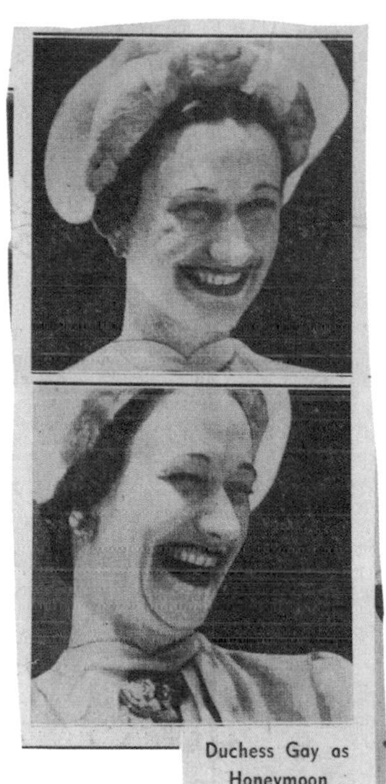

Duchess Gay as Honeymoon Begins

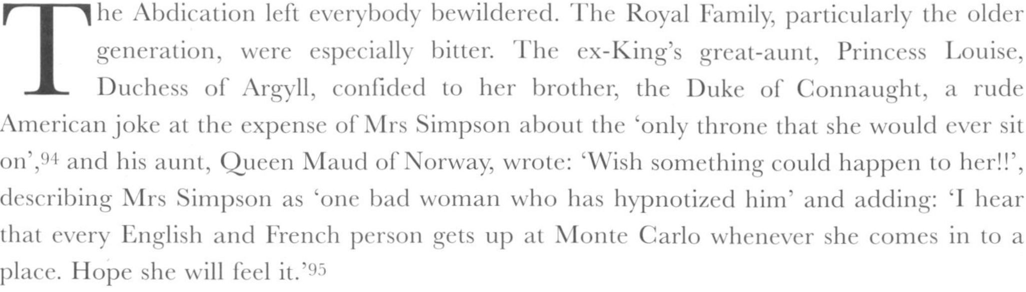

The Abdication left everybody bewildered. The Royal Family, particularly the older generation, were especially bitter. The ex-King's great-aunt, Princess Louise, Duchess of Argyll, confided to her brother, the Duke of Connaught, a rude American joke at the expense of Mrs Simpson about the 'only throne that she would ever sit on',[94] and his aunt, Queen Maud of Norway, wrote: 'Wish something could happen to her!!', describing Mrs Simpson as 'one bad woman who has hypnotized him' and adding: 'I hear that every English and French person gets up at Monte Carlo whenever she comes in to a place. Hope she will feel it.'[95]

The Duke of Connaught regretted the loss of the man 'who we all hoped would make a model though rather too modern king.'[96] Tommy Lascelles commented to his wife: 'He will be the most tragic might-have-been in all history. Nothing but his own will could have saved him, and the will was not there; no human being, other than himself — and of course, herself — could have averted this dreadful thing. The future, naturally, is obscure.'[97] And the traveller Freya Stark wrote to her mother: 'This business of the King leaves one quite stunned. What will he feel in two years time? And that unhappy woman? It is like a Shakespearian tragedy, so arbitrary in beginning, so ineluctable in its end.'[98]

In her place of exile in Cannes, Mrs Simpson listened to the ex-King's radio broadcast and hid her face. Though many refused to believe her, she always insisted that she had tried her best to prevent the Abdication, that it was the Duke's decision and his alone. As late as 1972 she told Lord Mountbatten: 'I spent a long time over a very bad telephone line from France begging him not to abdicate. I went so far as to say if he abdicated I wouldn't marry him.'[99]

In a letter to Lady Colefax written by Mrs Simpson on 18 December 1936, she said she had fought for time and implied that she believed she had in fact escaped.[100] Lord Brownlow, on returning from escorting her to Cannes, told Chips Channon his version, as Channon recorded: 'He is firm about one thing: he repeats and insists that Wallis did everything possi-

PREVIOUS PAGES, LEFT: *A Cecil Beaton portrait, 2 June 1937.* BACKGROUND: *Teasing inscription on a cookery book from the Duke to the Duchess.* RIGHT: *Press cuttings of the wedding photographs.* BELOW RIGHT: *December 1937, Cap d'Antibes refuge Wallis Simpson reading press reports of the Abdication crisis; with Lord Brownlow.* ABOVE: *March 1937, Wallis Warfield (as she was now styled) with Katherine Rogers, Château de Candé, Tours.* BELOW: *Old friends from America keeping Wallis company at Candé.*

ble to prevent the King's abdication, and he showed me a letter written in his own handwriting and dictated by Wallis, in which he authorises her solicitors to withdraw the divorce proceedings at Ipswich. This letter is signed by Perry [Brownlow], her solicitor Goddard and herself and is a valuable historical document.'[101]

But after the Abdication there could be no escape. Whatever Mrs Simpson may have wished in her heart, she now began preparing for her new life role — that of supporting the man who had made this albatross of a sacrifice for her.

For several months, due to the stringent divorce laws, the couple were not allowed to meet. Mrs Simpson, who had now changed her name by deed poll to Wallis Warfield, remained in France at Lou Viei, the home of Katherine and Herman Rogers. During these months she was joined by her Aunt Bessie, spent a weekend at Somerset Maugham's villa (where Lady Colefax was also a guest), and then in March moved to the Château de Candé, near Tours. Here she remained in the company of the Rogers', until the wedding. Another companion was the ex-King's cairn terrier, Slipper. He had accompanied his master into exile, and was sent on to her at Candé. Alas, on 6 April, Slipper was bitten by a snake and died, leaving his master and mistress inconsolable.

During the separation, Wallis began to face another role that she did not like, and which was to haunt her for the rest of her life. She wrote revealingly to the Duke: 'it has always been a lone game against the world for me and a woman always pays the most. . .'[102] In the perception of the general public she was the 'evil woman' who had 'stolen' the King. On 3 January 1937 she wrote to the Duke:

'It is all a great pity because I loathe being undignified and also of joining the countless

ABOVE: *Cecil Beaton (right) came to Candé, April 1937, to photograph Wallis, and so present a more sympathetic image of her to a hostile public.* BELOW: *After the Abdication, the Duke accepted the hospitality of Eugene de Rothschild at Schloss Enzesfeld, Austria, where he frenetically skied, climbed hills, played the bagpipes and talked till dawn. Friends came to help fill the five-month wait before he could rejoin Wallis. Early 1937, with Lord Brownlow (left), and 'Fruity' Metcalfe, his former equerry.*

titles that roam around Europe meaning nothing. To set off on our journey with a proper backing would mean so much — but whatever happens we shall make something of our lives. . . You must employ their [the new King and Queen's] means to accomplish your ends — and after Feb I should write to your brother a straightforward letter setting forth the reasons for him not to treat you as an outcast and to do something for me so that we have a dignified and correct position as befits an ex-King of England. . .'[103]

During this phase, Cecil Beaton visited her at Candé to take some portraits of her for *Vogue*, the purpose of which was to present a softer image of her to the world. He found her forthcoming about her plight. She told him that at times it had been hard not to hang herself from the antlers in the castle, and Beaton concluded that she was 'determined to love him though I feel she is not in love with him. She has a great responsibility in looking after someone who, so essentially different, entirely relies upon her.'[104]

Meanwhile the Duke of Windsor (as he was created in March 1937) remained in Austria, staying first at Schloss Enzesfeld, near Vienna, and later in a small hotel near Salzburg, before he was finally able to join Wallis on 4 May 1937. He had no shortage of time to think. At the time of the Abdication he had given little time to making serious arrangements for his future, but he believed that he had left England with some vital matters agreed either in writing or at any rate in principle. Others had been left to trust. He was therefore bitter that his wife was not to be allowed the title of 'Her Royal Highness'. On his departure, he had believed that

OPPOSITE: *Wallis Warfield by Beaton, Château de Candé, May 1937.* TOP: *Queen Mary robed for the Coronation of George VI on 12 May, 1937.* ABOVE: *Wallis Warfield and the Duke of Windsor pose for the press at the time of their reunion on 4 May, Candé, 1937.* BELOW RIGHT: *Pre-wedding photographs by Beaton.* OVERLEAF: *The Duke of Windsor skiing with his brother the Duke of Kent, Semmering, early 1937. The ex-King was distressed when his favourite brother did not come to his wedding a few months later.*

820

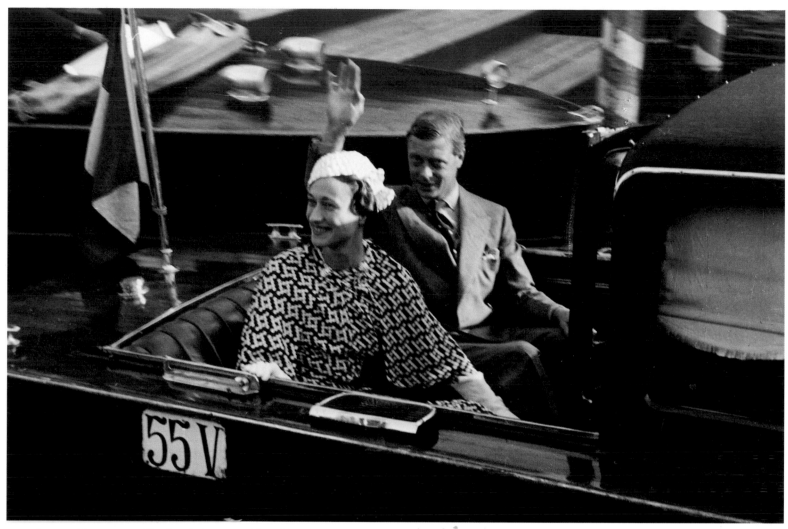

soon he would return to England almost as if nothing had happened. He even contemplated returning in the latter months of 1937. This could not be possible, he felt, until the Duchess was accorded her correct status. Whatever the rights of the matter, the Establishment by denying the Duchess her husband's status had found a way of effectively turning the marriage into a morganatic alliance, the very thing they had said was impossible for the King. For the next thirty-five years, the Duke insisted that the staff addressed his wife as 'Your Royal Highness', and old friends such as Lady Diana Cooper curtseyed to her 'to please him'.[105]

Over the years, and even since their deaths, the discussion has continued as to the validity of the Letters Patent denying the Duchess royal status. It soon became clear that official circles in Britain were prepared to do very little for the Duke and less still for the Duchess. They were genuinely terrified that the Duke and she would part and that Europe would be awash with Duchesses of Windsor 'floating about the cafés of Budapest'. The British Establishment was much more interested in protecting the new King, falling in behind him and presenting him as a stable successor after the shock of the Abdication. The best way to do this was to keep the ex-King as far away as possible from the workings of the realm. The Duke of Windsor underestimated the ways of officialdom, not realising that he was to be an out-

OPPOSITE: *A relaxed moment at the wedding rehearsal. The bridal couple with 'Fruity' Metcalfe. Only nineteen guests were present at the wedding of the ex King and no member of his family attended.* ABOVE: *They began their honeymoon in Venice before travelling north.* LEFT: *The Duke and Duchess at Schloss Wasserleonburg, Carinthia. They were visited there by many English friends holidaying in the area and by local noble families.*

THE DUKE OF WINDSOR'S SENSE OF TRIUMPH WHEN HE FINALLY MARRIED WALLIS SIMPSON IS EVIDENT IN HIS INSCRIPTION ON THIS BOX CONTAINING A SLICE OF THEIR WEDDING CAKE. THE BOLD CAPITALS IN 'OUR WEDDING CAKE' ARE EMPHASISED BY THE REPEATED 'WE'. (HE LOVED TO LINK THEIR INITIALS IN THIS SIGNIFICANT WAY). ON THEIR WEDDING DAY, A CHEST IN THE LITTLE LIBRARY AT THE CHÂTEAU DE CANDÉ WAS COVERED WITH A DAMASK CLOTH TO MAKE AN ALTAR. WHILE THE ROOM WAS TRANSFORMED WITH AN ABUNDANCE OF FLOWERS, THE DUKE BUSTLED ABOUT MAKING ADJUSTMENTS AND ENSURING THAT EVERYTHING WAS PERFECT. IT WAS NOT WESTMINSTER ABBEY, BUT HE WAS CONTENTED.

cast. He could not view the situation objectively and he always believed that some of his old friends had simply betrayed him and were being disloyal.

Besides the Establishment — the Court and the Government — there was also the Duke's family. He knew that he had broken their rules and that they were displeased with him. But he had no idea to what lengths this was to be taken. He found himself generally ostracised, and from the day of the Abdication there were some members of the family who referred to him in the past tense, as though he no longer existed. In the early weeks of the new reign, he used to telephone his brother, King George VI, with suggestions and ideas. In due course, Walter Monckton was delegated to tell the Duke that these calls must stop. There was much wrangling over money, and even quite near the event the Duke expected that his brothers would attend his wedding as his 'supporters'. They did not. He remained on good terms with his sister, the Princess Royal, who remained affectionate. Sadly, he even fell out with the Duke of Kent.

21

Ex-King Edward VIII of England posed for wedding picture with wife. Another 1937 wedding: Franklin Roosevelt Jr.—Ethel du Pont.

ABOVE: *Cecil Beaton's photographs of the Windsors' wedding were in fact taken the day before the ceremony, on 2 May 1937. They were widely reproduced in the press, as in this cutting, though Beaton was annoyed that wedding pictures by a lesser-known rival photographer named Soper reached America first.* RIGHT: *A selection of photographs from the Windsor albums taken at the time of the wedding, the honeymoon and during 1938; third row, left: the Revd Robert Anderson Jardine, the Anglican priest who defied his bishop to solemnise the Windsor marriage; centre left: the little library in the Château de Candé which was got up as a chapel for the ceremony; top right corner: snapshots showing the couple on their honeymoon in the company of friends in Austria; bottom row, centre: two photographs of the Duchess with friends at the Château de la Maye, the Windsors' Paris home near Versailles for a few months in 1938; bottom right corner: photographs taken at or near La Cröe, where they spent their summers from 1938 to 1949.*

The attitude of the new court was not so much one of vindictiveness to the Duke (although 'that woman' was allowed no quarter) as of lack of confidence in itself. Queen Elizabeth was worried that the new King was a less glamorous figure than his brother in the eyes of the people, and realised that the former King needed to be kept in the background. Regrettably the Duke of Windsor did not seem to appreciate this. Alec Hardinge, who had gone on to be the new King's Private Secretary, saw the benefits in King George VI travelling widely in his kingdom to become known to his people. The more the people saw their new king the less of a spectre his brother would be. Neither King had wanted the job much. And George VI was far from well prepared for it. But there was an important difference between King George and King Edward: the new King was determined to do his duty. In this he had no need of his elder brother's advice, which he soon saw as interference.

The wedding of the Duke and Duchess of Windsor was celebrated, to the Duke's great joy, in a contrived bridal 'chapel' at the Château de Candé on 3 June 1937. The Duke's old friend, the raffish 'Fruity' Metcalfe, was best man, and there was a handful of guests but no members of the Royal Family present. After the wedding, whatever the Duke's hopes and expectations may have been about the opportunities for royal employment, in practice the couple were thrown together for life, apparently with the sole task of displaying a united front and proving to the world that it had all been worthwhile. And the Duke had

much time to mull over his plight and plead for better treatment.

It was the Duchess's newly acquired duty to make a home for her husband, look after him and keep him happy. She proved a good *maîtresse de maison*, serving delicious food, doing her best to find him interesting company to enliven the long days of exile. She had married a man, whose every moment had been disciplined by the demands of affairs of state, a man who from the age of sixteen had been used to the considerable income of the Duchy of Cornwall, who was used to adulation wherever he went, accepted as a loved and respected symbol because of who he was, a man brought up in the relaxed and confident atmosphere of Edward VII's Sandringham, with the elegance and generosity of Queen Alexandra as an example, honed by the severity of his father combined with the increasingly formal dedication to duty of his mother. It was no easy undertaking for a not entirely willing bride in her middle years.

The honeymoon was spent at the borrowed Schloss Wasserleonburg, in Carinthia, with visits to Vienna, Salzburg, Venice and Yugoslavia, and a stay in a shooting lodge in Hungary.

At this time the Windsors still believed their exile was to be of brief duration. They were occupied in creating a temporary life until their envisaged return to England. The Duke hoped to find a role in the Royal Family equivalent to that of a younger brother of the Sovereign, with his wife at his side. It was only gradually that it dawned on him that this would not be possible: he and his wife could not return to Britain, as they might have hoped. The problem of what to do in the meantime, aggravated by worries over finance, affected many of their decisions. Towards the end of September the Windsors moved to Paris, settling temporarily at the Hotel Meurice, before moving to the Château de la Maye in Versailles in January 1938.

These were years when the threat of war hung over Europe, and it would have been unnatural for anyone who had witnessed the slaughter of the Great War not to dread a recurrence of fighting. In his lonely exile, the Duke of Windsor felt this keenly and desired to make a contribution to the reconciliation of Britain with Germany. But many of his actions were treated by the British government as interfering. In particular, the visit he and the Duchess made to Germany in October 1937, ostensibly to look into the welfare of the German people, but also to visit Hitler, proved a worry to the Foreign Office, and not the contribution to peace he had hoped. He could not understand that he had created a further cause for resentment by what was perceived as his desire to push himself forward. He still believed in the quixotic notion of himself as Edward the Peacemaker; as late as May 1939 he was to broadcast from the battlefield of Verdun, urging peace on the world's leaders.

In 1938, the Windsors began to establish a more settled life, first at Versailles and then at the Château de la Cröe on Cap d'Antibes, in the South of France. In October they moved their Paris home to 24 Boulevard Suchet, and much of their time was taken up in decorating these two houses. They took leases on both properties, but for only two years, since they were convinced that after that time Fort Belvedere would be their home, at least for part of the year.

The Windsors began a search for a temporary home, expecting to return soon to England. OPPOSITE: *The Duchess outside Cartiers, Cannes, 1938. In 1938, they took a lease on the Château de la Cröe, Cap d'Antibes, for use as a summer residence.* TOP LEFT: *Elsie de Wolfe, designer and friend of the Duchess, advised on the decoration at La Cröe.* ABOVE: *24 Boulevard Suchet, Paris, a two-year lease was taken on this house in 1938.* BELOW: *Beaton portraits - 1937 (left) and 1939.*

BELOW: *Watercolour by Serebriakov from the collection shows the little salon, 24 Boulevard Suchet. The very French interior was designed by Stéphane Boudin who later worked on the Windsor Villa.* ABOVE: *The dining room, La Cröe, with the Munnings portrait of the young Prince now hanging in the Windsor Villa library.*

Dina Hood, the Duke's secretary from 1938, gave an account of their lives at this time being entirely taken up with domestic matters. She described the Duke's devotion to the Duchess: 'Nothing was too good for her. He sought every way to make her happy. He himself was happy and lighthearted in her presence.'[106]

The Château de la Cröe was a beautiful white villa, not far from the celebrated Eden Roc and Hôtel du Cap, on Cap d'Antibes, nestling in glorious seclusion amongst the pine trees, with a long garden sloping down to the rocks and the sea of the Mediterranean beyond. A particular feature was the crescent-shaped terrace with six columns on its garden facade. The villa was owned by Lady Burton, widow of Sir Pomeroy Burton, and became known locally as the 'Château des Rois' since it was successively occupied by the Duke of Windsor, King Leopold of the Belgians and Queen Marie José of Italy. It had been built by the Burtons between 1930 and 1932, and in order to get the necessary land, they had to buy out no fewer than eighteen different owners, many of them long-established peasants.

The Château had a swimming pool cut into the rocks with attendant changing rooms and brightly canopied seats and terrace area, down near the sea. Both the Duke and the Duchess relished the favourable climate, and the Duchess observed: 'While I could not hope to reproduce on the Riviera the splendour of the life into which David had been born, at least he seemed happy in his new role as husband and man of the house.'[107]

The Windsors were in the South of France at an interesting time.

This was the doomed heyday of the Riviera, just a decade after its transformation from winter resort to summer paradise. The coast was peopled with fascinating figures who had settled there, from the actress Maxine Elliott (a former mistress of King Edward VII) to the writer Somerset Maugham. Casinos were thriving, sun-bathing was the rage, as was water-skiing on seemingly impossible boards, a new invention. Here they spent their summer.

Golf was now the Duke's main sporting passion, and since he never ate lunch, he was often out in the middle of the day. In the evening he occasionally surprised guests by donning one of his kilts and arriving from the terrace playing the bagpipes.

In November 1938, at the Hôtel Meurice in Paris, an increasingly rare encounter with the Duke's family took place: a visit from the Duke and Duchess of Gloucester. The Duchess of Gloucester recorded: 'some mention of the meeting did appear in the English papers and a lot of old ladies duly wrote furiously disapproving letters.'[108]

The Windsors might have continued in this manner, moving between Paris and the South of France, as they awaited their return to Britain, if the war had not intervened.

ON 20 NOVEMBER 1936 CECIL BEATON CALLED AT CUMBERLAND TERRACE, WALLIS SIMPSON'S HOME IN REGENT'S PARK, TO MAKE SOME DRAWINGS OF HER. ONE OF THESE WAS LATER TO HANG AGAINST A LOOKING-GLASS BACKGROUND IN THE DUCHESS OF WINDSOR'S BATHROOM. 'MRS SIMPSON PROVED AN EXCEPTIONALLY DIFFICULT WOMAN TO DRAW,' HE WROTE IN HIS DIARY. 'STILL, WE HAD A LOT OF FUN, DISCUSSING LONDON AND VARIOUS PERSONALITIES WE KNEW IN COMMON.' BEATON, WHO HAD MET WALLIS FIVE YEARS EARLIER, FOUND HER CHANGED: 'OF LATE, HER GENERAL APPEARANCE HAS BECOME INFINITELY MORE DISTINGUISHED. NOT ONLY IS SHE THINNER, BUT HER FEATURES HAVE ACQUIRED A REFINED FINENESS. SHE IS UNSPOILED.' A FORTNIGHT AFTER THE SKETCH WAS MADE, WALLIS SIMPSON FLED TO FRANCE AS THE ABDICATION CRISIS BROKE.

ABOVE: *The curved colonnade at the rear of the Château de la Cröe. The Duke often flew the Duchy of Cornwall flag above the house.* LEFT: *The dramatic view of the Mediterranean from the terrace. Certain of the Duke's possessions were brought over from Frogmore to furnish this house but most remained in storage at Windsor until the 1950s. The Duke and Duchess returned to this house in 1945, and it was their main residence from 1946-1949. In 1948, at the time of the Berlin Blockade, the Duke became nervous about the future of Europe and had most of the furniture packed up and sent to America. They lived in a few rooms until their lease ended in early 1949.*

To Our President
The Duchess of Windsor

with warr … ion of her
invaluable … ive interest
and partic … r efforts-
from the … the Executive
Committee, … ouncil—
Officers, supervisors and staff of the

Bahamas Red Cross

CHAPTER TEN

WAR AND THE WINDSORS

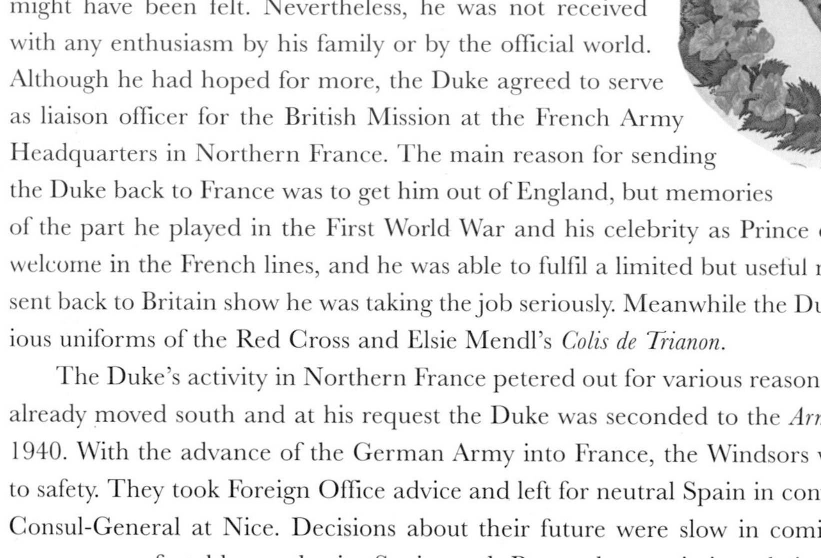

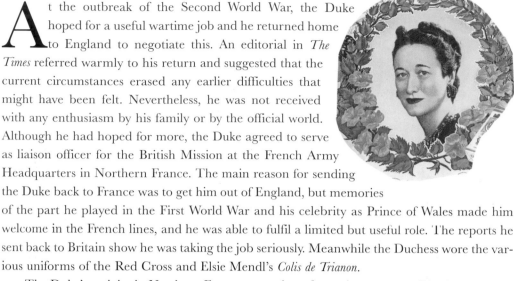

At the outbreak of the Second World War, the Duke hoped for a useful wartime job and he returned home to England to negotiate this. An editorial in *The Times* referred warmly to his return and suggested that the current circumstances erased any earlier difficulties that might have been felt. Nevertheless, he was not received with any enthusiasm by his family or by the official world. Although he had hoped for more, the Duke agreed to serve as liaison officer for the British Mission at the French Army Headquarters in Northern France. The main reason for sending the Duke back to France was to get him out of England, but memories of the part he played in the First World War and his celebrity as Prince of Wales made him welcome in the French lines, and he was able to fulfil a limited but useful role. The reports he sent back to Britain show he was taking the job seriously. Meanwhile the Duchess wore the various uniforms of the Red Cross and Elsie Mendl's *Colis de Trianon*.

The Duke's activity in Northern France petered out for various reasons. The Duchess had already moved south and at his request the Duke was seconded to the *Armée des Alpes* early in 1940. With the advance of the German Army into France, the Windsors were obliged to flee to safety. They took Foreign Office advice and left for neutral Spain in convoy with the British Consul-General at Nice. Decisions about their future were slow in coming, and they spent some uncomfortable weeks in Spain and Portugal negotiating their return to Britain. Paradoxically, the Duke, as an ex-King, was of great interest to the German government, yet

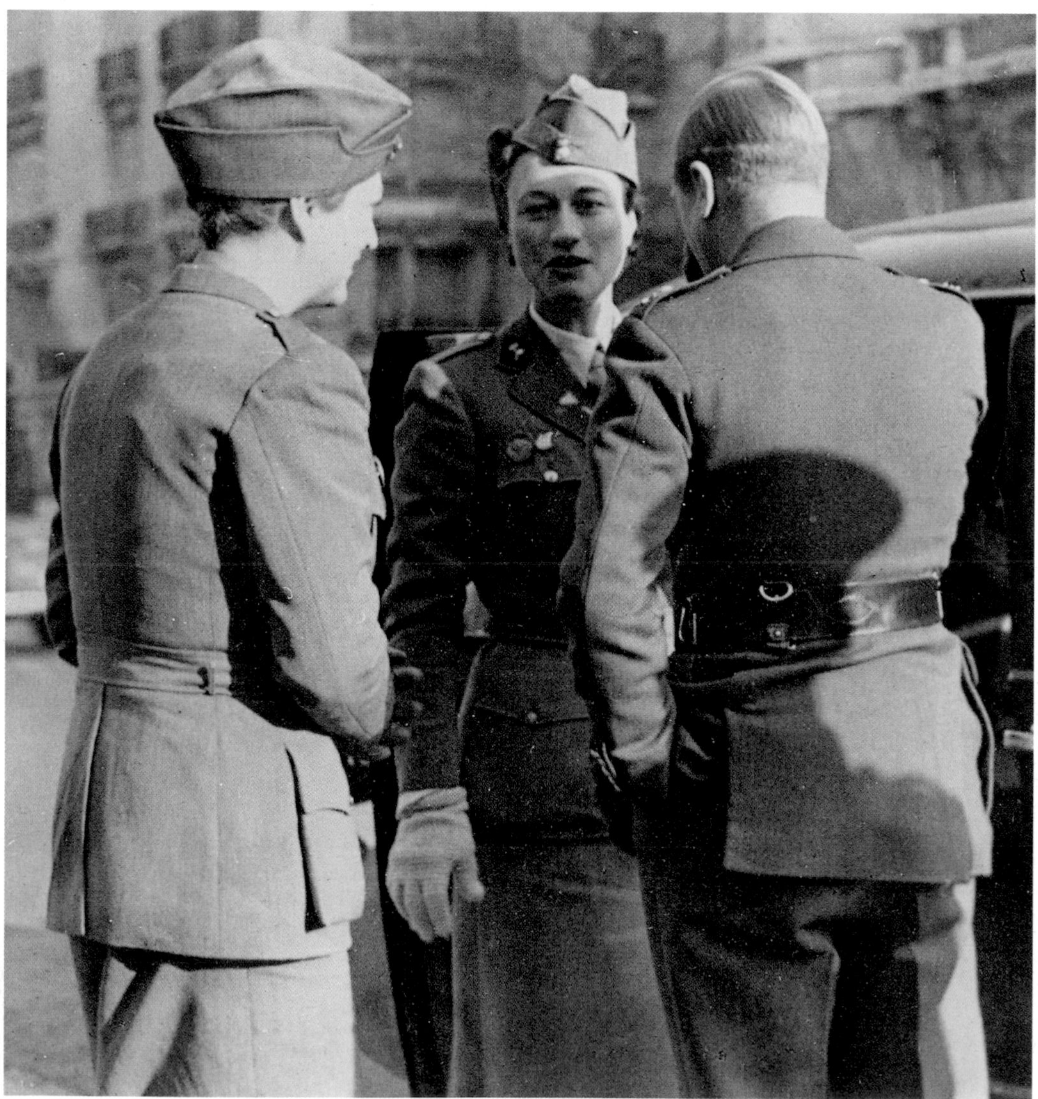

PREVIOUS PAGES, LEFT: *The Duke as Major-General appointed to the British Mission in Northern France, and the Duchess in French Red Cross uniform, March 1940.* BACKGROUND: *Commendation of the Duchess from the Bahamas Red Cross, 1940-1945.* RIGHT: *The Duchess's Bahamas Red Cross medal.* ABOVE: *Sussex 1939, the Windsors' first visit back to England. The Royal Family offered no hospitality so they stayed with 'Fruity' and Lady Alexandra Metcalfe.* TOP: *The Duchess as Red Cross worker.* TOP RIGHT: *US press cutting, 1943.* RIGHT: *The Duke, with the Duchess in the uniform of the* Colis de Trianon *which sent out gift parcels to the military.* OPPOSITE: *The Duchess dressed in her own version of utility wartime style.*

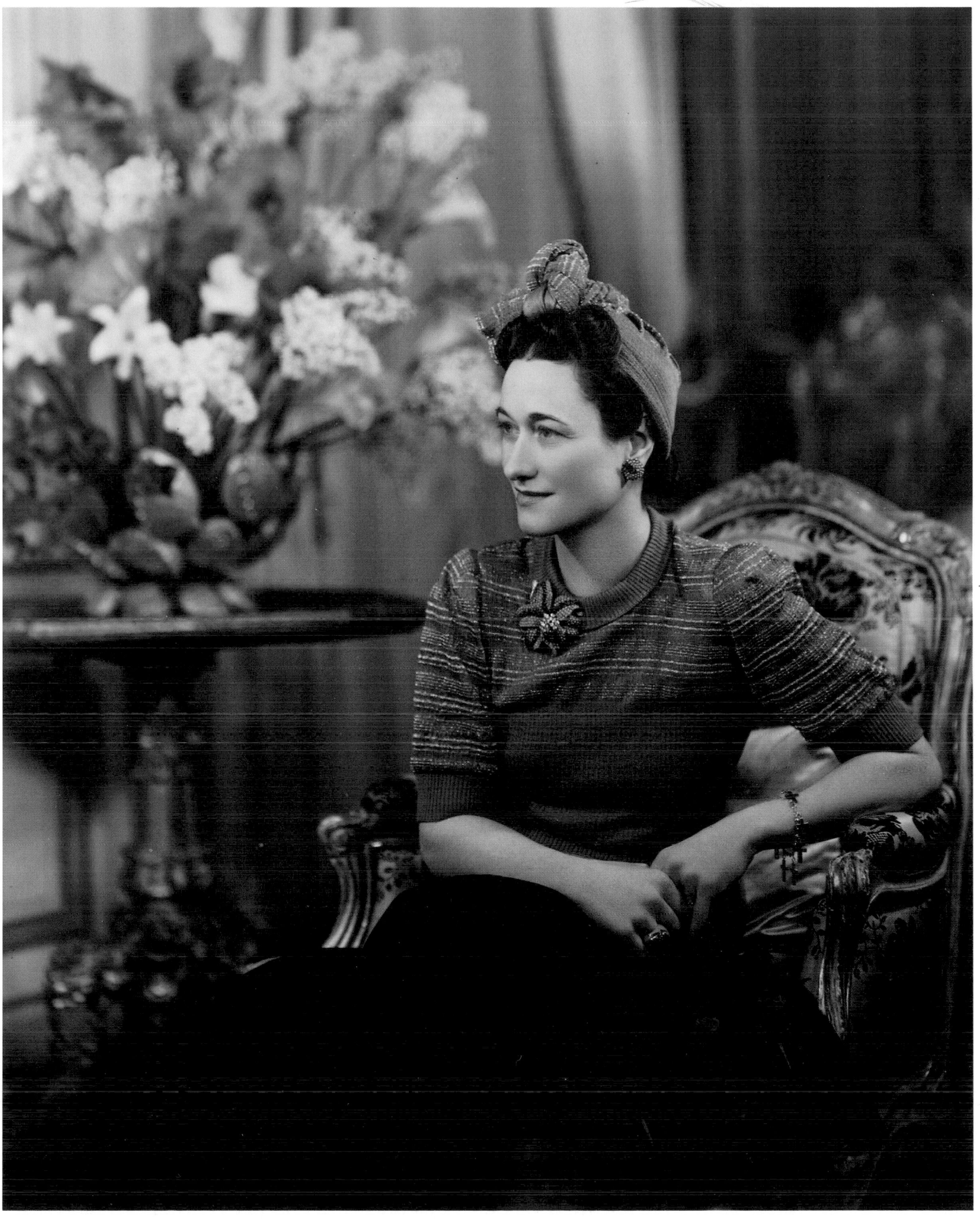

BELOW: *An American newspaper takes up the Daily Express crusade (no doubt prompted by Lord Beaverbrook) maintaining the right of the Duchess of Windsor to share her husband's royal title and therefore his status.*
RIGHT: *The Duke and Duchess attending a fund-raising event in the United States during their period in Government House, Bahamas, September 1943.*

WALLY

☆☆☆☆☆☆ april '39

Royal Title?

London—(U.P.)—The Daily Express urged editorially today that the title of royal highness be granted the Duchess of Windsor so the duke could return with her to England.

Duchess

Asserting that "it is a universal rule for the wife to take the status of her husband," the newspaper said Earl Baldwin had refused to allow Edward a morganatic marriage as king but that now a morganatic marriage has been forced upon him as duke.

"This petty injustice," it said, "is a poor return for the service he gave his country."

of very little interest to the British. He was still unwelcome in his own country. A solution was eventually found with his appointment as Governor-General and Commander-in-Chief of the Bahama Islands.

The Duke served as Governor from 1940 to 1945, with the Duchess at his side. They came to the islands feeling rather bitter about their treatment by the British Government, pained by the deepening rift with the Royal Family, and discontented at being cut off from events in Europe. The Duke believed that the appointment was an unsuitable one for him, but for all that he took it seriously and settled down to demonstrate that he was worthy of something better in the future. The Duke explained to Lord Halifax, the British Ambassador in Washington, that he did not intend to force himself on England against the King's wishes and would stick things out in the Bahamas, but he had little idea what he would do after that. Halifax advised him to avoid publicity and accept the situation, both public and private, and suggested that the passage of time would go a long way towards smoothing out the many difficulties. Halifax commented: 'He took it all very well, but of course thinks it wholly unreasonable.'[109]

The Duke had felt relaxed about one thing, at least — that as the Governor's wife, the status of the Duchess was a settled matter. But a memorandum had preceded him to the Caribbean from the Secretary of State for the Colonies. A distinction was to be made between husband and wife; no one was to curtsey to the Duchess and she was to be addressed by the lesser, non-Royal titles of 'Your Grace' or 'Duchess'.

They arrived in Nassau, the islands' capital, in the draining

---

WITH THE DUKE AND DUCHESS IN THE BACK OF THEIR BUICK, AS THEY MADE THEIR ESCAPE FROM FRANCE IN JUNE 1940, WERE THREE CAIRN TERRIERS: POOKIE, PREEZIE AND DETTO. DOGS WERE ALWAYS IMPORTANT TO THE WINDSORS. THEIR EARLY LETTERS ARE FULL OF REFERENCES TO THE 'EANUMS' (A WORD MEANING SMALL AND ENDEARING IN THE PRIVATE LANGUAGE OF THE LOVERS), AND AFTER THEIR MARRIAGE THE EVER-PRESENT PETS TOOK THE PLACE OF CHILDREN. POOKIE HAD BEEN ACQUIRED BY THE DUKE DURING HIS LONELY WAIT IN AUSTRIA IN EARLY 1937. AFTER A SUCCESSFUL CAREER IN THE BAHAMAS — WINNING THIS CUP AS 'MOST POPULAR DOG' AT THE BAHAMAS FAIR DOG SHOW IN FEBRUARY 1941 — POOKIE RETURNED TO FRANCE WITH HIS MASTER AND MISTRESS. BY THE TIME POOKIE DIED IN THE EARLY 1950S, AND WAS LAID TO REST IN THE DOGS' GRAVEYARD AT THE MILL, PUGS HAD TAKEN THE PLACE OF CAIRNS AS THE WINDSORS' FAVOURED BREED.

humidity of an August day in 1940, and were conducted to their official residence, Government House. This was badly in need of repair, and the Duke and Duchess had to borrow various houses while the Duchess set about turning the residence into a real home. Her refurbishment received an unexpected accolade in the memoirs of the Duke's aunt, Princess Alice, Countess of Athlone, who visited the Bahamas in 1946, and remembered the house in the days of the Duke's predecessor, Bede Clifford: 'Government House had been much improved since the Cliffords' day by the Duchess of Windsor,' she wrote.[110]

In 1941, the Windsors purchased a 57-foot cabin cruiser, which they called *Gemini*. They used it to visit most of the outlying Bahama islands.

The Duke and Duchess of Windsor reviewing troops at Nassau

The Duke was well trained for many of the duties which are the lot of a colonial Governor. The Duchess wrote: 'David, with his long experience in official life, was able to fit himself easily into his duties as Governor; and somewhat to my surprise and pleasure I was soon at home with those activities which by custom devolve upon the Governor's wife.'[111] It was to be the nearest the Duchess ever came to an official role. Initially uneasy in public life, she took on the presidency of the Red Cross and used the Duke's money to start infant welfare clinics. Later, as thousands of British and American servicemen arrived at the newly built air bases, the Duchess organised a canteen and social events for them.

As Governor-General, the Duke was judged by John Dye, the US consul in Nassau, to be a success. Dye spoke approvingly of the Duke's commitment to the job. He admired his sensi-

LEFT: *The Duke of Windsor with the Duchess at his side, being given an open-air welcome at the dockside, Nassau. His appointment as Governor-General of the Bahamas began in August, 1940; he served for five years.* RIGHT: *Set above the town of Nassau was Government House, where the Windsors took up residence after refurbishment had been carried out.* BELOW: *The Duke and Duchess taking tea on the first-floor veranda of Government House, early 1945.*

ABOVE: *The Duke of Windsor in the Council Chamber at Government House, Nassau, with members of the Executive Council (ExCo) of the Bahamas, all local men; also his three advisors, officials from the Colonial Service; and (right foreground) Captain Gray Phillips, his Private Secretary. This was a farewell meeting in 1945.*

RIGHT: *One of the Government House staff with the Windsors' family of dogs; by 1945, other terriers apart from the favourite cairns had been added to the group. In the background is the statue of Christopher Columbus, with Hog Island in the distance.*

ble and businesslike approach, and was surprised that only a few months after his arrival the Duke had got such a good grasp of local conditions.

Not only had he a grasp of local conditions, the Governor also showed a genuine determination to improve them. His sympathy with social hardship was still in evidence, and he made clear his intention to develop agriculture and relieve native unemployment. The Colonial Office was insisting on reform of race relations, whilst the Bahamian establishment used its effective powers to resist. Thus a Royal Prince, whose first rule of behaviour had previously been to stand outside politics, now had to carry out government policy, however unwelcome to sections of the local population, and to take public criticism for it. There is no reason to believe that the Duke

was a particularly enlightened man in matters of race, but he showed himself to be diligent in his task.

The Windsors were discomforted to find that they had become effective tourist bait for American visitors from the mainland only 180 miles away. Indeed the winter season after their arrival saw the best business the islands had ever known. Since the couple considered this role undignified, especially at a time of great austerity in Britain, they decided to attend only events that were in aid of charity.

The Duchess made no secret to her friends that she considered the Bahamas a place of relative unimportance, and regarded the time she and her husband spent there as a period of exile, equivalent to Napoleon's sojourn on Elba or St Helena. But they worked hard at their job. So much so that the Duchess's health deteriorated. The climate was enervating, except in the winter months. Previous Governors had been able to seek relief from the sticky heat by visiting the United States, but the Windsors had limited freedom in this respect. They needed permission from the Government in London before they could cross to America, and this was only grudgingly granted.

It was in 1942, during his time in Nassau, that the Duke was devastated by the news that his favourite brother, the Duke of Kent, had been killed in a flying accident in Scotland. His death was a grievous blow. The rift since the Duke's wedding had kept them apart for several years, but the two brothers had been very close.

Clearly, the British Government had hoped that by sending the Windsors to the Bahamas,

ABOVE: *The Duchess took on the presidency of the newly formed Bahamas Red Cross. She also set up three baby clinics which she helped to finance.* BELOW: *The Duchess fulfilling her role as Governor-General's lady, judging at a baby show, 1942.* TOP LEFT: *The Duchess opened a social club for British and US servicemen on Nassau Island. It provided a canteen, reading rooms, bar and showers.*

OVERLEAF: *The Empire State Building, New York, August 1944. Aunt Bessie Merryman was in New York to celebrate her eightieth birthday with the Windsors and their friend, Mai Douglas.*

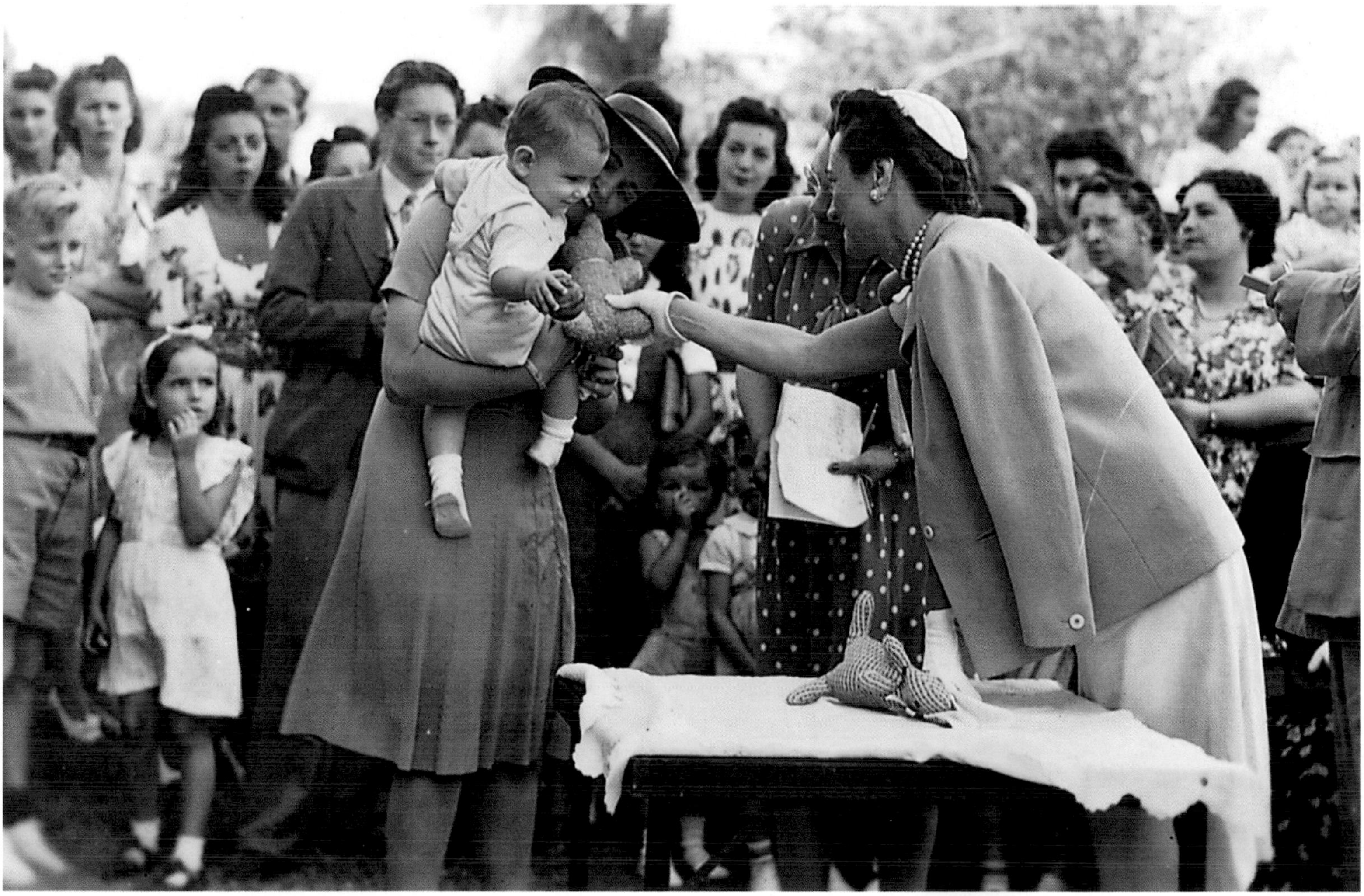

AYS SYSTE
AMERICAN AIRWAYS

they had put them safely at a distance for the duration of the war. The Abdication dust could thus be allowed to settle and the new King to establish himself in this difficult period. What the Government had not considered was that the Duke would take the job so seriously, that he would make a contribution towards persuading the United States from its isolationist position — nor that he would become an object of interest to various shady characters in the Caribbean.

FAR LEFT: *The Duke leaving the Bahamas for Miami after successfully quelling a riot amongst construction workers, June 1942. Left of him, Sir Harry Oakes, whose murder was to cast a shadow over the Duke's incumbency as Governor.* BELOW LEFT: *March 1941, a Red Cross charity match, Nassau, the Duke and Duchess with top golfers.* ABOVE: *Old friends, Katherine Rogers and Mai Douglas, with the Duke and Duchess, Hatchet Bay, Eleuthera Island, 1941.*

Questionable figures such as Axel Wenner-Gren, Harold Christie and Maximino Comacho lurked in the Bahamian sunshine. Their activities had attracted investigation by the authorities, and the Duke's name has been tarnished by association with them. It was natural, however, that the ex-King/Governor should meet most of the rich and powerful men circulating in the area. But in dealing with these characters the Duke of Windsor, who all his early life had been protected by courtiers and other advisers, was somewhat ill-equipped. He was not much helped by the Foreign Office in London, which showed itself to be ambivalent about him. Old rumours about his supposed pro-German leanings, as well as his now reduced status, made British officials less than open when it came to briefing him about their suspicions concerning his acquaintances. The Duke of Windsor had not been left in safe waters, as had been hoped, but dropped in a sea of sharks.

MINNEAPOLIS
Sports
STAR JOURNAL
Sunday, March 16, 1941
PAGE 3

Associated Press Wirephoto.

ROYALTY There was plenty of it in the British Red Cross relief golf match at Nassau, Bahamas. Left to right are: Bobby Jones, still regarded as the greatest golf machine of all time; the Duchess of Windsor, the Duke and Tommy Armour.

There were other problems to confront. Not everyone on the islands approved of the Governor. One who did not welcome him was Etienne Dupuch, the influential proprietor of the *Tribune*, one of the islands' leading newspapers. Dupuch had not approved of the Duke's marriage, but more importantly he perceived the Duke as a man who was given to 'shooting his mouth off',[112] and as a coloured man, Dupuch had taken exception to what he understood were the Duke's views on race. Dupuch was sensitive and the Duke handled him tactlessly, so a running battle ensued between the newspaper man and Government House over the next five years. Nevertheless, by the time the Duke and Duchess left the Bahamas, the Duke's achievements there had gained Dupuch's respect.

Inevitably, when the Windsors did manage to get permission to visit the States, they

attracted a great deal of interest there. Apart from giving the couple a break and a chance to see friends, these visits served a useful function, as the Windsors were seen visiting British servicemen in American hospitals, drawing the attention of the as yet neutral Americans to the wartime plight of Europe, and setting up CCC work camps for unemployed Bahamians on the mainland. However, it was the lifestyle of the Windsors that the newspapers most often reported and criticised. In particular, their luggage was of perennial interest. The supposedly excessive number of suitcases and trunks was to become a focus for the criticism that was levelled at them over the years. But they faced an awkward dilemma. They could easily be accused of extravagance (especially when there was a war on), yet it is quite probable that had they lived more austerely, they would also have been criticised for falling short of the dignity expected of a former sovereign.

One undeniable gaffe, which casts a shadow over any appraisal of the Duke's years in the Bahamas, was the precipitate action he took following the murder of Sir Harry Oakes. Sir Harry was a very rich man, who had made his fortune prospecting the second richest gold mine in the Western hemisphere. He had moved from Canada to make his home in the Bahamas. In July 1943, he was found murdered in his bed with four deep holes in his temples, as if made by a four-pronged instrument. There was also evidence that his body had been set on fire, possibly while Sir Harry was still alive.

ABOVE: *The new Governor-General did not stand on ceremony and was happy to get about Nassau under his own steam, 1940.* ABOVE LEFT: *Press cutting of the Duke and Duchess probably on a visit to Miami in the early 1940s.* BELOW: *The Duke and Duchess off duty on the beach with friends. They had a cabaña on Cable Beach where they would go at weekends.* OPPOSITE: *The Duke at the Cable Beach Golf Club early in 1945, with Harold Christie, a member of ExCo. Christie was a local property dealer with a less than perfect reputation.*

The Duke badly mishandled the events that followed. First, he declared local press censorship on the case, news of which was of course soon out on the mainland. His decision to bypass the local police was probably a wise idea, but to assign the case to two detectives who had been responsible for his safety on a visit to Miami was ill-advised. He ought, it was claimed, to have brought in the FBI or the CID. The two detectives committed so many blunders that the murder has remained unsolved. The Duke took no part in the investigation, but as was often to happen, his reputation received disproportionate damage.

In September 1944, the Duke of Windsor met the Prime Minister, Winston Churchill, who was visiting Washington, and arranged for his resignation from the Governorship to take effect a few weeks before his five-year appointment was up. During his period in office he had done his best to improve democracy and better social conditions, he had initiated work schemes, resolved a race riot, introduced a policy of fair pay to the islands, and he had assisted good relations with Britain's ally, the United States. He failed in much of what he tried to do thanks to the opposition of the local oligarchy — the 'Bay Street Boys' — rich men with vested interests, who were determined that he should fail and had the power to ensure that he did.

The Duke was fifty-one in 1945, and he still hoped to be given a useful job on his return home. But he was horrified when the post of Governor of Bermuda was suggested. As the Duchess wrote: 'David could see that this would be exchanging one military backwater for

ABOVE: *The Duke on an airfield construction site, Oakes Field, Bahamas, 1942.* BELOW RIGHT: *The Duke of Kent was killed on a routine RAF flight in August 1942. The Duke of Windsor felt huge remorse, since they had never repaired the rift created in 1937. His loss brought the Duke and Queen Mary closer.* BELOW: *She sent him this signed photo of her doughty wartime work with her 'wooding squad' at Badminton.*

another. Bitterly disappointed, he declined the Bermuda offer and decided to finish out his war service where he was. It was clear now beyond all question that David's family were determined to keep him relegated to the farthermost marches of the Empire.'[113]

There is no doubt that it was a preoccupation of the King and the British Government to make sure that the Duke of Windsor did not return to live in Britain after the war, though he would have liked to do so. Indeed, it was the George VI's view that his brother, as an ex-King, could never live in Britain again as an ordinary citizen. In a letter to him about this time the Duke wrote that he understood the position:

'I can see your point of view and am therefore prepared to put your feelings before my own in this matter . . . I have suffered many unnecessary embarrassments from official sources uncomplainingly during the last nine years, but I have reason to believe . . . that it is now your desire that these should cease.

'The truth of the whole matter is that you and I happen to be two prominent personages placed in one of the most unique situations in history, the dignified handling of which is entirely your and my responsibility. . . It is a situation which we cannot escape and one that will always be watched with interest by the whole world. I can see no reason why we should not be able to handle it in the best interests of both of us, and I can only assure you that I will continue to play my part to this end.'[114]

At one time the Duke had set his heart

on a roving ambassadorial commission in the United States, but what he now proposed on his return to Europe was that he should simply have some role in improving Anglo-American relations. This request for a job with official status was refused on the grounds that it was wrong for the Duke to have a job created especially for him. The idea of the Windsors residing permanently in America and acting quite unofficially on behalf of Britain was approved, however. The Duke finally abandoned the notion, because only official recognition would give him diplomatic status and therefore the tax break which would make the project possible.

The Duke was by nature an optimistic man, and often felt hopeful about his future, even when negotiations did not seem promising. There was one way in which the truth about his future prospects was made plain to him. Normally even the most junior of outgoing Governors could expect to be received at Buckingham Palace, but there was no audience at the Palace for either the Duke or the Duchess on their return from the Bahamas. Having declined the Bermuda offer, the Duke was not to be offered an official job of any kind for his country, not was he to be officially thanked for the job he had completed.

The Abdication had isolated him from his family and from the British Establishment. The war had set this isolation in concrete. Accordingly, the Duke felt all the more bitter as he ruminated on how he was to plan his empty future.

BELOW: *The Duke at a duck shoot, Andros Island, September 1943, in company with his equerry, James Drury (right), and some of the 'Bay Street boys'.* ABOVE: *The Duke and Duchess relaxing on a visit to a spa with friends, Blue Ridge Mountains, Virginia, October, 1943.* LEFT: *After attending many farewell events, the Windsors left the Bahamas quietly at dawn, 3 May 1945, on the* Jean Brilliant. *They are disembarking here at Miami.* OPPOSITE, TOP RIGHT: *The Windsors spent the summer of 1945 in the USA and Canada. With the Wesson brothers, General Truscott, James Cagney and war correspondents, Lee Carson and Lowell Bennett at a broadcasting studio, New York, May 1945.*

Wallis Windsor

Palm Beach –
1947

CHAPTER ELEVEN

SEASONAL MIGRATIONS

PREVIOUS PAGES, LEFT: *1955, the Duke meeting some old friends at Palm Beach station on his annual visit.* BACKGROUND: *Inscription by the Duchess in a book.* RIGHT: *Clapperboard used in filming* A King's Story. ABOVE AND BELOW: *Back in France, the Windsors carried out official duties. Officials reacted to them with greater or less enthusiasm.*

The Duke of Windsor had been given no job, nor did he create one for himself. One of the sternest criticisms of his later years was that he did not use his potential patronage to do something for other people. Instead he resigned himself to the life of the idle rich. With little of consequence to do, the Duke lived out his chosen fate, growing old with the Duchess, as they pursued their seasonal migrations from one continent to the other, in company with other members of their social set. The pattern soon became established and varied very little in the years from 1945 until he became seriously ill in 1971. But it was punctuated by the occasional semi-official engagement, and the focus of public attention turned to the Duke and Duchess whenever a member of the Royal Family died or married, or when the new Queen was crowned in 1953. On those occasions the media remembered the Windsors and wondered where they would be on the day of the ceremony.

It took the Duke of Windsor many years to realise that he was not to be called upon to serve his country in any capacity, however small. In the interim he expended a lot of energy

OPPOSITE, TOP RIGHT: *The Duke in London, 1945. Queen Mary and her son; at their first meeting for nine years the warmth is muted but evident.* LEFT: *Post-war, the Windsors extended their acquaintance among French society. The Bal Lambert, Paris, 1949.* BELOW: *The Duke and Duchess with the Baron de Cabrol at La Cröe, 1945. Fred and Daisy Cabrol were among their closest friends over the ensuing years.* BELOW LEFT: *The Duchess with Preezie outside 85 Rue de la Faisanderie, which they leased in 1949. Although they never really liked the house, they lived there for four years.*

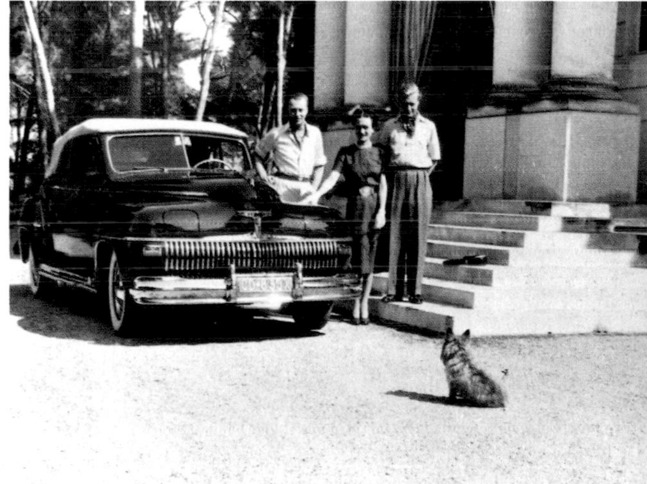

pleading with the court and with ministers of the crown for something worthwhile to do. Indeed it was only when his niece came to the throne as Queen Elizabeth II and he saw that the attitude of the court relaxed not a jot, that he finally resigned himself to the life of an exile.

When the Duke sailed away on that cold December night of 1936, he had not imagined that he was condemning himself to a life permanently away from Britain. Although there was always some contact with Buckingham Palace, the Duke found himself relying on his own resources, unprotected by the machinery of government and the court, without their advice and briefing, though he had never been trained for such an eventuality. In such circumstances there must have been many times when he felt exposed. It is understandable that he sought the company of rich and powerful men, and chose to overlook how unsuitable some of these might be as friends of a former sovereign.

On their return from the Bahamas, the Windsors went to live again at the Boulevard Suchet. When their lease here ended in 1948, they accepted the offer of Commandant Paul-Louis Weiller to live at number 85 rue de la Faisanderie, a mansion he owned but used only for entertaining. This was to be their Paris home until 1953. With their return to Paris the Duke and Duchess began to cultivate elements of French society. Old friends came to stay from England, although post-war exchange controls made travel difficult, and inevitably at this time they saw less of

4
8
12
3
7
11
2
10
1
5
9

their old American diplomatic and military friends. Their new circle began to include a few members of the French aristocracy.

In the early years after the war an annual pattern of travel was not yet established. In the summer of 1945, the Windsors went for a holiday in Locust Valley, Long Island, where they stayed with close American friends, Mrs George Baker (Edith Baker) and Charles Cushing, before returning to France and settling for a while at the Château de la Cröe. There were many idle hours in the sun, but the Windsors also accepted invitations to attend a number of local ceremonies, troop inspections, wreath layings and other such events. The Earl of Dudley, the Duke's closest friend from the old days, and other old friends — the Moncktons, the Seftons, the Buists and Sir John Aird — remained occasional visitors.

These guests languished in considerable comfort in the garden and by the pool. Scattered about were cushions with self-deprecating slogans inspired by the interior designer Elsie de Wolfe, who was a great influence on the Duchess's style: 'IT NEEDS A STOUT HEART — TO LIVE WITHOUT ROOTS' and 'SMILE AT THE POOREST TRAMP — AS YOU WOULD AT THE HIGHEST KING'.

The Duke took steps to break the isolation from his own family, when he spent a few days in London staying with his mother, Queen Mary, at Marlborough House in October 1945. The King came down from

OPPOSITE: *Contact prints showing the Duke and Duchess at Château de la Cröe, by the pool and in the grounds, summer 1945.* ABOVE: *The Duchess talks to Preezie and Pookie by the pool.* LEFT: *The pool at La Cröe, a gouache by Baron de Cabrol.* BELOW: *The Duke and Duchess in the baking heat of the rocks around the lower pool at la Cröe.*

ABOVE: *April 1950, Palm Beach, the Duke cool and elegant with Connie Mack, retired baseball star.* TOP: *Cool and elegant again, this time at a barbecue in Havana, Cuba, April 1948.* RIGHT: *The Duchess with journalist Elsa Maxwell and Lorna Mackintosh, April 1948. Elsa and Wallis organised 'The Veterans' Ball' together in 1953. When the Windsors were not invited to Queen Elizabeth II's Coronation later that year, Elsa joined fellow journalists in jeering at them. Wallis and Elsa did not speak for five years.*

Balmoral especially to see his brother. But the Royal Family would not relent with regard to the Duchess, whom they still judged quite unacceptable to the British people. For this reason they felt more than justified in keeping the Windsors, as a couple, at a distance. It made no difference that a Gallup poll of British public opinion in 1939 had revealed that 61 per cent of those polled said that they would like to see the Windsors back in Britain, with only 18 per cent against.

The Duke particularly disliked cold weather, so he and the Duchess began to visit Florida every January for golf at Palm Beach and duck-shooting at Edith Baker's Horseshoe Plantation, Tallahassee. Here they were happy in the circle of companions, little known to the outside world, who were their closest post-war friends. These included golfing pals such as Milton 'Doc' Holden and Christopher Dunphy. There was also the New York Central railroad tycoon, Robert Young, and his wife Anita, and Herbert 'Tony' Pulitzer, a former RAF officer who had been known to the Windsors in the Bahamas. Pulitzer had been a good friend to the Duke in the period of shock and sadness after the tragic death of his favourite brother, the Duke of Kent.

After his close wartime connection with the United States, the Duke became increas-

ingly interested and involved with American life. He also became noticeably more Americanised and gradually lost the manner of the naval prince and officer of years gone by, though his respect for the American informality was combined with his old-fashioned British courtesy. His wardrobe had its idiosyncracies, some of them transatlantic in origin and some inherited from the era of King Edward VII: his Savile Row elegance combined with some very loud tartans, the thick knot of his tie, his stylish shoes, and his occasional cloak or large overcoat with astrakhan collar. Yet together they added up to a version of the archetypal Anglo-American gentleman, a rather rare breed today.

In this context his remark to Robert Harris: 'I have always considered myself a Southerner by marriage' becomes more understandable.[115] He even talked with the twang of an American accent, while the Duchess's Southern drawl took on something of an English patina. In

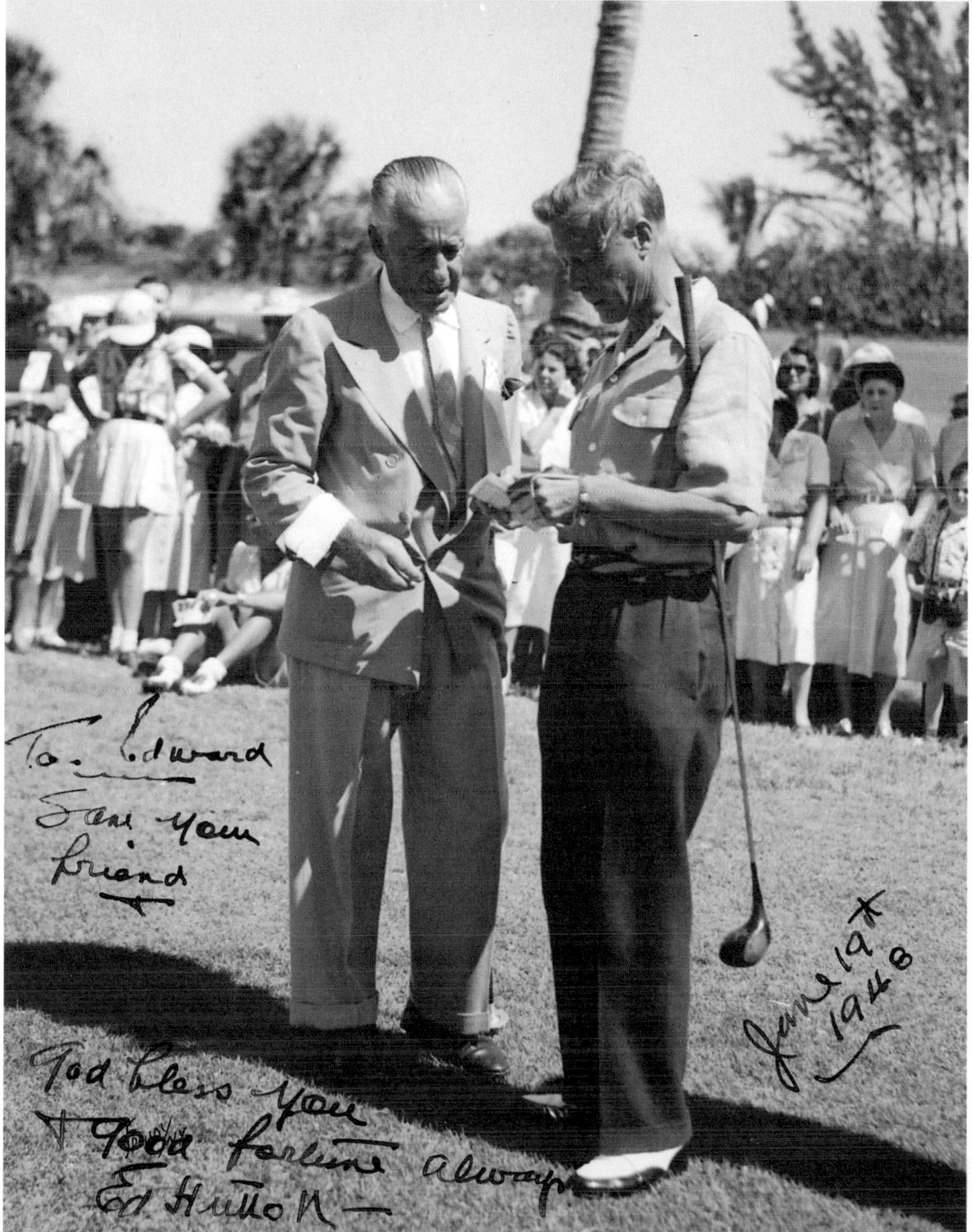
To Edward
God bless you
Good fortune always
Ed Hutton —
June 19th
1948

TOP LEFT: *In August 1952, the Duke and Duchess were given an audience with Pope Pius XII at his summer residence, Castel Gandolfo.* LEFT: *The Duke with Ed Hutton at a pro-am golf tournament, Seminole Country Club, Palm Beach, June 1948.* TOP: *Venice, 1955; the Duke's suit has a conventionally elegant Savile Row cut, but the white bow tie and the two-tone shoes are unusual.* ABOVE: *His green cord dinner jacket has Beaufort Hunt buttons, January 1960. In the evening he often wore midnight blue, rather than black, with a red carnation. The photographs on these pages show clearly the Duke's individuality and the understated, elegant rightness of his dress sense.*

RIGHT, BELOW AND BOTTOM LEFT: *The Duke and Duchess in Italy, September 1949, where they took the waters at Montecatini and spent some time with friends at Brunate, near Lake Como.* BOTTOM RIGHT: *A reunion with the Metcalfes: a photograph taken by Lady Alexandra Metcalfe of the Duke and Duchess, with her husband, 'Fruity', son David, and twin daughters, Davina and Linda, 1947.* OPPOSITE: *The last time the Duke ever visited EP ranch, his property in Canada. The Duchess is braving the cold cheerfully but the Duke has a melancholy look, 1950.*

America they were widely entertained and when in France they spent some time returning hospitality at La Cröe. In this new life the Duke held two types of men in particularly high esteem — the tycoon and the professional golfer. Had he been born in another orbit, he might have aspired successfully to a life in big business.

On their winter trips to the States, the Windsors would rent a regular apartment at the Waldorf in New York and from there take off for West Virginia and Long Island, and visit Nassau and Palm Beach, where the Duke played golf. The Duke and Duchess sought to establish an annual pattern of winter in America, spring and autumn in England and summer in France. They were still hoping for permission to make a home at least part of the time at Fort Belvedere. To this end they they paid brief visits to England, staying with the Dudleys in Sunningdale (where the Duchess's jewels were stolen in October 1946) or with the Metcalfes at Little Compton Manor in Gloucestershire. They were testing the water to see how their visits were received in official circles.

Most summers until 1949 were passed at La Cröe, and in 1948 unusually they spent Christmas there. In the late summer they travelled again, visiting Florence, Venice (where they had honeymooned in 1937), Lake Como and Montecatini (to take the waters). During these years there were a number of more adventurous foreign trips. April 1948 found them in Cuba, visiting a cigar factory at the behest of their old friend, Captain Ali Mackintosh, lunching with the President and consorting with Ernest Hemingway. In 1950 they went to Mexico and then attended Mardi Gras in New Orleans. At a ball there they bowed and curtseyed to the King of the Carnival and the Lord of Misrule, a curious role for an ex-monarch and his wife. They travelled to Texas as guests of officials of Shell Oil and then on to Canada, for a visit to the Duke's EP Ranch.

BELOW: *For many years a shooting party in Alsace in the autumn was part of the Windsors' annual programme. The Duchess endures the event dutifully while the Duke takes aim, Diebolsheim, Alsace, 1951.* RIGHT: *Biarritz 1951, the Duke and Duchess in a publicity shot for the Duke's memoirs,* A King's Story. *The book was published in at least ten languages. In the years after the Château de la Cröe was sold, summer in Europe tended to mean a cruise on the Mediterranean or a rented villa in Biarritz.*

In general the Duke of Windsor did not care to spend his time with the other ex-Kings of Europe. In January 1949, however, he played golf in the South of France with another monarch in exile, King Leopold of the Belgians. Leopold had been expelled from Belgium (now under the regency of his brother, Prince Charles) as a result of his controversial behaviour during the war, and lived in France with his second wife, Princess Liliane. Princess Liliane was almost as unimpressed with the Duke's game as the Duke had been with Crown Prince Hirohito's in 1922.

THE DUCHESS'S CYPHER, 'WW' UNDER A CORONET AND DELICATELY TRANSFIXED BY FOUR ARROWS, IS EMBROIDERED ON THIS IVORY SILK SATIN CLOTH WITH AN EXQUISITE APPLIED BORDER OF CHANTILLY LACE. THIS CLOTH WAS ONE OF TWELVE SUCH FINE PIECES TO BE FOUND AMONGST THE ITEMS IN HER VERY EXTENSIVE WARDROBE. FROM GIRLHOOD ONWARDS, IN LEAN TIMES OR AS A RICH WOMAN, WALLIS WINDSOR WAS A NATURALLY ELEGANT CREATURE WHOSE STYLE AND PRESENTATION WAS OF THE HIGHEST. AT VARIOUS PERIODS IN HER LIFE THE DUCHESS COMMANDED HER CLOTHES FROM MAINBOCHER, SCHIAPARELLI, VALENTINO, BALENCIAGA, DIOR, GIVENCHY AND SAINT LAURENT, AND LATTERLY, SHE NEVER FAILED TO BE NOMINATED TO THE BEST DRESSED WOMEN LISTS.

Repeating a successful old formula, in 1951 the Windsors joined Daisy Fellowes on her yacht, the *Sister Anne*, for a cruise, and later they rented a villa in Biarritz. During these years, from December 1951 until his eyesight grew bad, there were visits to Diebolsheim in Alsace, to shoot with Prince and Princess Alphonse de Caraman-Chimay. The Princess was a cousin of the Duke's old equerry, Lord Claud Hamilton.

On 6 August 1950, they were in Cannes for the wedding of Herman Rogers to his second wife, Lucy Wann. Wallis's old friend Katherine Rogers had died the year before. The Duchess had known Herman and Katherine Rogers for a long time, and she may have been upset by this new pairing. For whatever reason, Lucy treated the Duchess with caution.

An important focus of the Duke's attention at the beginning of the 1950s was the writing of his memoirs, *A King's Story*, published in March 1951. This was the result of a collaboration with Charles Murphy, his American ghost, and gave the Duke a chance to tell his side of the Abdication story publicly. It was generally well received,

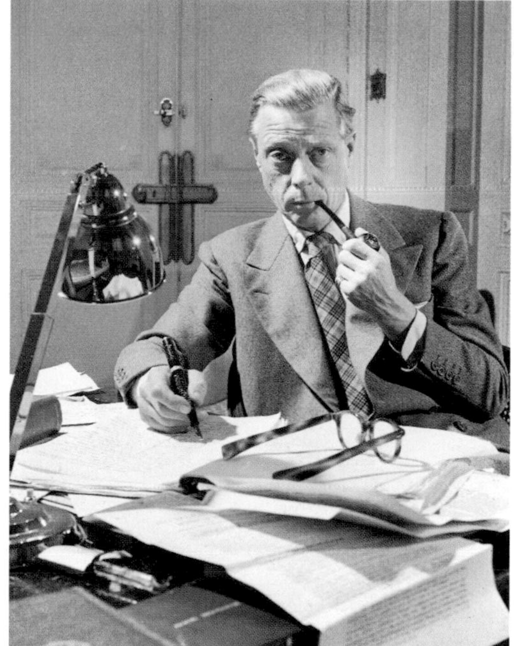

though there were murmurs of disapproval in some circles. Other books and articles followed, and later the Duchess wrote her version, *The Heart Has Its Reasons*, which was published in 1956. She had been reluctant to embark on the project at first, saying that she dreaded publicity and this would merely bring up an old and controversial issue.

The Duke thought that since at least two rather dubious biographies about her were about to be published, she should have her say first. But in the end they were swayed by financial considerations, since the decorating of their new Paris home was very expensive. Like the Duke, the Duchess employed first one ghost, then another.

The latter months of 1951 involved a certain amount of publicity for the Duke's book. He had intended to talk about his book in a speech to booksellers on 28 September in London. However, much to his annoyance, he was advised by Churchill and others not to address the gathering, since his brother, King George VI, was recuperating from a serious operation.

In February 1952, the Windsors were in New York as usual when the news reached the Duke that his brother had died and he found himself back in London alone for the State Funeral, an uneasy visit for him. He took part in the procession wearing the uniform of an Admiral and there were some who noticed that he walked out of line, a fraction of a step in front of the Dukes of Edinburgh, Gloucester and Kent. It was at this time that he heard that his allowance from the monarch was to be discontinued. Despite much discussion, it was some time before it was restored, although now halved in value. The Duke was by no means a poor man but he was thin-skinned about family slights and was becoming ever more alienated by tactless handling. After the burial he rejoined the Duchess in New York.

This process was repeated almost identically a year later when the Duke learned that his mother, Queen Mary, was dying. This time he and the Princess Royal sailed to London

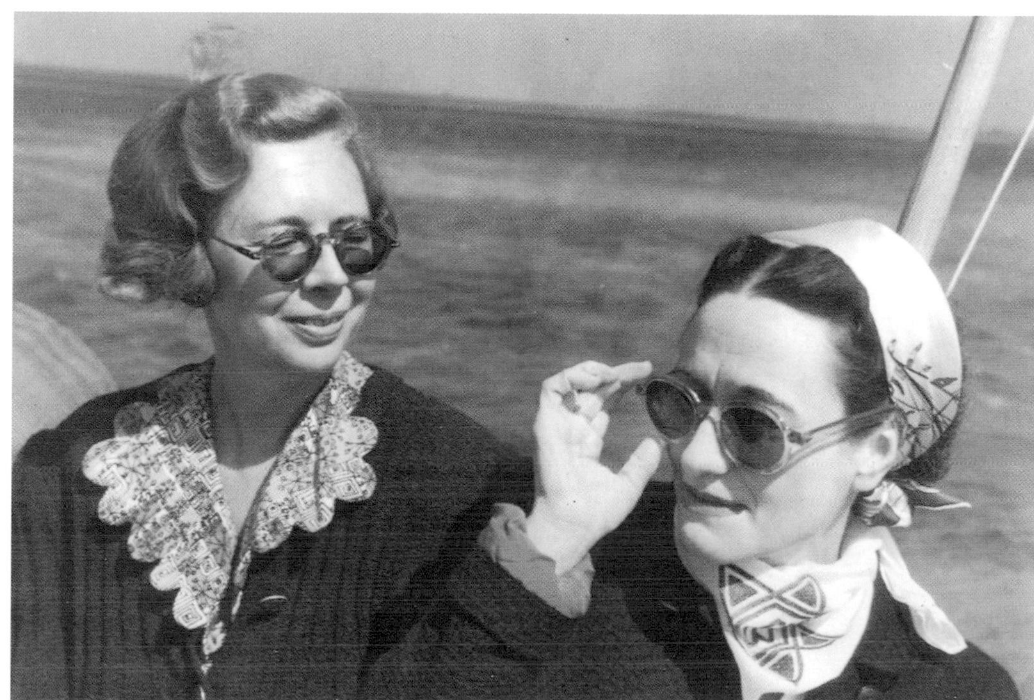

TOP LEFT: *Early 1949, the Duke at the Ritz Hotel, Paris, working on his memoirs. From 1946 to 1949 the Windsors had the largest suite at the Ritz as their Paris base, with the Château de la Cröe as their principal house.* LEFT: *The Duchess with Katherine Rogers on board a yacht, Florida, 1947. Katherine, Wallis's oldest, most constant friend, died of cancer a year or so later.* TOP: *The Duchess and the bereaved Herman Rogers, 1949.* ABOVE: *The evening of Herman Rogers's marriage to Lucy Wann, 1950. Herman and Lucy, another member of the Windsors' circle of friends, had both lost their spouses at the same time. The mood at the table seems uncelebratory; the Duchess may have had misgivings about this union.* OVERLEAF: *The Happy Hollow, Havana, Cuba, April 1948; left to right: the Duchess, Ernest Hemingway, his wife, Mary, and son, 'Bunby', with the Duke in the background.*

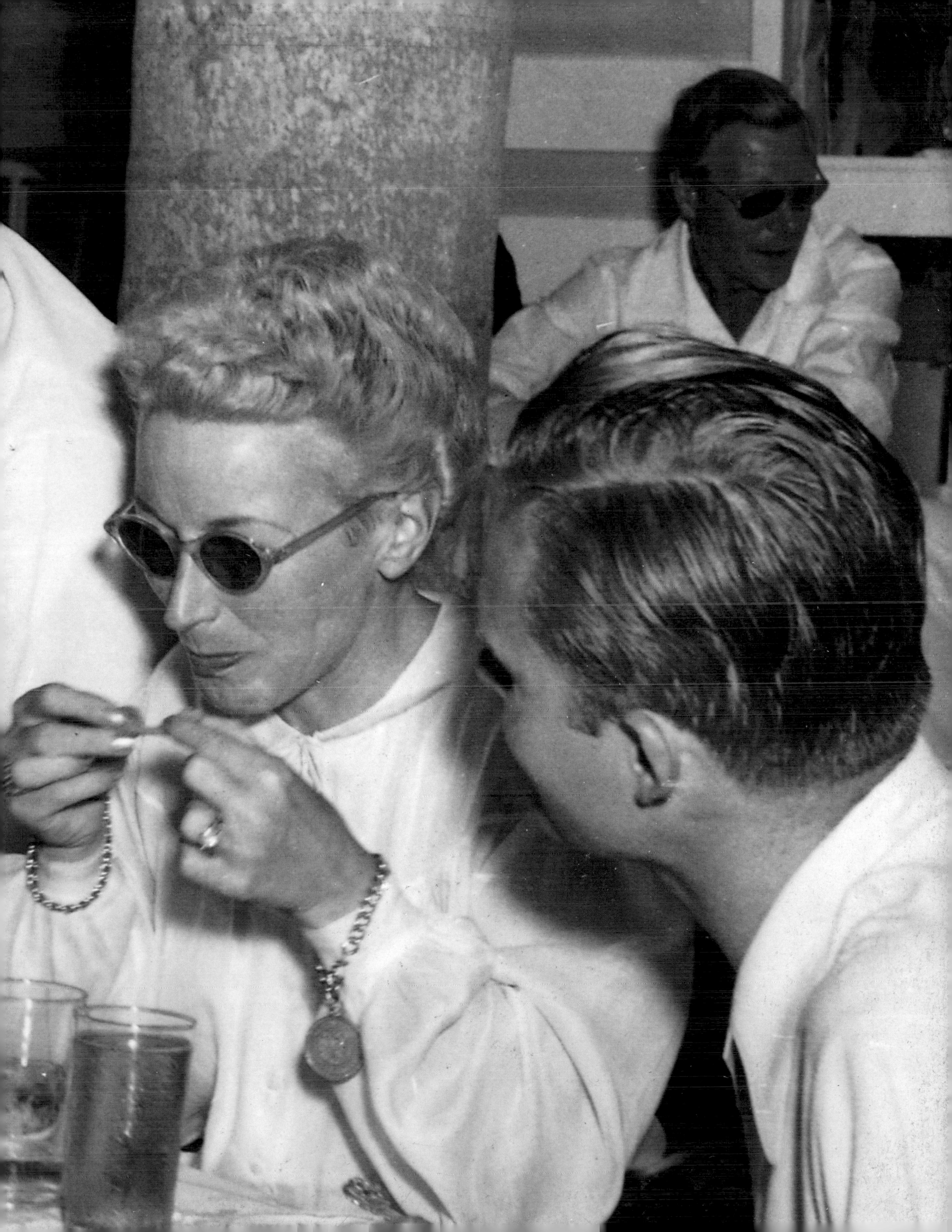

RIGHT: *The Duke and Duchess in the salon at the Windsor Villa, July 1956. In the acquisition of the house, the Windsors used the services of the lawyer Suzanne Blum for the first time. She was employed by the Paris branch of the Duke's lawyers, Allen and Overy.* BELOW: *The Duke with one of the pugs, the terrace at the Windsor Villa, 1959.* BOTTOM LEFT: *Outside the Mill, the Windsors' country house, at Gif-sur-Yvette, near Paris; the Duchess is standing with (second left) Stéphane Boudin, the interior designer, and (far right) Russell Page, the distinguished gardener who designed the Mill gardens, 1952.* BOTTOM RIGHT: *The Duke and Duchess at the Lido in Venice, 1961.*

together. This was the first time that the Princess had met her sister-in-law and she told her son, Lord Harewood, that 'she had found her charming.'[116] (Lord Harewood was one of the younger generation who stood 'in amazement at the moral contradiction between the elevation of a code of duty on the one hand, and on the other the denial of central Christian virtues — forgiveness, understanding, family tenderness.'[117]) After Queen Mary's funeral at the beginning of April 1953, the Duke of Windsor went back to New York.

The deaths of King George VI and Queen Mary caused the Duke genuine sorrow, and the loss of his mother severed the really important link with the centre of his family. In letters written during his stay in London to attend his mother's deathbed and funeral, he told the Duchess he was 'boiling mad' that she had been denied her 'rightful place as a daughter-in-law', and painted an unflattering picture of his stiff family, who still refused to receive his wife. 'But, he continued, 'let us skip this rude interlude and enjoy our lovely full life together far removed from the boredom, the restrictions and the intrigues of the Royal Family and the Court!'[118]

What is most evident is his complete and continued reliance on the Duchess and the durability of their marriage. It was now that

Plaza Stockings Always to the fore

DAILY GRAPHIC
DAILY & SKETCH

Thursday, February 28, 1952 ★★★★ A Kemsley Newspaper 1½d.

I'd rather have a Gin and VOTRIX

Duke of Windsor calls on Churchill

HER STORY MADE WOMEN SOB

This is the girl whose evidence at the Old Bailey yesterday made women weep. She is 11-year-old Frances Fletcher, of Turnpike-lane, Hornsey, N. Her beret and white-ribboned hair just showed over the witness-box rails as she told of—being punched on the nose by her father—being beaten "about 20 times" with a leather belt—being told "See how much more punishment you can take"—being burned with a poker. Her father, electrician Cyril Victor Fletcher, was jailed for seven years.

FULL STORY ON PAGE 5.

Name the six-year-old boy with the military air smiling good-bye to Britain before embarking at Southampton yesterday. Clue 1—the soldierly salute. Clue 2—his destination is Malaya. The answer is: Miles Templer, son of General Sir Gerald Templer, Malaya High Commissioner.

The Duke of Windsor spent half an hour with Mr. Churchill at 10, Downing-street yesterday.

As the Prime Minister said good-bye at the door the Duke raised his hat and smiled to a small crowd in the street.

Then he drove to Buckingham Palace.

★ ★

The Duke is staying with Queen Mary at Marlborough House.

They dined together last night.

Earlier yesterday he visited his doctor for treatment for a slight chill.

The Duke will sail for the U.S. to-day in the liner Queen Elizabeth.

Secrets of the fashion world

To-morrow's DAILY GRAPHIC will reveal the secrets of the fashion designers of Paris and London.

The DAILY GRAPHIC's unrivalled picture service will ensure that a full survey of the chic and the ungainly, the beautiful and the bizarre in fashions is presented.

Order your DAILY GRAPHIC from your newsagent—and don't miss this picture special.

TIMELY WORDS OF FAITH

In the day of my trouble I will call upon Thee: for Thou wilt answer me.
—Psalms 86, 7.

Does every day mirror your beauty?

It will if you light up your own good looks with the correct shade of Yardley Powder. To keep you lovely wherever you go, there are two forms of Yardley powder. For your dressing table, the familiar loose powder, superfine and subtly blended. For travel, the unspillable Feather Pressed, which clouds on to your puff easily, lightly, without spoiling your clothes or even your gloved finger tips . . .

YARDLEY POWDER

Loose—for your dressing table

Feather Pressed for travel

HP SAUCE

SUNDAY GRAPHIC

A Kemsley Newspaper

Plaza Stockings Always to the fore

THEY MOURN THEIR SQUIRE. Sandringham Estate workers file past the coffin of the late King in the church of St. Mary Magdalene, while four keepers mount guard. At the foot of the bier is the Queen's wreath.

EXTRA: 8 ROYAL PICTURE PAGES

The Duke's brother and unwilling successor, George VI, died in February, 1952. ABOVE: *From the Duke's collection of old newspapers: estate workers pay homage to their late sovereign, Sandringham parish church.* LEFT: *There was press interest when the Duke took the opportunity to visit his old friend, Prime Minister Winston Churchill.* BELOW: *The Duchess in teasing mood with the Marquès de Villa Verde (son-in-law of Generalissimo Franco) at a party in Madrid, January 1963.*

they put down firm roots in France, settling into a new life in a new house they bought in the country outside Paris, the Moulin de la Tuilerie ('the Mill'). Without realising it, and like so many expatriates, the Duke recreated in France much of the conventional life that he had been so keen to escape from in Britain. He lived a life with a fixed annual programme, as his father had, isolated from the general fray, with servants in royal livery, and royal ciphers on virtually everything he touched. And he was content.

For some time the Windsors had been at odds about the choice of town or country for their principal residence. The Duke preferred the country and the Duchess the town; according to the Duke's valet, Sydney Johnson, she always seemed happiest in New York. The Duke spent part of the summer of 1952 inspecting and preparing for the restoration of the Mill, which was to give him much pleasure. For some years to come the couple were preoccupied with the reconstruction of this house, and the creation of a garden. And in December 1953 they moved from the rue de la Faisanderie to a villa on the edge of the Bois de Boulogne, 4 Route du Champ d'Entraînement, their last home.

The choice of a town house in Paris and of the Mill marked their settling down. Number 4 in the Route du Champ d'Entraînement was a charming villa set in a small park and garden

BELOW: *The Duchess in animated conversation, England, 1954 – perhaps advising her companion that she could never be too rich or too thin.* RIGHT: *The Duchess of Windsor at the centre of a group of Society beauties gathered for a ball, December 1949; Helen Lyttle-Hull (right), Deenie Hutton (third right).* OPPOSITE: *The Duchess and Pugville's Imperial Imp II ('Impy') matching each other's paces at the Manhattan Savings Bank Dog Show, New York, February 1960.*

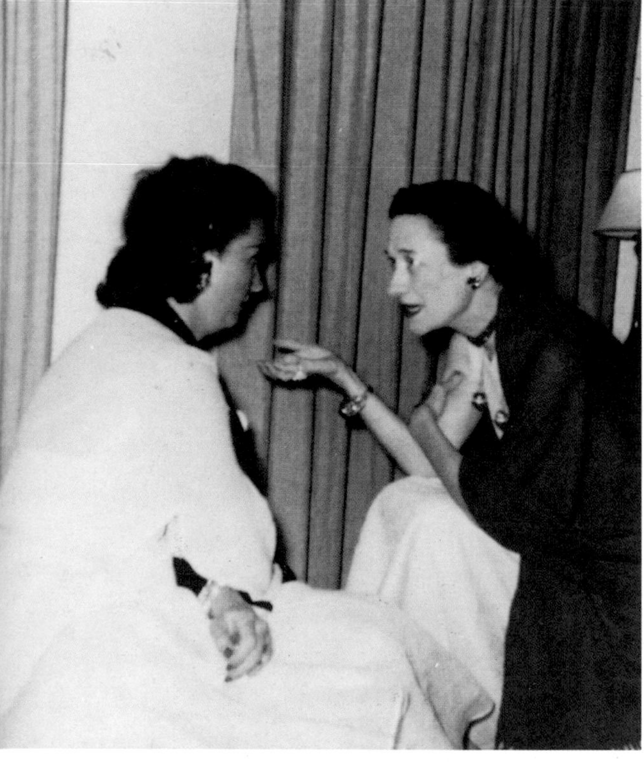

on the edge of the Bois de Boulogne near Neuilly. Under the guidance of the gifted interior decorator Stéphane Boudin, it was transformed into a grand palace in miniature suitable for a former King-Emperor. Boudin's skill lay in his ability to understand exactly what his clients required: the villa possessed every modern American comfort as well as formality of style. The striking feature of the house was the spacious, square hall with its fine staircase rising on the left, hung with tapestries, and the Duke's Garter banner (as Prince of Wales), suspended above the upper banisters to the right. The hall was kept dimly lit, bathed in honeyed colours like burnished gold. Facing the visitor was the entrance to the salon with bright light flooding in through tall french windows that led out to the terrace and garden. The elegant blue and silver salon, used by the Windsors for formal receptions, had double doors at each end. To the right was a small library, decorated in warm, autumnal colours, where Gerald Brockhurst's portrait of the Duchess hung. This comfortable room, the only one on this floor with a fireplace, was used as a downstairs sitting room. To the left was the ingenious dining room with its minstrels' gallery, mirrors and chinoiserie. An integral component of the decoration were the changing flower arrangements. Throughout the house were many portraits and photographs of Queen Mary, the mother whom the Duke described as having been so severe, and who never received the Duchess. It was almost a shrine to her.

The Windsors' everyday sitting room, the boudoir, was upstairs, placed directly above the salon and overlooking the garden. Their suites were ranged on either side, the Duchess's to the right and the

THIS SOLID BRASS BELL WAS ORIGINALLY PART OF THE FITTINGS ON BOARD THE ROYAL YACHT BRITANNIA, DESIGNED FOR GEORGE V AND BUILT ON THE CLYDE. SADLY, IN THOSE MORE EXTRAVAGANT TIMES, AFTER THE KING'S DEATH SHE WAS TOWED OUT TO SEA AND GIVEN NAVAL BURIAL IN DEEP WATER. THE DUKE OF WINDSOR WAS VERY ATTACHED TO THIS REMINDER OF HIS FATHER'S LARGE ELEGANT RACING YACHT AND DISPLAYED IT IN TWO OF HIS HOUSES. AT LA CRÖE HE HAD THE ROOF FITTED OUT LIKE THE DECK OF A SHIP. THE THREE ROOF TOP ROOMS WERE CALLED 'CABINS' AND THE BRITANNIA BELL AS WELL AS FAKE GUNS, TELESCOPE AND LIFEBELTS WERE ON DISPLAY THERE. LATER IT HUNG BY THE FRONT DOOR AT THE MOULIN DE LA TUILERIE.

ABOVE: *The Windsors celebrating their twenty-fifth wedding anniversary, on board the SS* United States, *June 1962.* RIGHT: *April 1948, the Windsors at the reopening of a hotel owned by a friend, Robert Young, the railway tycoon, at White Sulphur Springs. The Duke did a stint on drums with the Meyer Davis Band during the event.* BELOW: *The Duke at ease with his golfing pals: behind him, Lord Dudley, beside him, Bob Simons and behind, Charles Cushing, Palm Beach, 1955.* OPPOSITE: *A montage of photos of the Mill, parts of which dated back to the seventeenth century. Guests who could not be accommodated in the ten rooms of the main house were lodged in the further fourteen rooms created from the outbuildings. The property was intended for entertaining over long weekends.*

Duke's to the left. The Duchess had assigned to the Duke the larger of the two bedrooms. This was transformed for him into a very English room. The Duke's study formed part of this bedroom, which as near as was possible echoed his bedroom at Fort Belvedere. The splendid tapestry behind the bed, woven with the arms of a Tudor Prince of Wales, had hung over his bed at the Fort. The Duke and Duchess each had a further suite of small rooms extending along either end of the villa, along the sides of the gallery, which ran round the entrance hall at the upper level. The Duke had as extensive a dressing-room as the Duchess, and beyond this was his marble-lined bathroom, the room with the bath covered over and a grim-looking shower.

The Duchess's dressing room occupied similar space behind her bedroom. Beyond this was her bathroom, which was decorated with wall paintings and a number of gouaches by the Russian ballet designer, Dimitri Bouchène (whose works also adorned Greta Garbo's apartment in New York). The Duchess's bedroom was pale blue and silver, and displayed the influence of Elsie de Wolfe. It was very French and elegant, not American, chintzy and comfortable like the Mill.

This was the Windsors' home for most of their year. Here they entertained their friends to dinner parties with exquisite foods and wines, and often dancing in the hall after dinner. The editor of *Vogue*, Diana Vreeland, remembered the Duke calling her at the Crillon on a hot summer's day with the welcome invitation to drive the twenty minutes or so out of Paris and sit with them on the cool of the terrace.

The Mill was their country retreat half an hour's drive from Paris, much loved by the Duke, who threw himself into working on the garden with the same relish as he had tackled the Fort's as Prince, less loved by the Duchess, who was essentially more of a city person, much preferring a visit to the fashion collections, to rural life. The Mill had been the home of the painter, Drian, and was a group of several grey-stoned houses with tiled roofs and white shutters. The property was surrounded by a wall and could not be over-

05-31-6
05-31-12
05-31-5
05-31-11
05-31-4
05-31-10

LEFT: *Contact prints: the Duke and Duchess picnicking, mid-1950s.* ABOVE: *The Duke, possibly 1955.* BELOW: *September 1954, Munich, the Duchess in cahoots with Jimmy Donahue. At first, both Windsors enjoyed Donahue's company and were seen often with him. Later, gossip columnists fastened on the story, and Elsa Maxwell took the chance to make mischief. The friendship petered out after 1954 as Donahue got more out of hand. He died of alcohol and drug poisoning aged fifty-one.*

looked by the neighbouring houses. The Duke was particularly proud of his water garden, with its waterfalls and cataracts.

As ever, the house was staffed by liveried servants. The Duke's study was a converted barn, with huge french windows. It was a sort of museum filled with souvenirs of his travels, the maps of his world tours, side-tables made from regimental drums and a great number of military and royal memorabilia. The bedrooms of the house were not large, and in contrast to his Paris life, the Duke slept in a narrow bed in a low-beamed attic room which had no door, and was open to the stairs that led up to it.

James Pope-Hennessy stayed at the Mill in the 1950s and described the guest-room in which he was put: 'The room in the stables . . . was very pretty and convenient, and once more prepared or planned by a perfectionist; there was nothing on earth that you might conceivably want that wasn't there — every kind of writing paper, nail-file, brush, fruit, ice-water; the bathroom loaded with scent-bottles like a counter at a bazaar — a delicious sense of self-indulgence.'[119]

The summer of 1954 was spent once more on a Mediterranean cruise, this time with Jimmy Donahue amongst others on board, followed by visits to Austria and Southern Germany. Donahue, an heir to the Woolworth fortune, was something of a beau as far as the Duchess was concerned. An effeminate man and an excellent raconteur, he shared her taste for quick and witty conversation. Despite his somewhat *louche* reputation, he was ostensibly a safe admirer at a time in her life

when her morale may have needed a boost. For some years he was a regular nightclub companion of both the Windsors in New York, but his friendship with the Duchess and his increasingly outrageous behaviour caused the Duke concern, and attracted a fair amount of unfavourable gossip. Later he fell from favour and finally came to a tragic end in 1966.

And so the Windsors lived through the 1950s, occasionally spotted in London or in nightclubs such as El Morocco in New York for a New Year's Eve party. In 1956 the Duke put on his Garter robes at the Mill in order to be painted by James Gunn, a portrait that was a reminder of the earlier portraits of the wistful young Prince of Wales newly installed as a Knight of the Garter. The portrait disappeared without trace during the Duchess's long illness in the last decade of her life. Public interest in the Windsors was sustained by an interview they gave to the celebrated American journalist Ed Murrow on his television programme, *Person to Person*, to publicise the Duchess's memoirs.

BELOW: *The Duke posing in his Garter robes beside his portrait with the artist, Sir James Gunn, September 1955. This painting disappeared from the Windsor house during the Duchess's final illness.* RIGHT: *The Duke with Ed Murrow at the Moulin de la Tuilerie.* BELOW RIGHT: *The Ed Murrow* Person to Person *interview took place in September 1956 at the Waldorf Towers, New York, in the Windsors' usual suite, 28a.* BELOW LEFT: *Like the Murrow interview, the article in* McCalls *magazine was intended to launch the Duchess's autobiography,* The Heart Has Its Reasons. *The book was a great success in America.*

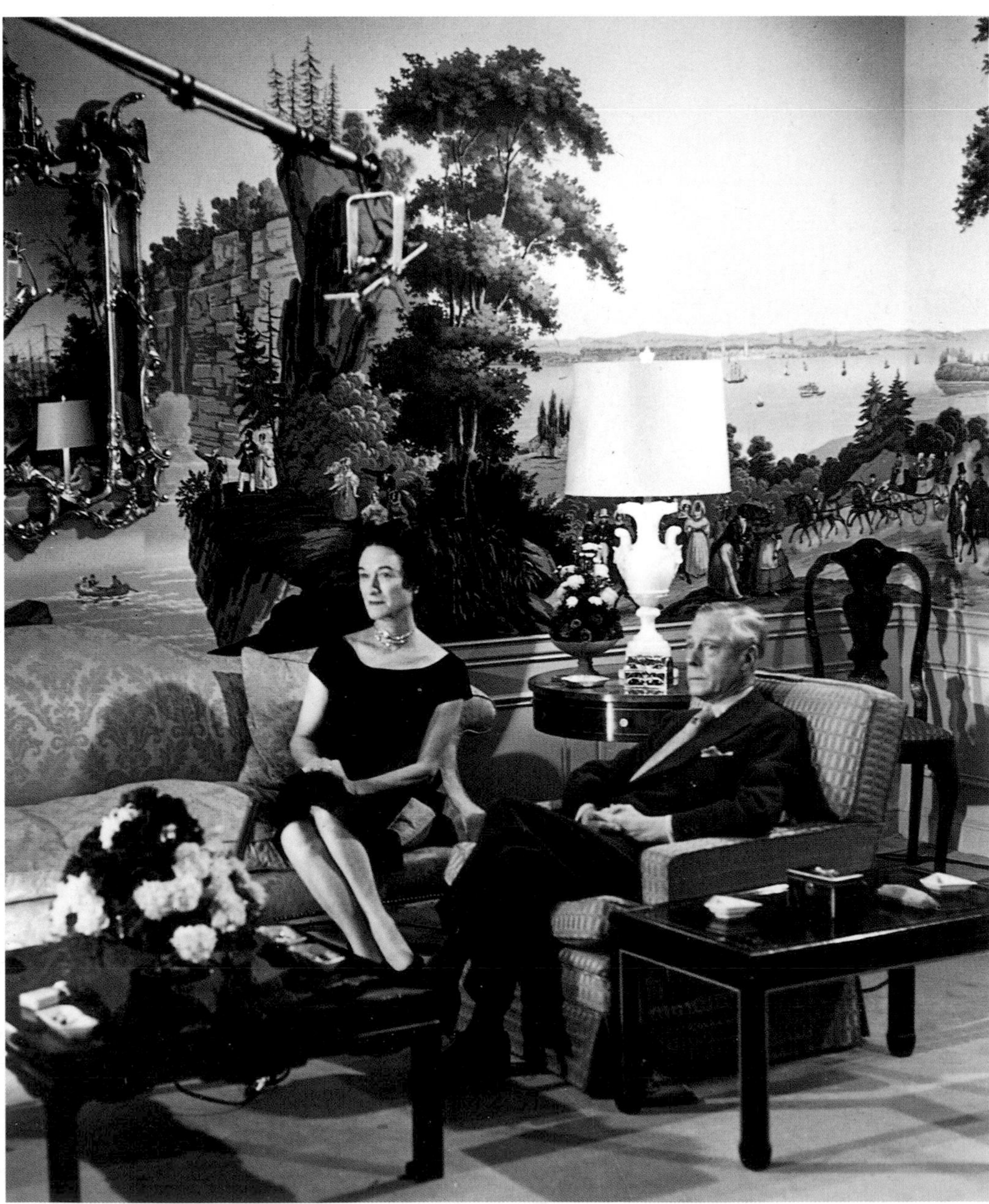

And so it went on, a ball here, a trip to Palm Beach, a spirited game of golf, a visit to Arizona (in March 1959), an interview with the well-known journalist Nancy Spain, visits to Deauville, the Lido, and St Moritz. And from 1962 onwards the Windsors headed south to Spain and even considered building themselves a palatial house near Marbella. They were no more idle or trivial in the way they spent their time than many people of their wealth and position; they were simply more conspicuous and, in the Duke's case at least, comparisons with what might have been were the chance for journalists to score an easy point.

In June 1964, the Duke celebrated his seventieth birthday. There then followed a series of events which brought him gradually back into the public eye. The first was the film of his book. Jack Le Vien, the film producer, had directed a documentary about the life of Sir Winston Churchill, called *The Finest Hours*. The Duke agreed that, if funds were raised, he would be prepared to take part in a film, based on *A King's Story*. He believed, with more prescience than he can have realised, that the story would be told more accurately if he and the Duchess took part while they were alive, rather than be played by actors, as would surely happen after their deaths. Thus, in August 1964, filming began on *A King's Story*, which proved to be a moving documentary, and a considerable success when released to the general public. Curiously, it was soon after this, that the Duke of Windsor began to become an old man, this despite his well-deserved reputation for a brisk outdoor routine and abstemious appetite.

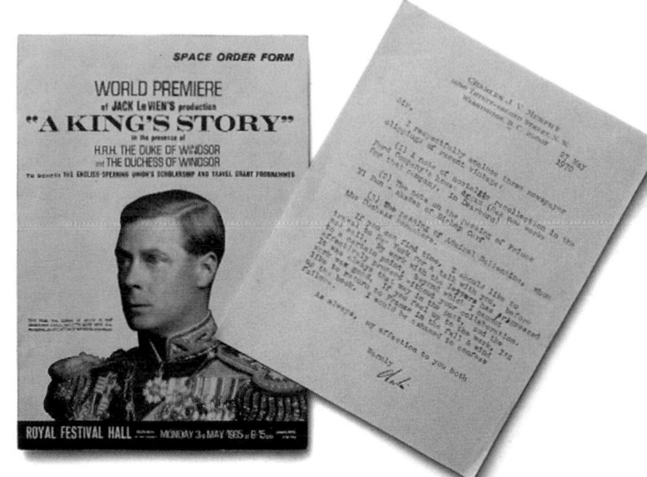

BELOW: *The Duke at the Mill filming Jack Le Vien's version of his book,* A King's Story, *August 1964.*
ABOVE: *The programme (left) for the London première of the film, May 1965, which the Duke and Duchess did not attend, and (right) a letter from Charles Murphy, who ghosted the book for him.*

Edward

Duke of Windsor

1965

CHAPTER TWELVE

GROWING OLD TOGETHER

The King and the Lady
A film that will astonish the younger generation
TIME & TIDE
THE BRITISH NEWS MAGAZINE
18–24 JUNE 1964
TWO SHILLINGS WEEKLY

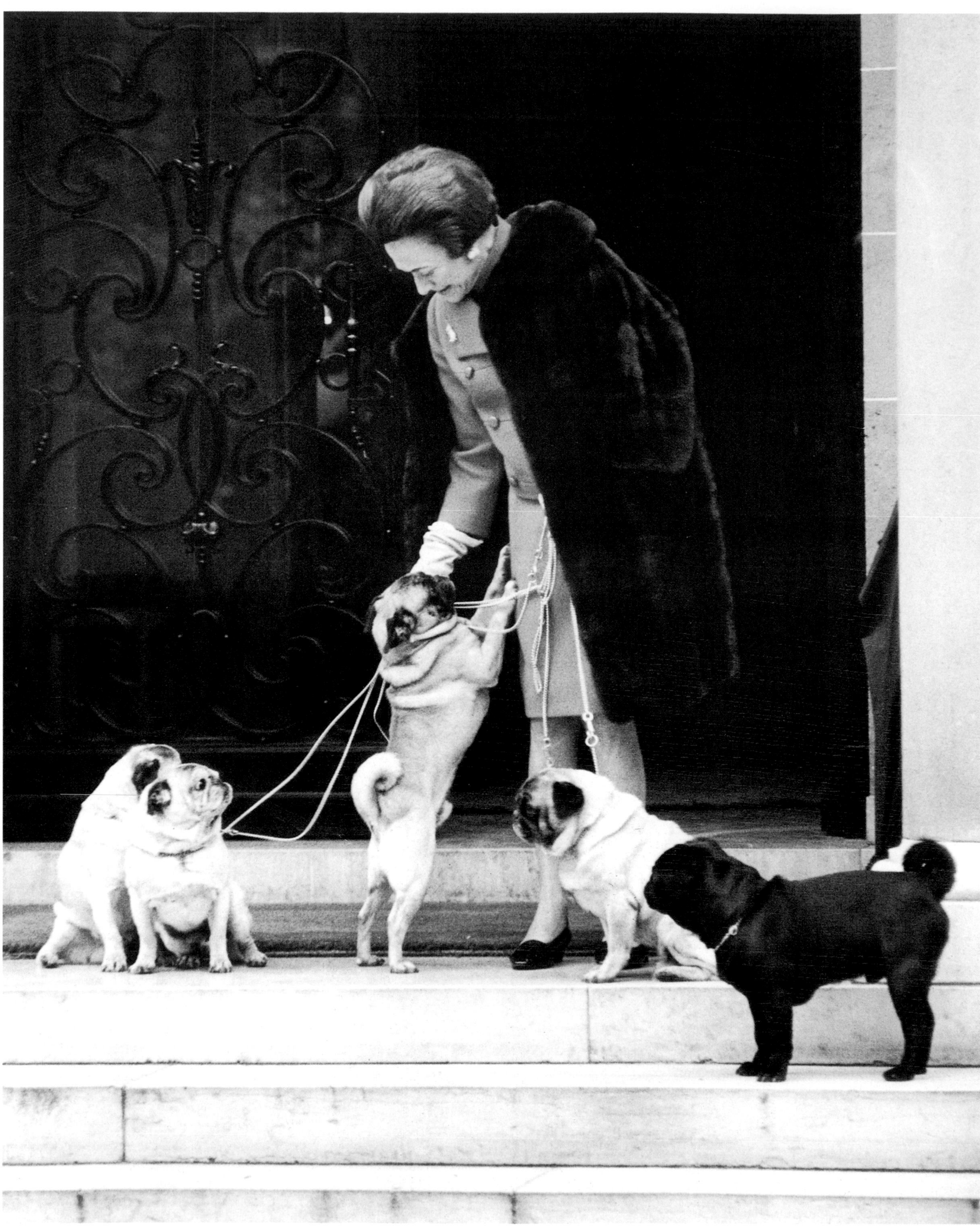

Severe ill health dogged the Duke of Windsor from the mid 1960s. He underwent an operation for open heart surgery in the United States at the Methodist Hospital, Houston, Texas, at the hands of Dr Michael DeBakey in December 1964 and then spent some weeks in London, undergoing a serious eye operation in the London Clinic in 1965. While he was there, the Queen paid him two visits, which had something of the nature of a formal reconciliation. As he recuperated, the Duke was invited to walk in the gardens of Buckingham Palace. It was during this time that the Duchess of Windsor was often photographed entering and leaving the London Clinic, dressed in her mink coat, or later, as the weather grew better in a Chanel suit. It was a time when the British public remembered that the Windsors still existed and realised that they were now an elderly couple, dignified and very much together.

The Duke was visited in hospital by his sister, the Princess Royal. She died suddenly ten days later on 28 March 1965, and her Memorial Service in Westminster Abbey on 1 April was the first public engagement in Britain to be attended by the Windsors together.

When the Duke emerged from the London Clinic, he looked frail and wore heavy dark glasses to protect his eyes. From now on press photographers with their flashes were particularly irksome. Following this period, photographs of the Duke show a frail figure, invariably protected by the dark glasses. The Duchess, on the other hand, remained remarkably elegant and seemed to defy the years. Their travelling did not diminish, and they sought the winter sun as usual in Palm Beach, following their normal annual peregrination.

Portrait photographs further reminded the world of the existence of the Windsors. The

PREVIOUS PAGES, LEFT: *The Duke and Duchess, Connecticut, 1965.* BACKGROUND: *The Duke's inscription on the photo.* RIGHT: *Cover of* Time and Tide, *with an article on the filming of* A King's Story, *June 1964.*
TOP: *The Windsors at a restaurant, Palm Beach, November 1956.* ABOVE: *The Duke with the Duchess and Dr DeBakey after the successful heart operation, Methodist Hospital, Houston, December 1964.*
LEFT: *Regent's Park, London, March 1965, the Duchess and Duke taking exercise after his retina operation. The Duke never quite regained his vigour after these set-backs.*
OPPOSITE: *The Duchess with her team of pugs in the doorway of the Windsor Villa, 1967*

FAR RIGHT: *The Windsors on their annual winter trip to the sun arriving at Palm Beach station, March 1958, and delighted to be met by their great friends Arthur and Susy Gardner, Milton Holden, Anita Young and Edith Baker. Their luggage was the object of perennial press interest.* ABOVE: *The Duke and Duchess attended the première of the film by Jack Le Vien (left) of the Duke's life story, Marbeuf Cinema, Paris, 1966.* BELOW RIGHT: *The Duchess looking composed and content, USA, 1968.*

Duchess was particularly pleased to be photographed by Lord Lichfield, commenting gamely: 'Patrick and I had our session — but you must remember it is an old face and even he can't put the clocks back . . .'[120] The photographs were taken in connection with an interview by the journalist, Godfrey Winn. During a stroll round the garden of the Mill, Winn asked the Duchess about her life. Predictably, she spoke about fashion, though she claimed that it was never her main interest. She welcomed the arrival of off-the-peg clothes, sweaters and shoes from Marks and Spencer, and costume jewellery, and told him that 'the hemline should stay firmly anchored on the knee.' On a more personal note, she said that both she and the Duke would have liked to have had children, and she spoke of their life together:

'Yes, we have made our own private happiness, somehow. And we have come through, despite all that our critics said at the time. But it has not been easy for either of us. And every day of my life I can't help remembering, however hard I try to forget, all that he gave up for me. This came home with a compelling new force when I saw the completed film. His film.'[121]

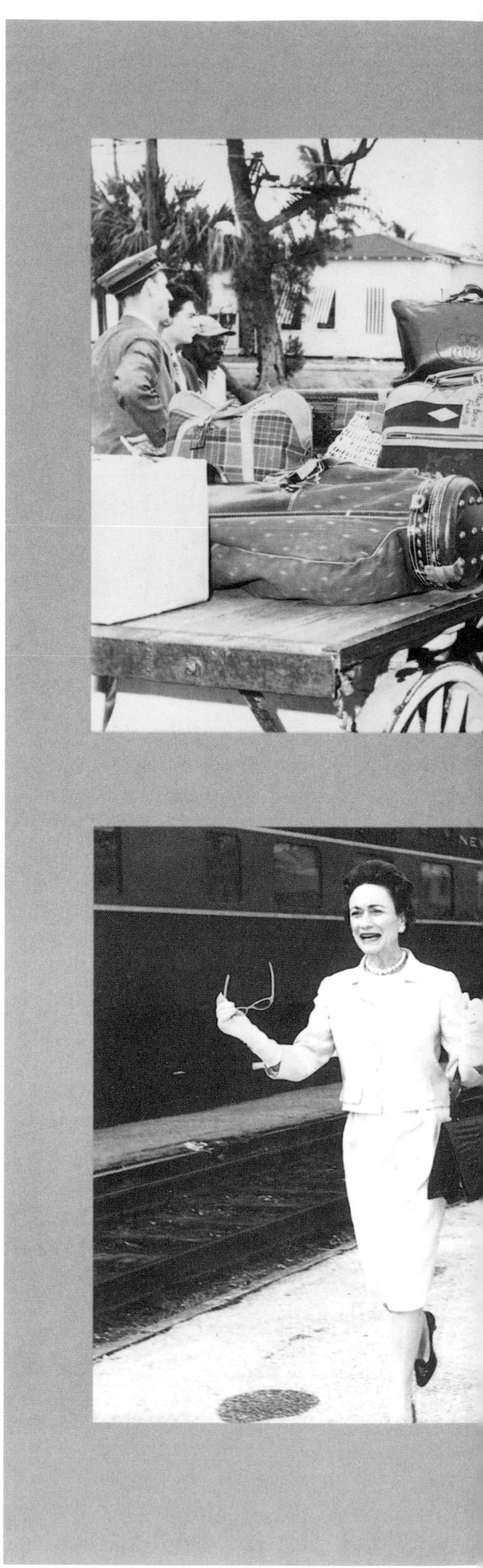

On 3 June 1967, the Windsors celebrated their thirtieth Wedding anniversary. In New York there was the gala film première of *A King's Story*, attended by celebrities such as Senator Edward Kennedy and his mother, Rose. It was a benefit for the New York Hospital for Special Surgery, and so moved were some of the guests that they left the cinema in tears. The Windsors then left for London, where they attended the unveiling of the Queen Mary memorial at Marlborough House on 7 June, the only time they were seen together in public with the Royal Family. The camera clicked as the Queen greeted her uncle and his wife, and courtiers stood back in amazement as the Queen Mother leaned forward to kiss him.

In July 1968, a scene from Julie Andrews' film, *Darling Lily*, was filmed at their Paris house, and the Windsors came to meet the star on the set. They enjoyed the company of film stars and invited Elizabeth Taylor and Richard Burton to both their homes. A month later, the Duke visited Britain for the last time, to attend another funeral at St George's Chapel, that of his sister-in-law Princess Marina. So trim was his figure that he wore the same morning coat as at his wedding. The Royal gathering in the Deanery, following the service, was the last occasion when the Duke was amongst his family. It was the only time he ever had a conversation with Princess Anne. He asked her why she did not hunt and she replied simply: 'Bloodsports'. (A few years later she and Prince Charles overcame this worry and took to the field.)

In 1969 the Windsors made friends with Nathan Cummings, President of Consolidated Foods in America. Cummings

ABOVE: *The Duchess has the President's attention, New York World Fair, May 1964; left to right: Charles Engelhard, Lyndon Johnson, Jayne Engelhard, Ladybird Johnson, the Duke.* TOP RIGHT: *The Duchess is still conscious of the camera, while the ageing Duke no longer notices the cigar ash on his trousers, New York, 1967.* BELOW: *Julie Andrews on location for the film, Darling Lily, July 1968. The Windsors allowed the façade of their house to be used as a location for the film.* OPPOSITE: *The Duke and Duchess watching a ticker-tape parade on Broadway, New York, 1970.*

had heard that the Duchess could not get bagels in Paris and so sent her a giant deep-freeze. Thereafter the Duke undertook some public openings for Cummings, which did no harm to his bank account. The Duke was always shrewd enough to take advantage of financial advice from experts. Cummings and the Duke liked to drink whisky together at the Waldorf Hotel, and Mrs Cummings later recalled life at the Mill, where the Duchess always ensured the food came from the kitchen piping hot, where a late breakfast was followed by a long lunch and high tea, with the Duke handing out the cups himself with a shaky hand.[122] The highlight of the Duke's day was cocktail hour, since his self-imposed rule was that he never took a drink before seven in the evening. It was clear to visitors that the drinking hour sometimes seemed to him a long time in coming.

In January 1970, an interview was broadcast on British television in which the Duke and Duchess spoke to the political journalist, Kenneth Harris. The conversation was filmed in the salon of their house in the Route du Champ d'Entraînement, sometimes with both Duke and Duchess present, sometimes just the Duke. As ever he averred that he had no regrets, though he wished he had been able to do a job of some kind in later life. He supposed that those who had prevented him were now 'under the ground'.[123]

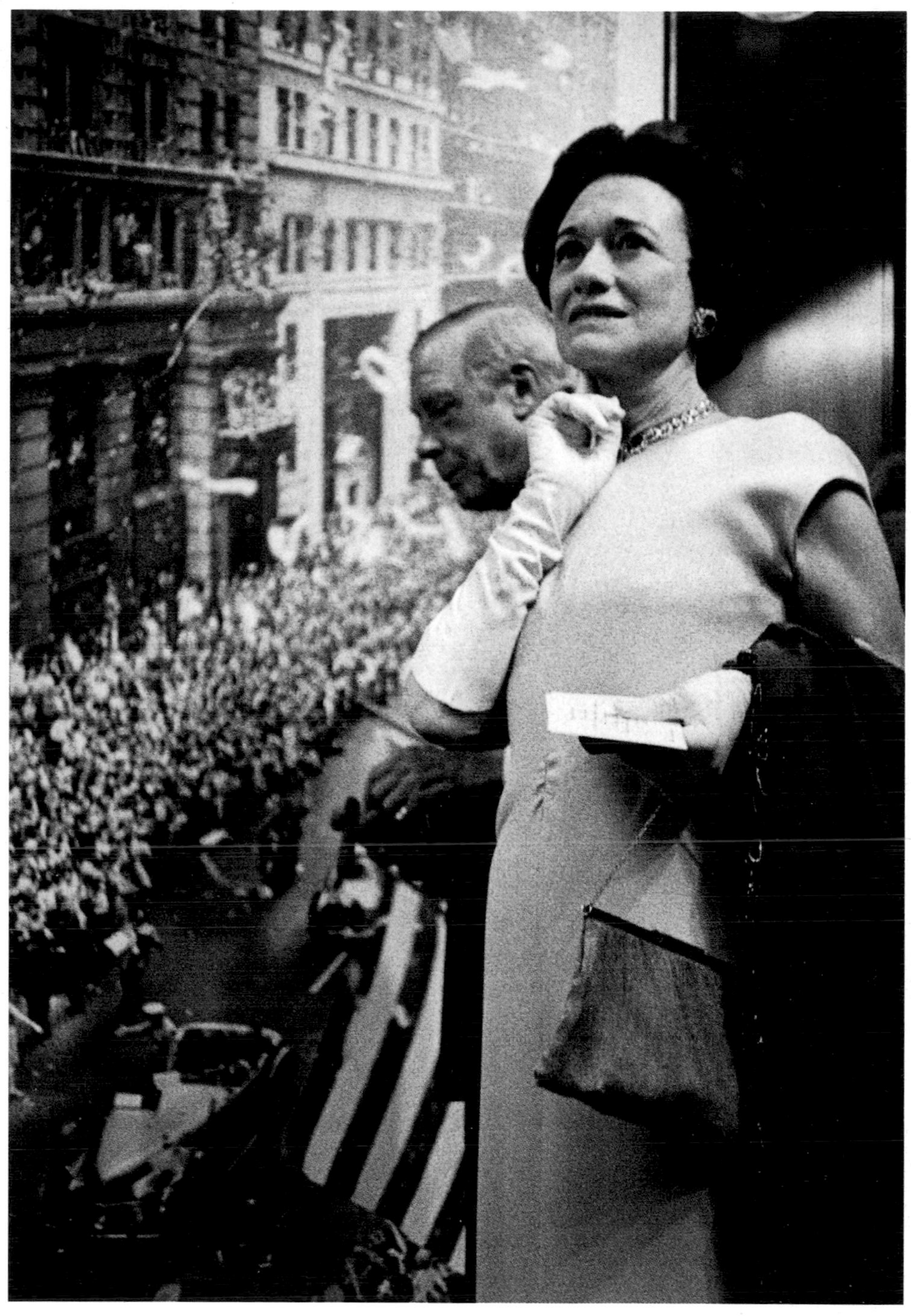

BELOW: *Lord Mountbatten and his daughter, Lady Brabourne, resuming their friendship with the Windsors after many years, receive the Duke and Duchess at Broadlands, June 1967. The main purpose of their English visit was to attend with the rest of the Royal Family the unveiling of a plaque commemorating Queen Mary at Marlborough House. The Duke squints increasingly in strong daylight.* RIGHT: *The Duke, who called himself a 'Southerner by marriage', and the Duchess were gratified when President Nixon and his wife gave a dinner in their honour at the White House, April 1970.* BOTTOM: *This portrait of Emperor Hirohito and the Empress was given to the Duke at the time of their visit to the Windsors in October 1971. The Emperor and the ex-Emperor had not met since 1922.*

Lord Mountbatten came to Paris early in 1970 and dined alone with the Duke. Though he recorded that the Duke 'repeated for the third time how much he had enjoyed the dinner with me';[124] Mountbatten omitted to mention that the Duke also took the opportunity to berate him for refusing to be his best man in 1937. After all the years he still felt let down by his travelling companion of the 1920s and had taken to referring to his cousin as 'Tricky Dicky'.[125] Mountbatten found the Duke's eyesight much better, and noted that though his hip was giving him trouble, he was still able to play nine holes of golf.

In April 1970, the Windsors received their greatest official accolade in the United States, when they were the guests of honour of President and Mrs Nixon at a grand dinner at the White House.

Old age encroached gradually. The Duke kept his dapper figure, and the newspapers published occasional photographs of the Duchess attempting some new dance more suited to the very young. Her preoccupations were largely social and domestic, with financial worries over the rate of exchange of the franc in France, which she occasionally called 'this miserable country'.[126] She kept good care of herself, telling Barbara Cartland: 'I wash my face a lot with Dr Lazlo's soap and I use Dr Bergman's products. As a vitamin product I take Geriatric Pharmaton from Switzerland.'[127] Always a zealous adherent to a strict diet, she also underwent a regular massage, both of which iron disciplines helped to keep her trim.

The Windsors were scarcely ever apart in their later years. Witnesses observed that the Duke would look worried if the Duchess was absent for long. Certainly he spent long periods in the study that was part of his bedroom, looking over his financial portfolio and dealing with his correspondence. There were times when he would call his Private Secretary there for a chat, John Utter invariably finding the Duke in a cloud of smoke from his pipe. One afternoon the Duke told him he had had two pieces of bad news, the first was a letter from the Duchess of Gloucester telling him that his brother had suffered a bad stroke, and the second was that the Duchess was downstairs in the hall, discussing some expensive improvements to the house with Monsieur Boudin, of Jansen. He was always reluctantly indulgent of the Duchess's decorative extravagances.

The Duke and Duchess were well served by their staff. Gregorio Martin, their Spanish chauffeur, still works at the house today. He admired the Duke greatly and spoke fondly of his kindness and sympathy and his great courtesy. The Duchess was quicker-witted than the Duke; she knew how to express herself amusingly, but she could never resist a bitchy remark, even about her good friends. Theirs was a marriage where the two partners were different in most ways, and yet it worked. Monsieur Martin observed that of the two, the Duke was the more devoted, while the Duchess could be very irritable with her husband.[128] Sydney Johnson, the Duke's faithful valet for thirty years, went further, recalling that the Duchess had an unpredictable temper and often made her husband cry. Nevertheless, his devotion to her never wavered. His favourite term of endearment for her was 'Peaches'.

Cecil Beaton, ever the observant onlooker, called in for tea at the house in the Bois, in September 1970:

'The Duchess appeared at the end of a garden vista, in a crowd of yapping pug dogs. She seems to have suddenly aged, to have become a little old woman. Her figure and legs are as trim as ever, and she is energetic as she always was, putting servants and things to right. But Wallis had the sad, haunted eyes of the ill. In hospital they had found she had something wrong with her liver and that condition made her very depressed. . .

'Wallis tottered to a sofa in a small, overcrowded drawing-room. Masses of royal souvenirs, gold boxes, sealing wax, stamps and seals; small pictures, a great array of flowers in obelisk-shaped baskets. These had been sent up from the Mill, which will be sold now the Duke is not able to bend down for his gardening.

EDWARD VII, THE DUKE OF WINDSOR'S GRANDFATHER, SMOKED CIGARS IN HUGE QUANTITIES AT ALL TIMES OF DAY, EVEN BEFORE BREAKFAST. HIS FAVOURITE CIGARS WERE THE VERY LARGE CORONA Y CORONA OR HENRY CLAY'S TSAR. HE USED THIS CASE AS A YOUNG MAN, LATER PASSING IT ON TO HIS GRANDSON. THE DUKE OF WINDSOR STARTED HIS SMOKING CAREER AT SIXTEEN AND HIS HOUSE IS LITTERED WITH THE ATTRACTIVE ACCOUTREMENTS OF THE THEN FASHIONABLE HABIT: CASES, ASHTRAYS, HOLDERS AND BOXES FOR CIGARETTES, CIGARS AND MATCHES, AS WELL AS A SELECTION OF PIPES. THIS CROCODILE SKIN CASE ADORNED WITH THE PRINCE OF WALES FEATHERS WAS OFTEN IN HIS BREAST POCKET.

One of the Fairchild Business Newspapers

Women's Wear Daily

THE RETAILER'S DAILY NEWSPAPER

TWENTY CENTS

Chains' Sales Up For March, April

ARTS & PLEASURES

Passion Play's Locale A Blend of Old and New

A CHAT WITH THE DUCHESS

THE DUCHESS OF WINDSOR IS EVERYTHING YOU EXPECT . . . AND MORE.

Haggarty's Calls Parley Of Creditors

Full Orders In Children's Off Target

Creslan looked into sweater-shirts

Romanova by andrex THE NEWEST IN DOUBLE KNITS

ANDREX INDUSTRIES CORP.

BELOW: *The Duke loved country life. He is seen here in the Mill garden, looking relaxed, in a cloud of tobacco smoke, with Princess Dmitri Romanov (formerly Sydney born Sheila Chisholm), whom he had known through her successive marriages, as Lady Loughborough and Lady Milbanke.* ABOVE: *The Duchess wears a Givenchy suit to be photographed for* Women's Wear Daily *of May 1970. In the interview she predictably talks about entertaining and fashion, but also reveals that she runs a dog charity which cares for and rehouses strays. She is praised for her charm of manner and for her youthful looks. The Duchess is over seventy here but her reputed three face-lifts have served her well: she now looks more attactive than she did twenty years before.*

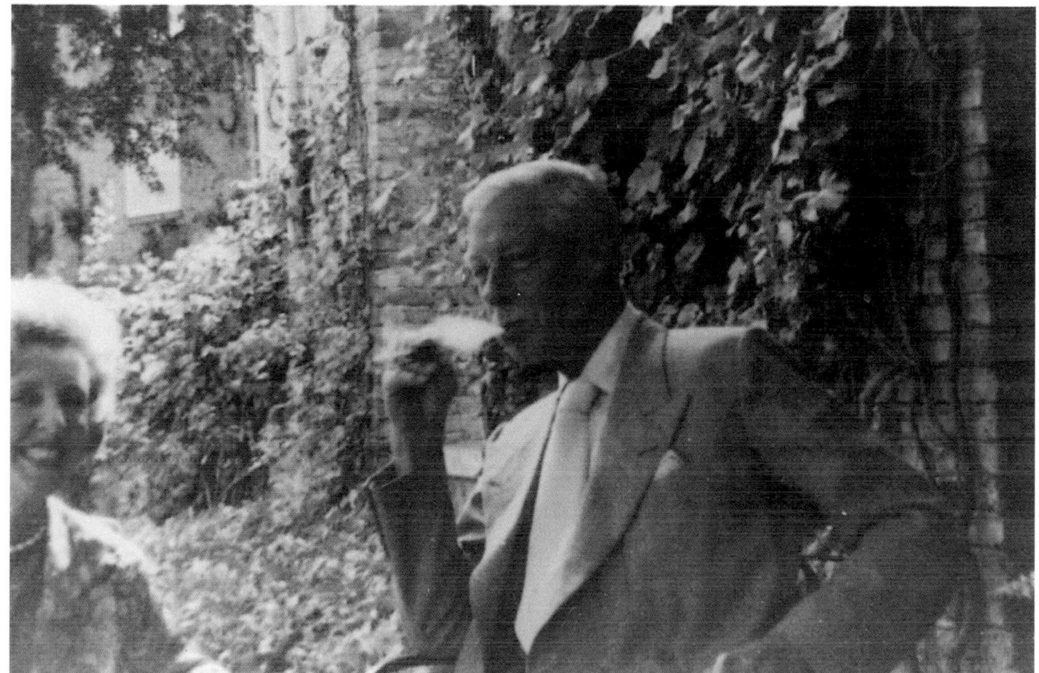

'We talked easily as old friends do. Nothing much except health, mutual friends and the young generation was discussed. Then an even greater shock; amid the barking of the pugs, the Duke of Windsor, in a cedar-rose-coloured velvet golf-suit, appeared. His walk with a stick makes him into an old man. He sat, legs spread, and talked and laughed with greater ease than I had ever known . . .

'But they are a happy couple. They are both apt to talk at once, but their attitudes do not clash and they didn't seem to have any regrets. . . An hour passed quickly enough. . .'[129]

The Duke had two royal visits in October 1971. The first came unexpectedly from Prince Charles, who had longed to reverse the situation whereby the Windsors were kept at arm's length. He wanted his family to invite the Windsors for the weekend. He told them that he felt sorry for his great-uncle, who might well wish to return to Britain, and that he thought it would be fun to get to know the Duchess. This move was met without enthusiasm.

But the Prince took the opportunity to pay an impromptu Saturday evening visit to the Windsors, after a day in the country with the Ambassador, Sir Christopher Soames. He left a vivid account of it in his diary. Having circumnavigated some 'dreadful American guests', the young Prince managed a quiet word with his great-uncle in his study:

'He seemed in very good form, although rather bent and using a stick. One eye was closed most of the time, as a result of his cataract operation, but apart from that he was in very talkative form and used wide, expansive gestures the whole time, while clutching an enormous cigar. . .

ABOVE: *The Duchess with her hairdresser, New York, 1968. Alexandre tended the Duchess's hair for thirty years, until her health declined. She made his reputation when she discovered him at Cannes and brought him to Paris.*
BELOW: *Two of many sketches in the Villa of hair styles created by Alexandre for the Duchess. Several of the Duchess's hair-pieces are in the collection.*

'While we were talking the Duchess kept flitting to and fro like a strange bat. She looks incredible for her age and obviously has her face lifted every day. Consequently she can't really speak except by clenching her teeth all the time and not moving any facial muscles. She struck me as a hard woman — totally unsympathetic and somewhat superficial. Very little warmth of the true kind; only that brilliant hostess type of charm but without feeling. . .'[130]

Perhaps the Prince felt their circumstances were a little undignified, and he may have been a touch disdainful about his elderly hosts, but his visit gave the Duke great pleasure and thereafter he held his great-nephew in high esteem. The Duchess was also grateful to the young Prince for the kindness that he showed her then and later.

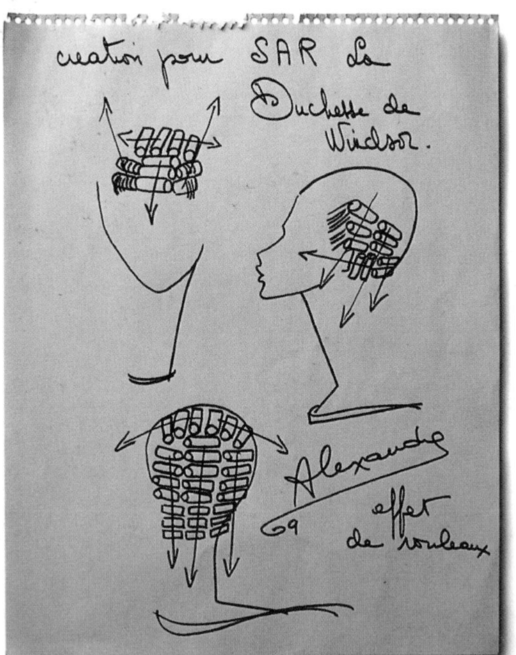

The following Monday, by long-standing arrangement, the Windsors received Emperor Hirohito and Empress Nagako at their Paris home. The Emperor was on a round of European state visits and particularly requested to see the man with whom he had played animated golf half a century earlier when they were both heirs to Empires. In a way it was appropriate that the two should meet again. Never could either have predicted the difficult roads that each man had been destined to follow. Photographs were taken of the Duchess and the Empress holding hands on the terrace. A signed photograph of the

Imperial couple was placed on a table in the salon and remained there. It was the last important public appearance of the Duke, and photographs of his frail features were flashed around the world.

Now the Duke went out less, but the Duchess made the occasional foray into the social world. One memorable excursion was to the Proust Ball at Ferrières, given by Baron and Baroness Guy de Rothschild. Other guests included Princess Grace of Monaco, Elizabeth Taylor and Richard Burton. The latter recorded his striking impression of the Duchess in his diary: 'She had an enormous feather in her hair which got into everything, the soup, the gravy, the ice-cream, and at every vivacious turn of her head it smacked Guy sharply in the eyes or the mouth and at one time threatened to get stuck in Guy's false moustache which was glued on.'[131]

The Burtons dined with the Windsors the following Monday, after which Richard Burton concluded: 'one of them — probably the old Duke — must die very soon, though it is she who is now nearly completely ga-ga.'[132]

Burton was near the mark. Early in 1972 it became clear that the Duke of Windsor was seriously ill from cancer of the throat, and there was no visit to the United States that winter. Stoically, he underwent a course of cobalt treatment and used to tell his private secretary: 'I am not really ill. It's just these drugs that make me feel so rotten.'[133] But those around him realised that he was dying. Since a state visit to Paris had been arranged for the Queen in May 1972, there was great anxiety about the Duke's condition. It had been hoped that the

ABOVE: *Golf at Palm Beach, May 1968. The Duke and his old friend, Christopher Dunphy (beside him) are getting a little frail; with Winston Guest (centre).* TOP LEFT: *The Duke keeps up his photography, Long Island, July 1968.* BELOW: *Elizabeth Taylor and Richard Burton visiting the Windsors, with whom they became friendly in 1967. They are in the garden of the Mill, autumn 1968, with Linda Metcalfe.* OVERLEAF: *The Duchess and the Duke photographed in New York, June 1971, by Karsh of Ottawa, who did not try to conceal their years. The Duchess kept a Karsh portrait of the Duke on her dressing table.*

ABOVE: *Baron Guy de Rothschild beside the Duchess at a ball, given by the Baronne at Château Ferrière-en-Brie, December 1971. The party was attended by Elizabeth Taylor, Richard Burton and Grace Kelly, among others.* BELOW: *It was an irony that on the only occasion that the Duchess entertained the Royal Family she did so alone, since the Duke was in his sick-room upstairs. The Duchess was nervous. Here she bids farewell to the Queen, who was on a state visit to Paris with Prince Philip and Prince Charles.*

Queen, who was on friendly terms with her uncle, would be able to pay him a visit. His death would have caused all sorts of problems in the circumstances. Every medical care was given to preserve him, and so the Queen had the chance to visit her uncle one last time at his house in the Bois.

On that afternoon the royal party, which included the Duke of Edinburgh and the Prince of Wales, took tea with the Duchess in the library. One present recalled that their elegant hostess sat under her portrait, looking just as good as she had when it was painted some thirty years before, and they talked of everything imaginable except the one thing on all their minds — the poor man dying in his room upstairs. Another recalled that the Duchess was so nervous that her cup rattled in the saucer, and the tea was not helped by the sudden arrival of some unruly pugs that leaped onto the table and had to be removed by liveried footmen.

To receive the Queen, the Duke insisted on leaving his bed, being dressed and seated in a chair in the boudoir. In order to sustain him, a number of tubes were rigged up, attached to him and concealed behind the chair. A man of great courtesy, the Duke could do no less for his Sovereign than rise to greet her. His physician watched horrified while his patient stood with supreme physical effort as the Queen entered, and gave her a bow from the neck. Somehow the tubes did not become detached.

The last meeting had taken place and the world observed the pictures of the Duchess escorting her royal visitors to their car. Ten days later, in the middle of the night, on 28 May, the Duke of Windsor died. His frail widow was woken and told the news.

In the days that followed the full panoply of the royal burial procedure wound into action with the moving magnificence for which Britain is well known. The Duke's body was flown to RAF Benson and conveyed to Windsor Castle. It lay in state for two days, and many thousands of members of the public queued to pay their respects. The empty nave of St George's Chapel with the solitary catafalque in the middle, covered with the Duke's standard and some lilies from the Duchess, was a splendid sight, and anyone who witnessed the scene and the reactions of the sad crowds could not fail to be moved. There were even old

BOTTOM: *The Duchess, flanked by Lord Mountbatten and the Duke of Kent, beside her husband's grave at Frogmore. This was her last visit to England, in 1973, a year after his death.* LEFT: *The Duchess at a reception in Paris, c. 1975. Behind her, John Utter, her secretary.* BELOW: *One of the last photographs of the Duchess, taken in the boudoir of the Windsor Villa, 1975.*

soldiers who walked by, almost marching. One dropped some flowers surreptitiously, wishing to make the tribute, but not wanting to appear sentimental.

During these days, the Duchess was not well enough to leave Paris. But she arrived at Buckingham Palace on the Friday, greeted by Lord Mountbatten. She lunched with the Queen, who was very kind to her throughout her stay. On the Saturday the Duchess was photographed at the palace window watching the procession return from the Trooping the Colour ceremony where a Highland lament had been played in the Duke's honour.

That evening the Duchess visited St George's Chapel, accompanied by Prince Charles and Lord Mountbatten, and attended the Duke's lying-in-state on what would have been their thirty-fifth wedding anniversary. At one point she stood alone in the almost empty nave, as Prince Charles described: 'a frail, tiny, black figure, gazing at the coffin and finally bowing briefly. . . As we stood she kept saying 'he gave up so much for so little' — pointing at herself with a strange grin.'[134]

Throughout the week tributes poured in to the Duke, and flowers arrived in quantity at Windsor Castle. The obituaries were published and the historians made their comments. James Pope-Hennessy, recorded some perceptive observations in the *Sunday Times*:

'Nineteenth and early twentieth-century British royalties certainly had a well-developed sense of duty, but there went with it an unexpressed conviction that it was very good of them to do so much "for the people". Through this attitude the Duke of Windsor, when Prince of Wales, broke as through a crash-barrier.

'He set out, and set out successfully, to modernise the conception of British monarchy. And it was this vivid sense of what he had tried to do and what he had done that gave him, later in his life, a feeling that he had been ungratefully treated both in 1936 and after.

'So far as the Abdication of December, 1936, was concerned, the Duke's fervent conviction that he had never had a choice to make and that there had been no alternative to marrying Mrs Ernest Simpson and abandoning the throne, stayed with him for ever. The fact that this view conflicted with that of his whole family, most of the country and all of the Empire did not shake him in the least.'

Pope-Hennessy concluded: 'He was not a great man, but he was an astonishingly human one.'[135]

On Monday 5 June the Duke's funeral took place in the presence of almost the entire Royal Family, including King Olav of Norway, though the Duke's only surviving brother, the Duke of Gloucester, was too ill to attend. The Queen sat next to the Duchess of Windsor and guided her through the service, the Royal men followed the coffin in procession through the chapel. There were many representatives of Government and regiments, and old friends. In

RIGHT: *South Terrace, Château de la Crõe, January 1949.* BELOW: *Photographed in Madrid, 1962.*

the congregation sat Lord Brownlow, bowed with age, the man who had accompanied Mrs Simpson on her drive through France. There was Fruity Metcalfe's widow, Lady Alexandra Metcalfe, Cecil Beaton, who had taken the wedding photographs, and Lady Diana Cooper, who had been one of the party on board the *Nahlin*.

After the service the Duchess of Windsor joined the Queen and the Royal Family for lunch. Afterwards a small group of mourners, including the Queen Mother, drove to Frogmore for the committal. Every member of the Royal Family was at the steps of the Castle to bid the elegant and brittle widow farewell. Age as well as grief had blurred her mind and she frequently appeared not to know that her husband was dead. She flew back to France that afternoon. A year later, on 11 July 1973, she made a secret visit to Windsor for her only ever visit to the Duke's gravestone at Frogmore.

In the House of Commons the Prime Minister, Edward Heath, paid tribute to the dead Duke, and recalled that, when he was Prince of Wales, he had visited the communities most afflicted by the depression and brought them a message of sympathy and reassurance, if not hope. He said: 'There must be men and women on Tyneside, and in Liverpool and South Wales, who are remembering today the slight, rather shy figure, who came briefly into their lives, and sometimes into their homes, in those grim years.'[136]

The Prime Minister spoke of the efforts made by the then Prince of Wales 'to make the monarchy less remote, less formal, more accessible, and more closely enmeshed in the social fabric of the country.' He expressed his sympathy to 'the wife for whose love King Edward was content to give up his patrimony and who has repaid his devotion with an equal loyalty, companionship and love. His death', said Mr Heath, 'has been above all her loss and to her the House will wish to extend its profound sympathy.'[137] The Duchess's name was added to the Commons motion of sympathy, *nemine contradicente*.

The Duchess of Windsor was already ailing at the time of the Duke's death. She was suffering from arterio-sclerosis, and this had been the cause of some worry to the Duke for some time. The shock of his death did not help her condition, and friends noted that she often repeated herself and lost the thread of the conversation. She felt disorientated. The Duke had managed everything, to the point that she no longer knew even how to write out a cheque.

Her staff felt sorry for her. Gregorio Martin said she was desperate because she knew that she had crossed many a widow off her social list and had no illusions as to what would now be her fate. She was lonely without the Duke, having been so wholly dependent on him, and, not unnaturally, she was all the more concerned about the world's perception of her. It distressed her that she was still cast in the role of the woman who stole the King. As she became more frail her natural timidity increased and she worried ceaselessly about her security.

The early years of the Duchess's widowhood included a certain amount of travel and a few parties. Then, increasingly, there were accidents that put the Duchess in hospital. She began to fall in her home as early as November 1972 and she was in hospital for some weeks the following January. Despite these setbacks the Duchess spent three summers in Biarritz and continued to visit New York for two more winters. Lord Mountbatten paid numerous visits to her during the first years of her widowhood, but he seemed to be primarily concerned with advising her about the disposition of her fortune. This distressed her greatly. Eventually he was kept away altogether.

In those early years the Duchess was still supported by the Duke's staff. Although never grateful to him, she depended on John Utter, who remained as her private secretary. The Queen gave him a CVO in December 1972, and the press, having nothing better to write about, speculated that the Duchess might marry him. She often telephoned to him several times during the weekend. He occasionally escorted her to a party or accompanied her on a journey, although she was not an easy companion. John Utter was 'retired' in 1975. Her personal secretary, Johanna Schütz, a Swiss girl, stayed with her well into her illness, until 1978. She travelled with her each year to the United States, and was with her on her last voyage back to France aboard the *Raffaello* in July 1975. The butler, Georges Sanègre, and his wife stayed until the Duchess's death, as did Gregorio Martin and his wife, Maria (two of the staff who have remained at the house in the service of Mohamed Al Fayed). Sydney Johnson, who entered the Windsors' employment in the Bahamas, left the Duchess after the Duke's death. He returned to the house fifteen years later as a member of Mohamed Al Fayed's staff, and died in service in 1990.

Gradually, the Duchess's affairs fell into the hands of the indomitable Maître Suzanne Blum, who assumed complete control and who finally dismissed Miss Schütz. After that Maître Blum became prominent as the Duchess's lawyer, spokeswoman and in her own words: 'the defender of the moral rights and interests of the Duchess of Windsor'. Much has been made of the idea that Suzanne Blum was in some sense a friend to the Duchess. She was never more than the lawyer, and in the Duke's lifetime, was politely asked to luncheon

ABOVE: *On board Daisy Fellowes's yacht,* Sister Anne, *July 1951.* BELOW: *South Terrace, Château de la Cröe, January 1949.*

The love that shook an empire is what they called it when King Edward VIII gave up the throne of Britain in December, 1936, for marriage in 1937 to Wallis Warfield Simpson, "the woman I love."

TOP: *Perennial press interest in the Windsor romance.*
ABOVE: *Cover of* Life *magazine, May 1950.*
TOP RIGHT: *A letter from a fan inscribed 'FOR THE WORLD'S IDEAL LOVERS' with no address – it was delivered to the Windsors, January 1951.*
OPPOSITE: *Portrait by Dorothy Wilding, May 1943.*

once a year. The Duchess was frightened of her forceful legal advisor: the staff observed that she became extremely agitated when a visit from the lawyer loomed. However, it is clear that Maître Blum controlled the Duchess's affairs in the last years of her life, authorising the publication of various books, as if by the wish of the Duchess, and issuing statements and writs on all who purportedly offended her client. She tried hard to stop the television film, *Edward & Mrs Simpson*, starring Edward Fox and Cynthia Harris, which was serialised in 1979, though by then the Duchess was beyond awareness of any film.

On 13 November 1975, the Duchess collapsed with a severe haemorrhage from a stomach ulcer, brought on by her reliance on nips of vodka as her only form of sustenance. She remained in the American Hospital in Neuilly, returning home a virtual wreck in the early summer of 1976. Photographs taken by paparazzi with long lenses showed her in her garden, an emaciated figure with her head hanging to one side. Then she disappeared completely from public view, a bed-ridden figure, cared for round the clock by nurses.

In those long years a wall of security fell around her and her old friends were not allowed to see her. Printed cards were sent

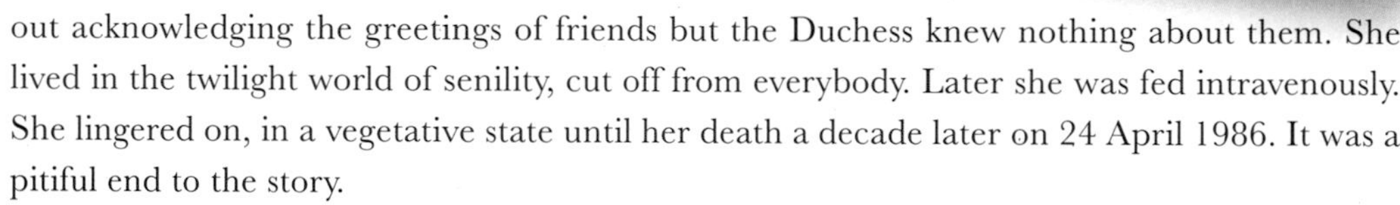
out acknowledging the greetings of friends but the Duchess knew nothing about them. She lived in the twilight world of senility, cut off from everybody. Later she was fed intravenously. She lingered on, in a vegetative state until her death a decade later on 24 April 1986. It was a pitiful end to the story.

The Duchess was a few weeks from her ninetieth birthday when she died. By an agreement made with the Queen many years earlier, her body was flown back to England. There was a private funeral at St George's Chapel attended by the the Queen, Prince Philip, the Queen Mother, the Prince and Princess of Wales and other members of the Royal Family. The press did their best to make it appear a dismal affair, but it was exactly the same as the private funerals for members of the Royal Family such as Princess Marina (though by a curious error on the part of the Dean of Windsor the Duchess was not mentioned by name).

A bearer party of the Welsh Guards, the Duke of Windsor's regiment, carried the coffin into the quire, the Dean of Windsor conducted the service and afterwards the Queen and the Royal Family followed the coffin out through the nave and into the April sunshine.

The Duchess of Windsor was buried beside the Duke in the Royal Family's private burial ground at Frogmore, a garden with a lawn and trees, nestling behind Queen Victoria's mausoleum a few minutes' drive from the Castle in the Home Park. Here, after fourteen unhappy years, the couple's earthly remains were reunited.

On the day the Duchess of Windsor died, her friend, Lady Diana Cooper, then aged ninety-three and herself to die within two months, was interviewed on the BBC Radio programme, *The World At One*. She was asked to sum up the Abdication drama. 'What man ever gave up so much for one woman!' she said.[138]

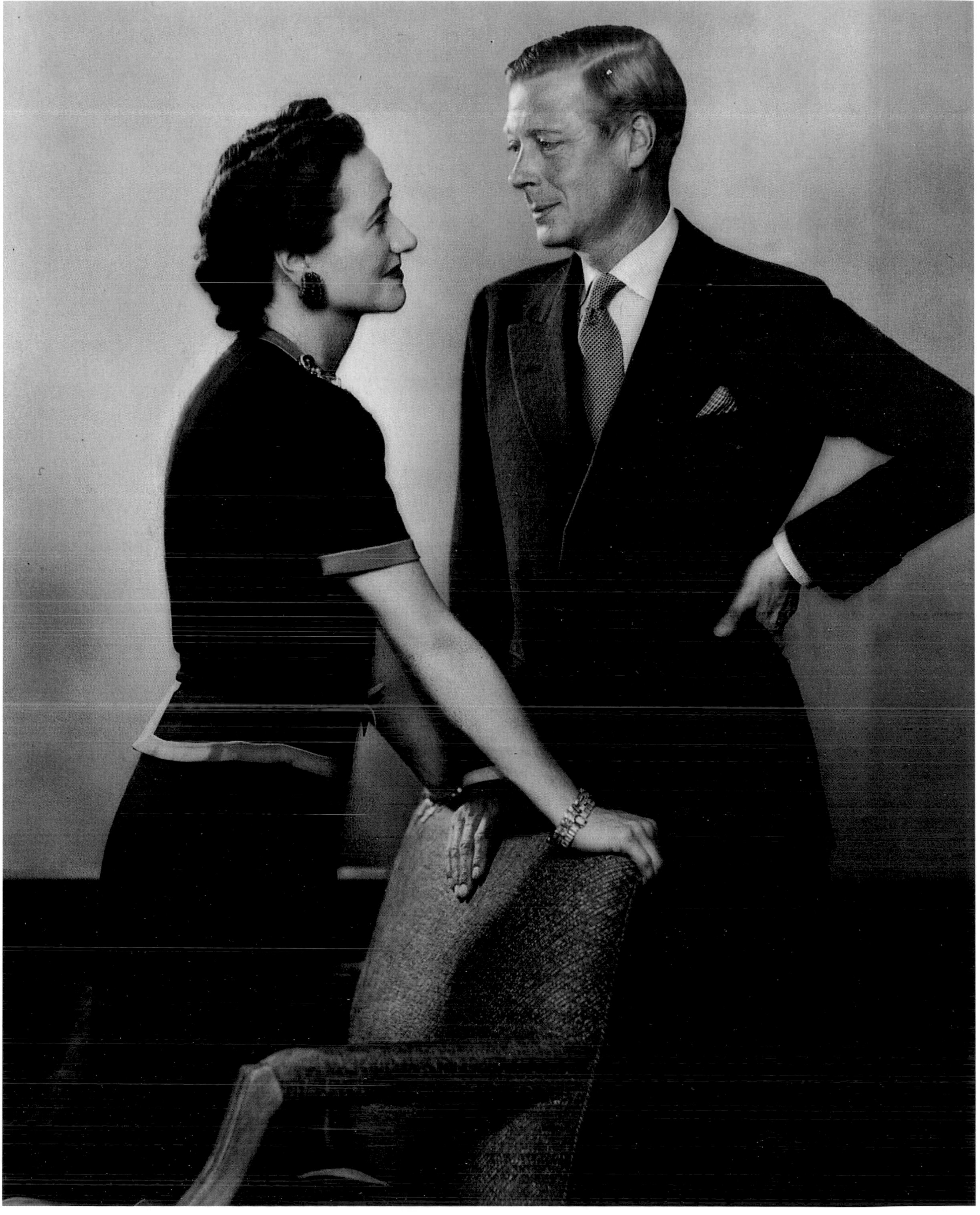

EPILOGUE

In 1979, the Ritz Hotel in Paris was going through a difficult time. Mohamed Al Fayed bought it and set in motion the vast project of returning it to its former magnificence. It was an enjoyable exercise for him and involved very substantial investment. It is Mr Al Fayed's well-known business acumen combined with a characteristic blend of courage, romanticism, a love of history that drives him to undertake such projects. He has shown the same dash and enthusiasm in his restoration of the Harrods building in Knightsbridge.

The City of Paris and the French nation were grateful for his gesture. Paris, an important meeting point in Europe, needs impressive hotels such as the Ritz as settings for its important guests and its wealthy travellers. In recognition of his work in the Ritz Hotel and for his humanitarian action in supporting the Georges Pompidou Foundation, a charity for the handicapped and destitute, young and old, he was awarded both the *Médaille de Paris* in 1985 and the *Légion d'Honneur* in 1986.

When the Duchess of Windsor died in 1986, Mr Al Fayed did not hesitate. The Windsors' once splendid house near the Bois de Boulogne stood, sad and shabby, empty of a tenant although it still held almost all their possessions. The Windsor Villa, owned by the City of Paris, cried out for an imaginative response. The Mayor of Paris, Monsieur Jacques Chirac, at once thought of Mohamed Al Fayed and entrusted the lease of the house to him.

Someone less sensitive to the Villa's place in history than Mr Al Fayed might have decided that the house was best served by giving it a 'new look' – in the best of late-twentieth century design. Instead, he chose the painstaking task of reinstating the entire setting in which the Duke and Duchess of Windsor lived out their final decades. Through this enterprising gesture, these two figures from history, jointly celebrated for one striking moment in their lives, can now be better understood; a picture of their life and an archive of their possessions are now permanently on record.

For this achievement, Mohamed Al Fayed was given the rare award of the Grande Plaque de Paris – presented to only fifteen other individuals since its institution. In his presentation speech Mayor Chirac (President Chirac since May 1995) gave the following address.

ABOVE: *The Windsor Villa restored to its former glory was, in 1989, the setting for the presentation of the* Grande Plaque de Paris, *a rarely awarded commemorative medal struck at the time of the Bimillennium of the City of Paris.* BELOW: *Mr Al Fayed shows Monsieur and Madame Chirac some of the items on display in one of the basement Museum Rooms, with Joe Friedman, the Curator.* OPPOSITE ABOVE: *Mohamed Al Fayed outside the Windsor Villa.* OPPOSITE BELOW: *Mayor Chirac presents the* Grande Plaque de Paris *to Mohamed Al Fayed.*

MAYOR JACQUES CHIRAC'S SPEECH PRESENTATION OF THE *GRANDE PLAQUE* FROM THE CITY OF PARIS, DECEMBER 1989

'Dear Friend, Mr Al Fayed, Ladies and Gentlemen,

The event which brings us together today in this historic place, still charged with so much emotion, is exceptional.Exceptional, first, because of the enthusiasm, warmth and especially generosity, of the person who is receiving us, a man to whom Paris owes so much.

Dear friend, dear Mr Al Fayed, you are a business man, as everyone knows, but you are also a man of feeling and a man of taste. Your love for Paris is well known as is your love for London. It was ten years ago that you took over the Ritz Hotel, a prestigious symbol of the French way of life. The Ritz was then experiencing difficult times. But because of your talent and determination, it has found, once again, the quality which has made it the best hotel in France, and probably the best hotel in the world.

This is also a very special occasion because of this other jewel of Paris which you feel passionate about, the Windsor Villa – this fairytale place, redolent with history, where the Duke and Duchess of Windsor settled in 1953, happy at last to have found a peaceful haven after sixteen years of exile. All those who frequented the house at that time, assure us that the Villa Windsor lived through its finest hours, thanks to the talent of the hostess, the Duchess of Windsor. She managed to recreate around her husband, around them both, the refined and elegant atmosphere of the English Court which Edward VIII had given up for her sake.

In 1986, the Duchess died, and with her the last symbol of a great love story which set the whole world dreaming. Through you, Mr Al Fayed, a fragment of the history of Paris and that of England has been restored, reinstated – indeed rescued – from what would have been without your intervention, a disastrous loss. When I handed over the Villa Windsor to you, I had already experienced the quality of your restoration at the Ritz. Today, after two years of difficult and hard work, you have again demonstrated your extraordinary capacity to mobilise energies and talents to restore this home to its past splendour. Once again, permit me, dear friend, to address to you, as well as the restorers and curators, led by Mr Joe Friedman, my sincere and warm thanks for the remarkable work which you have accomplished.

Dear Mr Al Fayed, I wanted to mark this moment with some gesture. The City of Paris at the time of its second millennium, thirty or forty years ago, produced a special plaque which it awards only rarely, and only to those who have served Paris with great understanding, sincerity and affection. I would like now to present to you this commemorative plaque of the Bimillennium of Paris for your contribution to our city has placed you amongst the most eminent of our fellow citizens.'

NOTES

1 The Duke of Windsor writing in the *Daily News* (New York), December 1966, reprinted in the *Sunday Express* in 1967.
2 Peter Quennell (ed.), *A Lonely Business. A Self-Portrait of James Pope-Hennessy* (Weidenfeld & Nicolson, 1981), p. 219.
3 Lord Birkenhead, *Walter Monckton* (Weidenfeld & Nicolson, 1969), pp. 125-126.
4 Lord Brownlow to Cecil Beaton, recorded in Beaton's unpublished diary, early 1937 (Cecil Beaton papers, St John's College, Cambridge).
5 Wallis Simpson to Cecil Beaton, 1937 (Beaton Papers).
6 Michael Bloch, *The Secret File of the Duke of Windsor* (Bantam Press, 1988), p. 345.
7 HRH The Duke of Windsor, *A King's Story* (Cassell, 1951), p. 10.
8 Ibid., p. 13.
9 Ibid., p. 45.
10 HRH The Duke of Windsor, *The Crown and The People 1902-1953* (Cassell, 1953) p. 41.
11 *A King's Story*, p. 82.
12 Ibid., p. 25.
13 Ibid., p. 26.
14 *A Lonely Business*, pp. 218-219.
15 Ibid., p. 226.
16 *A King's Story*, p. 189
17 James Pope-Hennessy, *Queen Mary* (Allen & Unwin, 1959), p. 180.
18 *A Lonely Business*, p. 214.
19 *A King's Story*, p. 99.
20 Philip Ziegler, *King Edward VIII* (Collins, 1990), p. 32.
21 *Queen Mary*, p. 511.
22 Ziegler, *Edward VIII*, p. 80.
23 *Queen Mary*, p. 511.
24 J. Bryan III and Charles J.V. Murphy, *The Windsor Story* (Granada, 1979), p. xvii.
25 Ibid., p. xvi.
26 *A Lonely Business*, p. 225.
27 HRH The Duke of Windsor, *A Family Album* (Cassell, 1960), p. 4.
28 Alexander Hardinge's game book 1909-1926 (unpublished).
29 James Lees-Milne, *The Enigmatic Edwardian. The Life of Reginald, 2nd Viscount Esher* (Sidgwick & Jackson, 1986), p.160.
30 *A King's Story*, p. 59.
31 *The Enigmatic Edwardian*, p. 214.
32 Ibid., p. 238.
33 Ziegler, *Edward VIII*, p. 44.
34 *A King's Story*, p. 109.
35 Ibid., p. 113.
36 Ibid., p. 120.
37 *The Enigmatic Edwardian*, p. 283.
38 Quoted in *A King's Story*, p. 128.
39 *Speeches by HRH The Prince of Wales 1912-1926* (London, 1927), p. 4.
40 Ziegler, *Edward VIII*, p. 108.
41 Duff Hart-Davis (ed.), *In Royal Service - The Letters and Journals of Sir Alan Lascelles* (Hamish Hamilton, 1989), p.65.
42 Ibid., p. 64.
43 Prince of Wales to Sir Godfrey Thomas, 25 Dec 1919, quoted in Ziegler, *Edward VIII*, p. 122.
44 *A King's Story*, p. 142.
45 Quoted by Alastair Forbes, *Times Literary Supplement*, 1 November 1974, from Lilli Palmer, *Dicke Lilli, Gutes Kind* (Droemer Knaur, Zurich, 1974), p. 298. Cf. English translation: *Change Lobsters – and Dance* (Macmillan, New York, 1975), p.211.
46 *In Royal Service*, p. 74.
47 Philip Ziegler, *Mountbatten* (Collins, 1985), pp. 54f.
48 *A King's Story*, p. 154.
49 Ibid., p. 178.
50 Ibid., p. 199.
51 Ibid., pp. 199f.
52 Ibid., p. 210.
53 Ibid., P. 220.
54 *In Royal Service*, p. 76.
55 *A King's Story*, p. 221.
56 *In Royal Service*, p. 4.
57 Alistair Cooke, *Six Men* (Bodley Head, 1977), p. 75.
58 Ziegler, *Edward VIII*, p. 97.
59 Ibid., p. 100.
60 *In Royal Service*, p. 50.
61 Ibid., p. 59.
62 Ibid., p. 118.
63 Ibid., p. 120.
64 James Fox, *White Mischief* (Jonathan Cape, 1982), p. 259.
65 Lady Diana Cooper, *The Light of Common Day* (Rupert Hart-Davis, 1959), p. 162.
66 The Duchess of Windsor, *The Heart Has Its Reasons* (Michael Joseph, 1956), p. 13.
67 Baltimore press cutting (undated), Windsor Collection, Paris.
68 *The Heart Has Its Reasons*, p. 65.
69 Ibid., p. 94.
70 Cecil Beaton's diary, 20 November 1936.
71 *The Heart Has Its Reasons*, p. 146.
72 *A King's Story*, p. 255.
73 The Duke of Windsor to Kenneth Harris, BBC Interview, January 1970.
74 Adela Rogers St Johns, *The Honeycomb* (Doubleday, New York, 1969), quoted in Michael Pye, *The King over the Water*, p. 22.
75 Robert Rhodes James (ed.), *Chips: The Diaries of Sir Henry Channon* (Weidenfeld & Nicolson, 1967), p. 30.
76 *Chips*, pp. 51, 54.
77 Kenneth Young (ed.), *The Diaries of Sir Robert Bruce Lockhart*, vol. 1, 1915-1938 (Macmillan, 1973), p. 321.
78 *The Times*, 21 January 1936.
79 His Majesty's Speech to His Peoples (BBC), 1 March 1936.
80 *Cape Times*, 17 July 1936.
81 *Chips*, p. 35.
82 Derived from a letter from Sir Alan Lascelles to Christopher Sykes, 1 December 1974 (Sykes Papers, Georgetown University, Washington).
83 See John Evelyn Wrench, *Geoffrey Dawson and Our Times* (Hutchinson, 1955), pp. 339-342.
84 Private notes by Hardinge on the Abdication.
85 Robert Rhodes James, *Victor Cazalet: A Portrait*, (Hamish Hamilton, 1986), p. 186.
86 Lord Beaverbrook, *The Abdication of King Edward VIII*, edited by A.J.P. Taylor (Atheneum, New York, 1966), p.120.
87 Michael De-la-Noy, *The Queen Behind the Throne* (Hutchinson, 1994), p. 83
88 *The Diaries of Sir Robert Bruce Lockhart*, vol. 1, p. 361.
89 Pope-Hennessy, *Queen Mary*, p. 575.
90 Hardinge notes on the Abdication.
91 Queen Mary to Hardinge, 12 December 1936.
92 *A King's Story*, pp.413-414
93 Ibid., p. 415.
94 Elizabeth Longford (ed.), *Darling Loosy* (Weidenfeld & Nicolson), p. 309.
95 John Van der Kiste, *Edward VII's Children* (Alan Sutton, 1989), p. 176.
96 *Darling Loosy*, p. 307.
97 *In Royal Service*, p. 201.
98 Lucy Moorhead (ed.), *Freya Stark, Letters*, vol. III (Compton Russell, 1976), p. 63.
99 Philip Ziegler (ed.), *From Shore to Shore* (Collins, 1989), p. 253.

NOTES

100 Michael Bloch (ed.), *Wallis & Edward Letters 1931-1937* (Weidenfeld & Nicolson, 1986), pp. 222-223.
101 *Chips*, p. 101.
102 *Secret File*, p. 44.
103 Ibid., p. 39.
104 Hugo Vickers, *Cecil Beaton* (Weidenfeld & Nicolson, 1985), p. 198.
105 Lady Diana Cooper to the author.
106 *Secret File*, p. 162.
107 *The Heart Has Its Reasons*, p. 312
108 HRH Princess Alice, Duchess of Gloucester, *The Memoirs of Princess Alice, Duchess of Gloucester* (Collins, 1983), p. 117.
109 *Secret File*, p. 232.
110 HRH Princess Alice, Countess of Athlone, *For My Grandchildren* (Evans 1966), p. 271.
111 *The Heart Has Its Reasons*, p. 346.
112 Etienne Dupuch, *Tribune Story* (Benn, 1969), p. 83.
113 *The Heart Has Its Reasons*, p. 355
114 *Secret File*, pp. 260f.
115 The Duke of Windsor to Kenneth Harris, BBC Television, January 1970.
116 Lord Harewood, *The Tongs and the Bones* (Weidenfeld & Nicolson, 1981), p. 18.
117 Ibid., p. 17.
118 *Secret File*, p. 330.
119 *A Lonely Business*, p. 212.
120 The Duchess of Windsor to Diana Vreeland, 17 February 1967.
121 The Duchess of Windsor to Godfrey Winn, July 1966: *Woman*, 2 October 1966, p. 87.
122 Mrs Nathan Cummings to author, 26 February 1990.
123 Harris interview, BBC Television, January 1970.
124 *From Shore to Shore*, p. 190.
125 Johanna Schütz to author, November 1976.
126 The Duchess of Windsor to Diana Vreeland, 24 November 1968.
127 *Barbara Cartland's Book of Beauty and Health* (1972).
128 Gregorio Martin, 1994
129 Cecil Beaton's Diaries: *The Parting Years* (Weidenfeld & Nicolson, 1978), pp. 110-111.
130 Jonathan Dimbleby, *The Prince of Wales* (Little, Brown, 1994), pp. 178-179
131 Melvyn Bragg, *Rich: The Life of Richard Burton* (Hodder & Stoughton, 1988), pp. 390-391.
132 Ibid., p. 393.
133 John Utter to author.
134 Dimbleby, p. 180.
135 *Sunday Times*, 4 June 1972.
136 *Daily Telegraph*, 6 June 1972.
137 *The Times*, 6 June 1972.
138 *The World At One* (BBC Radio 4), 24 April 1986.

Permission to publish extracts from the following is gratefully acknowledged: the writings of Cecil Beaton, by permission of The Literary Executors of the late Sir Cecil Beaton; © 1988 *The Secret File of the Duke and Duchess of Windsor* by Michael Bloch published by Bantam Press, All Rights Reserved; Jonathan Dimbleby, *The Prince of Wales*, by permission of Jonathan Dimbleby; *In Royal Service, the Letters and Journals of Sir Alan Lascelles*, by permission of A.P. Watt Ltd on behalf of The Estate of Sir Alan Lascelles; Philip Ziegler, *King Edward VIII*, by permission of HarperCollins Publishers and Philip Ziegler; and Peter Quennell (ed.), *A Lonely Business: A Self-Portrait of James Pope-Hennessy*; Lord Birkenhead, *Walter Monckton*; and Robert Rhodes James (ed.) *Chips: The Diaries of Sir Henry Channon*, by permission of Weidenfeld & Nicolson.

All the archive photographs are from the Duke and Duchess of Windsor's own collection, except page 229 (bottom right) by the late Elizabeth Johnston (© Hugo Vickers). Windsor Villa Restoration Project: pages 7, 9 (top left, top right), 10 (bottom left, bottom right), 11 (top left), 13 (top left, bottom right), 14 (lower top left), 16 (lower top right), 22 (top left, bottom left), 29 (top left).

The publishers are grateful to the following for permission to publish photographs: Associated Press Ltd, 11 (top right); Camera Press, 204, 226, 227; Condé Nast, 193 (top); *Daily Express*, 197 (top) and 217 (bottom left); National Archives of Canada (Roloff Beny Archive), 204 (top left); Sotheby's London (Cecil Beaton Archive), 158, 162 (right), 163, 168 (left); Tony Linck /*Life* Magazine /©Time Warner Inc., 201 (top left); Philippe Halsman /*Life* Magazine /©Time Warner Inc., 232 (below left).

Photographs by Fritz von der Schulenburg: pages 6, 7, 8, 9 (bottom right, bottom left), 10 (top), 11 (bottom right), 12-13, 13 (lower top right), 14 (top left), 14-15, 16 (top left, top right, bottom right), 17, 18-19, 20, 21 (top right, bottom left, bottom right), 22 (bottom right).

Note on the Photographs

The collection of photographs included a large group of re-photographed photographs, with red crayon inscriptions identifying the names of persons and places. They may be connected with preliminary research for the writing of the Duke and Duchess's memoirs, or for the making of the film version of *A King's Story* in 1964. The red markings are visible on some of the photographs reproduced in this book.

INDEX

INDEX

INDEX